Florida Paper Money

Florida Paper Money
An Illustrated History, 1817–1934

RONALD J. BENICE

Edited by Fred Reed

McFarland & Company, Inc., Publishers
Jefferson, North Carolina, and London

The present work is a reprint of the illustrated casebound edition of Florida Paper Money: An Illustrated History, 1817–1934, *first published in 2008 by McFarland.*

Ronald J. Benice also wrote *Alaska and Yukon Tokens: Private Coins of the Territories*, 3d ed. (McFarland, 2010)

LIBRARY OF CONGRESS CATALOGUING-IN-PUBLICATION DATA

Benice, Ronald J.
Florida paper money : an illustrated history,
1817–1934 / Ronald J. Benice ; edited by Fred Reed.
p. cm.
Includes bibliographical references and index.

ISBN 978-0-7864-6605-4
softcover : 50# alkaline paper ∞

1. Paper money — Florida — History.
I. Reed, Fred L. II. Title.
HG627.F5B46 2011   769.5'59759 — dc22   2007007205

BRITISH LIBRARY CATALOGUING DATA ARE AVAILABLE

© 2008 Ronald J. Benice. All rights reserved

No part of this book may be reproduced or transmitted in any form or by any means, electronic or mechanical, including photocopying or recording, or by any information storage and retrieval system, without permission in writing from the publisher.

Front cover: Civil War 2, State of Florida, 20 Dollars, 1861 essay (author's collection)

Manufactured in the United States of America

*McFarland & Company, Inc., Publishers
Box 611, Jefferson, North Carolina 28640
www.mcfarlandpub.com*

To Doris

Table of Contents

Photographic Credits	ix
Preface	1
Introduction	3
1—Republic of the Floridas	5
2—Territorial Notes	8
First Issue	8
Second Issue	9
3—Civil War Currency	11
1861 Dated Issues	11
1862 Dated Issues	20
1863 Dated Issues	24
1864 Dated Issues	30
1865 Dated Issues	32
4—Florida Currency During Reconstruction	35
Interim Currency 1865–1870	35
1870 Currency Issue	36
Redemption and Destruction of Notes	40
5—Obsolete Notes and Scrip	41
Alafia	41
Apalachicola	42
Bay Port	60
Brooksville	61
Brunswick & Florida Steam Boat & Stage Line	62
Cedar Keys	63
Cork	64
Dutton	65
Ellaville	66

Fernandina	68
Fort Blount	73
Hernando County	74
Highland	75
Iola	76
Jacksonville	79
Key West	92
Madison	93
Magnolia	93
Manatee	96
Marianna	96
Micanopy	100
Millview	101
Milton	103
Montgomery, Alabama	103
Monticello	107
Ocala	109
Orange Springs	109
Panama	113
Pensacola	115
Quincy	127
St. Augustine	128
St. Joseph	131
Silver Springs	138
Starke	138
Tallahassee	139
Tampa	164
6—Advertising Notes	166
7—Financial Panic and Depression Scrip	174
1873	174
1907	174
1933	176
8—College Currency	184
Florida Normal College, White Springs	184
Bibliography	187
Index	191

Photographic Credits

American Numismatic Society: 103, 109 bottom
Daniel G. Cassidy: 65 bottom, 125 bottom, 157 top
C.R. Clark: 138 top
Florida Historical Society: 137 bottom
Florida State Archives: 5, 12 top, 22 center, 34, 57 bottom, 107 bottom
Richard Frey: 71 bottom, 134 bottom, 136 center
Heritage Currency Auctions of America: 114 top & center, 175 top, 176
Linda and Russell Kaye: 97 bottom, 119 center & bottom, 120, 145 bottom, 146
Lyn Knight Currency Auctions: 67 top
Museum of Florida History (from the collections): 110 top, 179 bottom, 183
Philip A. Pfeiffer: 117 center & bottom, 126 top
R.M. Smythe & Co.: 54, 63, 126 bottom, 127 top, 131 top, 136 bottom
Society of Paper Money Collectors: 59 top, 60, 62 bottom, 66, 92 bottom
State Historical Society of Wisconsin: 39 bottom
State Library of Florida: 9 top
P.K. Yonge Library of Florida History, (courtesy of the Department of Special Collections, George A. Smathers Libraries), University of Florida: 137 center
William Youngerman Inc. Boca Raton: 74, 78 bottom, 88 bottom, 92 top, 101, 102, 108, 138 bottom, 155 bottom

Additional illustrations from the author's collection

Preface

This is a catalog of Florida paper money from colonial days through the Great Depression. It encompasses governmental issues of the Republic of the Floridas, Territory of Florida, and the State of Florida, as well as scrip issued by cities and counties. Included, of course, are obsolete bank notes and scrip issued by banks, railroads, insurance companies, merchants and individuals. Federal currency issues, namely National Bank Notes, are not included.

My research on Florida paper money started from scratch. For more than 10 years I have delved into archives, legislative records, libraries, museums and historical societies. I have uncovered significantly more information about Civil War era currency than appears in Criswell's *Confederate and Southern States Currency* and significantly more information about the issues and issuers of obsolete notes and scrip than appears in either Freeman's *Florida Obsolete Notes and Scrip* or Cassidy's *Illustrated History of Florida Paper Money*. I had an advantage over my predecessors in that many local histories were published subsequent to their research, and Internet search tools enabled me to locate source materials in unlikely remote locations. I also made some lucky finds in the Florida State Archives. I have corrected errors in the three works mentioned above, and no doubt have included a few of my own.

The section on obsoletes and scrip includes about 520 notes compared with approximately 349 in Freeman and 382 in Cassidy. Time and technology helped me here. Significant holdings unknown to my predecessors have come on the market. Auction catalogs now have many photographs of notes so that different designs for the same denominations from the same issuer could be recognized. The sale of the American Bank Note Company archives released proofs of many previously unknown notes.

I have indicated rarities of notes using the Sheldon scale familiar to most collectors:

> R8: 1 to 3 known
> R7: 4 to 12
> R6: 13 to 30
> R5: 31 to 75
> R4: 76 to 200
> R3: 201 to 499
> R2: 500 to 1250
> R1: more than 1250

The rarities assigned are estimates, no formal census having been conducted. They represent a consensus of opinion among knowledgeable collectors and dealers, as well as an analysis of 30 years of auction records and inventories of collections owned by individuals and museums.

I have followed tradition by listing obsolete currency issued by banking institutions ahead of non-bank scrip for each town. Wherever possible, I have identified portraits of the real and mythological characters or allegorical representations appearing on the notes. Many of the characters have multiple names and some of the allegories are subjective interpretations, but I aimed for consistency with Roger Durand's publications (see Bibliography). Census data and local historians have helped me decipher many signatures that had eluded previous catalogers.

The decision on what to include as obsolete "paper money" and what to exclude was admittedly subjective. Notes issued by banks that are payable to bearer on demand certainly qualify for inclusion. Unlike Haxby (*United States Obsolete Banknotes 1786–1866*), however, I include certificates of exchange and negotiable certificates of deposit from these institutions. At the other end of the spectrum, cancelled checks and three-party exchange certificates do not qualify. In between falls a wide range of paper that, however worded, amounts to promissory notes. Those that are payable to bearer and intended to circulate are included in this catalog; those that are two-party transactions or for single use are not. Punch cards and coupon books have been excluded.

Many of my sources are cited in the text or in the extensive bibliography. In addition to those, I would like to acknowledge numerous helpful communications with Hugh Shull and Bill Youngerman. John Yasuk provided valuable assistance on state notes, and Roger Durand helped with identification of vignettes.

Most of the notes pictured in this catalog are from my personal collection. The photographs of the Treasurer, Comptroller, three Governors and Gregor MacGregor were provided by the Florida State Archives. The photograph of Governor Reed was provided by the State Historical Society of Wisconsin. I would like to thank Heritage/Currency Auctions of America, R. M. Smythe & Co. and Lyn Knight Currency Auctions for permission to use illustrations from their auctions. Bill Youngerman has generously provided images of notes in his collection. Other photographs were provided by the American Numismatic Society, Florida Historical Society, State Library of Florida, Museum of Florida History, Society of Paper Money Collectors, University of Florida, Russell and Linda Kaye, Daniel G. Cassidy, C. R. Clark, Richard Frey, and Philip Pfeiffer.

My wife, Doris, is to be commended for her encouragement during the research and writing of this book and for her careful proofreading of the final manuscript. Finally, I'd like to thank my editor, Fred Reed, who converted my manuscript and images into this book.

Ronald J. Benice
Sarasota, Florida
June 2006

Introduction

Florida paper money ties together the history and the economic development of Florida from colonial days to the Great Depression.

The earliest dated piece of Florida paper money was issued in 1817 by a Scottish adventurer who captured a small corner of the state from the Spanish. A decade later the Territory of Florida issued small scrip and large engraved notes. The Territorial Legislature granted charters to a number of banks between 1828 and 1837 and authorized them to circulate paper money. The banks were corrupt and inevitably failed.

During the financial panic of 1837–1838 and ensuing nationwide depression of 1839–1843 many towns and merchants issued scrip to alleviate the shortage of gold and silver. When Congress and the Florida Legislature restricted the formation of new banks, banks in neighboring states filled the void by issuing paper money valid in Florida. Some Florida businesses issued scrip that purported to originate elsewhere.

After Florida seceded from the Union in 1861, it issued its own paper money. As the tide of the war declined, so did the quality of the paper money. Private issues, often on small pieces of low quality brown paper, were produced to provide change. During Reconstruction, Florida issued paper money despite the Constitutional proscription. Private scrip continued to circulate during the hardship years of Reconstruction.

The Financial Panic of 1873 saw new issues of scrip from merchants and company stores in the transportation, lumber and naval stores industries. Then during the Panic of 1907 Clearing House Associations issued scrip to keep local economies alive until the banks reopened. In 1933, during the Great Depression, the issuance of scrip by local banks and clearing houses was widespread.

This book describes all this paper money together with information about its rarity, its engravers and its issuers.

Introduction

Florida paper money ties together the history and the economic development of Florida from colonial days to the Great Depression.

The earliest dated piece of Florida paper money was issued in 1817 by a Scottish adventurer who captured a small corner of the state from the Spanish. A decade later the Territory of Florida issued small scrip and large engraved notes. The Territorial Legislature granted charters to a number of banks between 1828 and 1837 and authorized them to circulate paper money. The banks were corrupt and inevitably failed.

During the financial panic of 1837–1838 and ensuing nationwide depression of 1839–1843 many towns and merchants issued scrip to alleviate the shortage of gold and silver. When Congress and the Florida Legislature restricted the formation of new banks, banks in neighboring states filled the void by issuing paper money valid in Florida. Some Florida businesses issued scrip that purported to originate elsewhere.

After Florida seceded from the Union in 1861, it issued its own paper money. As the tide of the war declined, so did the quality of the paper money. Private issues, often on small pieces of low quality brown paper, were produced to provide change. During Reconstruction, Florida issued paper money despite the Constitutional proscription. Private scrip continued to circulate during the hardship years of Reconstruction.

The Financial Panic of 1873 saw new issues of scrip from merchants and company stores in the transportation, lumber and naval stores industries. Then during the Panic of 1907 Clearing House Associations issued scrip to keep local economies alive until the banks reopened. In 1933, during the Great Depression, the issuance of scrip by local banks and clearing houses was widespread.

This book describes all this paper money together with information about its rarity, its engravers and its issuers.

1
Republic of the Floridas

The earliest known dated and issued Florida currency was for Gregor MacGregor's independent Republic of the Floridas on Amelia Island.

General Gregor MacGregor, a grand-nephew of Rob Roy, was born in Scotland on December 24, 1786. He entered the British Army in 1803 as an ensign and left as a captain in 1810. In 1811 he sailed to South America and served in the Venezuelan Army of Liberation under Simon Bolivar, who promoted him to the rank of general. In 1812 Gregor married the daughter of Bolivar's sister.

MacGregor's next adventure was a campaign to free East Florida and West Florida from Spanish control. In 1816, he went to Baltimore and Philadelphia to get financial support and obtained a commission from representatives of Mexico, Rio de la Plata, Nueva Granada and Venezuela to first capture Amelia Island and then the rest of the Floridas. Proceeding south, he obtained significant additional funds in Savannah and recruited soldiers and sailors in Charleston and Savannah for $10 a month. Then on June 29, 1817, with a force of only 73 men, he captured Amelia Island from a surprised Spanish military detachment. He declared it free and independent, variously referring to it as the Green Cross Republic or the Republic of the Floridas.

MacGregor quickly established

Gregor MacGregor

a government, created an Admiralty Court to collect duties on goods brought ashore by privateers and pirates, opened a post office, started a newspaper, and issued currency. He tried unsuccessfully to sell Florida to the United States. In September, he sold the lands for $50,000 to Luis Aury, a pirate operating under the Mexican flag. U.S. President James Monroe decided that these events were not helping American negotiations to buy Florida from Spain, so he ordered troops to the area. On December 23, 1817, Luis Aury surrendered to the American Navy which returned Amelia Island to Spanish control.

During the brief life of the Green Cross Republic, Gregor MacGregor issued scrip, of which only one piece is known to have survived.

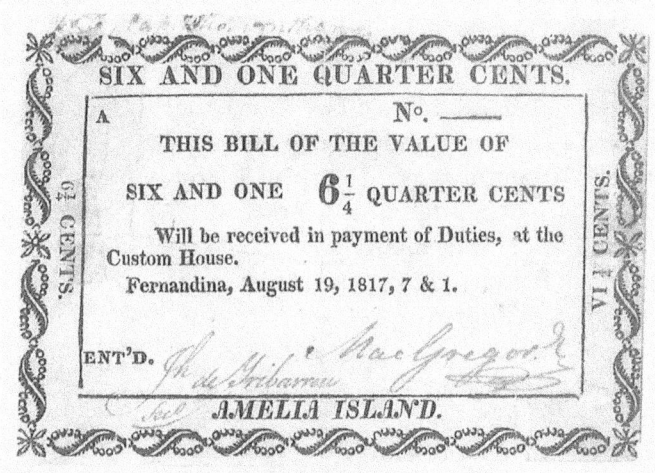

The sole surviving specimen of MacGregor's Amelia Island currency

The sole surviving specimen of MacGregor's Amelia Island currency is the earliest dated, issued piece of Florida currency. The note is hand signed by Gregor MacGregor and by his Secretary, Joseph de Yribarren. It was printed on Amelia Island using a printing press that MacGregor brought in to publish the newspaper, *El Telégrafo de las Floridas*, and other government forms. The numbers "7 & 1" after the August 19, 1817, date signify the 7th year of Venezuelan independence and the 1st year of Florida's independence. The back of the note is blank.

Amelia Island is located off the northeast coast of Florida, just below the Georgia border. Its only town in 1817 was Fernandina, now called Fernandina Beach. Amelia Island was named by General James Ogelthorpe of the Georgia Colony in 1734 to honor Princess Amelia, second daughter of King George II of England.

No records have survived to indicate which denominations or how many notes were issued. However, based on this 6¼¢ note and a $1 sketch in Colombia, it seems reasonable to assume that 12½¢ and 25¢ notes were also issued in 1817.

Several writers have alleged the existence of a second surviving specimen, a $1 note which has never been photographed or listed in any price list or auction catalog. The specimen reported to be in the National Archives of Colombia is a contemporaneous hand-drawn sketch of a $1 note of the same design as the 6¼¢ note. The specimen reported to be in the Pan American Union in Mexico City is a photocopy of the Colombia fac-

1. Republic of the Floridas

simile. The specimen in the National Archives of Scotland is a $1 note on the Bank of Poyais, printed by MacGregor in 1822 for his colony in Nicaragua and Honduras.

In 1839, MacGregor returned to Venezuela where the government restored his rank of General and granted him a generous pension. He died there on December 4, 1845, and was buried in Caracas Cathedral. His name is inscribed on the city's memorial to the leaders of the fight for independence. MacGregor's life and further exploits are described in greater detail in my March/April 2006 article in SPMC's journal, *Paper Money*.

2

Territorial Notes

On November 22, 1828, Governor Duval signed "an act to authorise the issuing of treasury warrants" which the legislature had passed three days earlier. "It shall be the duty of the Treasurer of the Territory to cause to be struck on good silk paper, the amount of ten thousand dollars in notes or warrants, from twelve and a half cents to five dollars, to bear interest at the rate of six per cent per annum each of which notes or warrants shall be signed by the treasurer and issued by him in payment of all audited accounts against the Treasury."

The notes were receivable in payment of debts to the territory and could be used to purchase public lands.

On November 22, 1829, another act declared "It shall be the duty of the Treasurer ... to issue Treasury warrants for all claims and demands ... provided nothing shall be construed to permit said Treasurer to redeem the Territorial scrip already out with the scrip now on hand unless the party presenting said scrip will deduct interest due thereon."

On February 13, 1831, the treasurer was authorized to continue issuing scrip under the 1829 rules. Unfortunately, no records or reports relating to the actual quantities, denominations, dates or serial numbers have survived.

First Issue

Simple typeset notes without vignettes or printer's imprint. Hand signed by Davis Floyd, Treasurer. Handwritten dates between January and June 1829 have been observed.

2. Territorial Notes

1. 50¢ R7
2. $1 .... R8
3. $2 .... R8
4. $3 .... R8

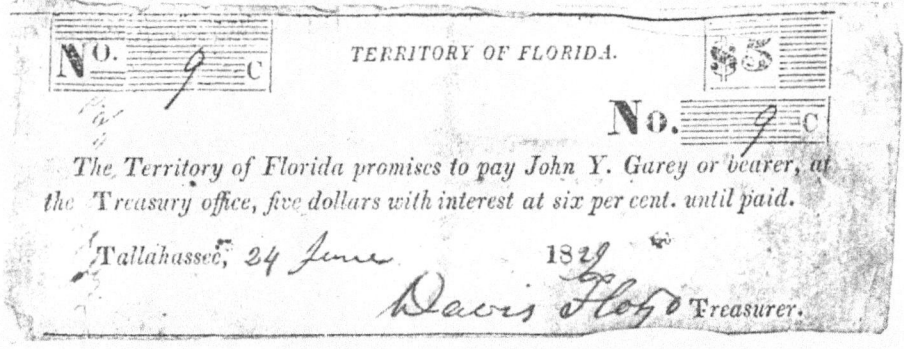

5. $5 .... R8

Second Issue

Engraved notes imprinted N. & S. S. Jocelyn, New Haven. Hand signed by Davis Floyd, Treasurer. Dates between January 8, 1830, and June 13, 1831, have been observed.

Caution must be exercised in drawing conclusions about quantities issued based on the absence of notes with high serial numbers. Each day that notes were issued, the numbering started over with 1. I have seen 20 different issue dates. I have seen 7 notes with serial number 1.

The majority of known surviving issued notes are in museums. Therefore, I am showing the actual rarity followed by the rarity currently available to collectors. Unissued notes are probably reprints made after the territorial period from the original plates, and are not included in the census used to determine rarity.

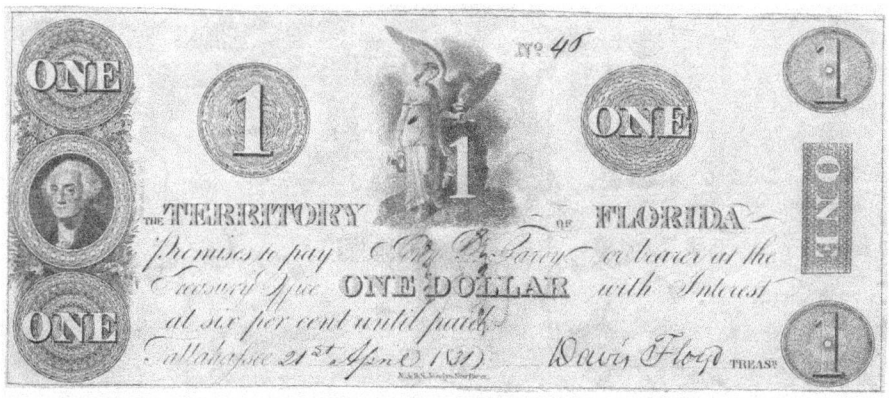

6. $1 .... **Hebe serving water to eagle** R5/R6

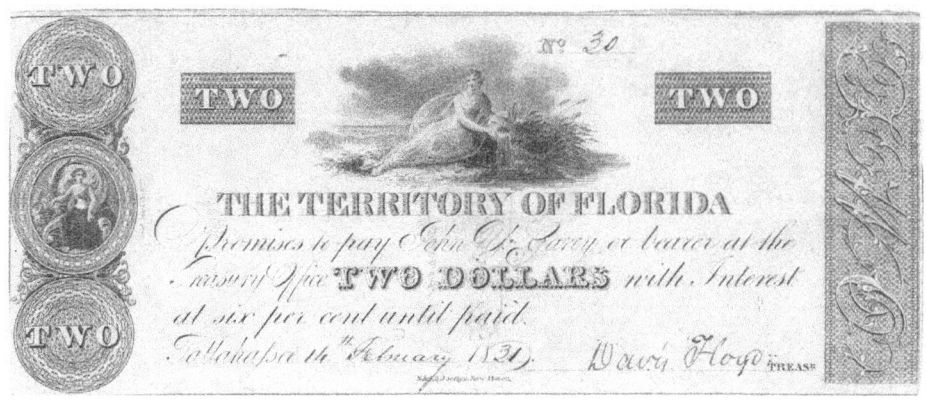

7. $2 .... Water goddess R5/R6

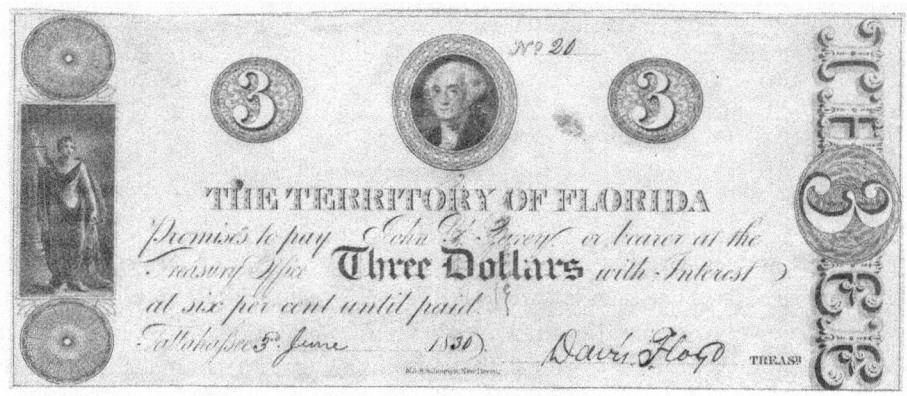

8. $3 .... Washington R5/R6

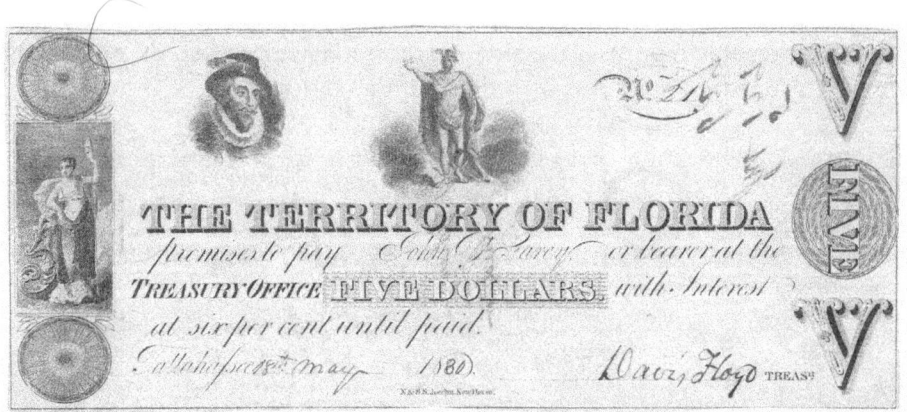

9. $5 .... Raleigh, Mercury.......................... R5/R6

3
Civil War Currency

The first catalog to include currency issued by the state of Florida was William Bradbeer's *Confederate and Southern State Currency* in 1915. He indicated quantities issued as "about" or "over" for all denominations aggregated in each year from 1861 to 1864.

In 1955, B. M. Douglas and B. H. Hughes published a *Catalogue of Confederate and Southern States Currency* that contained "estimated values of all Bradbeer types." Their introduction stated: "There is ample evidence that a few of the varieties listed by Bradbeer do not exist; at the same time it is definitely known that varieties not listed do exist." Unfortunately, they didn't tell us which notes were nonexistent or unlisted.

In 1957 Grover C. Criswell, Jr., and Clarence L. Criswell published the first edition of *Confederate and Southern State Currency*. They prefaced, "The numbering system set down by Mr. Bradbeer still remains the standard, and it is significant that it should be used as the basis of the new Criswell Numbering System." The descriptions of quantities issued each year were the same as in Bradbeer. Suffixes A and B were added to the Bradbeer numbers to accommodate previously unlisted varieties.

The present catalog presents what was legislated, what the executive branch reported, and what the evidence indicates actually happened. Since I am including varieties not previously listed, deleting notes Criswell listed that do not exist, and relocating the "Carpetbagger Notes" to their rightful place as early Civil War essays, Criswell's numbering system is no longer convenient. However, since these numbers have been widely used, I am including the Criswell numbers in parentheses after the new numbers wherever applicable. Hugh Shull's book *A Guide Book of Southern States Currency* continues the Criswell numbering scheme, noting the non-existent notes and chronological errors in Criswell. Rarities are shown in the standard Sheldon quantitative scale rather than Criswell's relative rarity scale. Notes are listed in increasing denominational order within each issue.

1861 Dated Issues

$500,000 authorized February 14, 1861, and issued 1861–1862
$340,000 authorized December 6, 1862, and issued 1863

Florida seceded from the Union on January 11, 1861, and joined the Confederacy on January 28, 1861. On February 14, 1861, the General Assembly passed Chapter 1097 of the Laws of Florida, "An act providing for the issue of Treasury Notes." It required the Governor to:

> cause to be engraved and printed in the best manner to guard against counterfeiting, notes for circulation in the similitude of bank bills, of the different denominations of ones, twos, threes, fours, fives, tens, twenties, fifties and hundreds in amount not exceeding five hundred thousand dollars. Said blank circulating notes shall be signed by the Governor and countersigned by the Treasurer.... Said circulating notes shall have expressed on the face of same to be "receivable by the State of Florida in payment of all dues and demands."

Governor Madison Starke Perry   Governor John Milton

Essays

Peter Hawes of New Orleans was engaged to design the new currency and produced two essays that conformed to the February 14 law. The full story of the essays can be found in my article in the March/April 2000 issue of *Paper Money*.

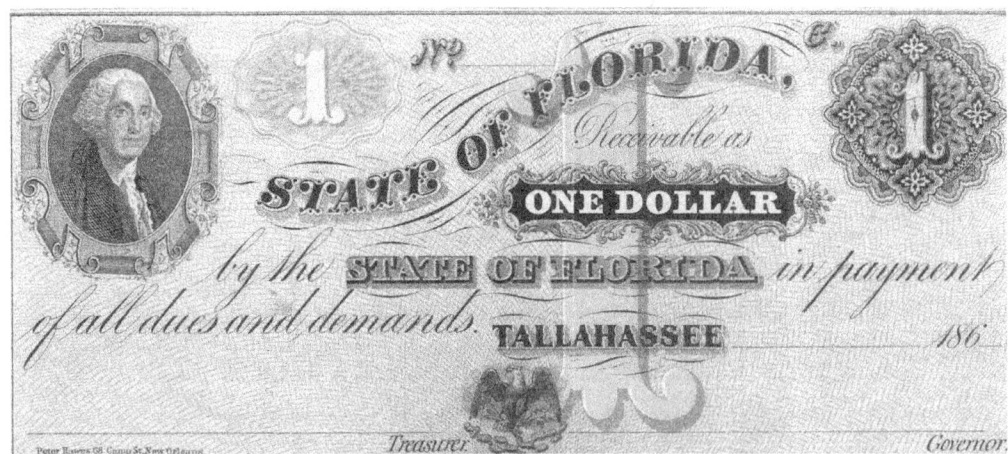

1. $1 (Cr. 67) R8

2. $20 (Cr. 67F) R8

Actual Notes

Actual notes did not appear until September and October of 1861 and were engraved by Hoyer and Ludwig of Richmond. Legal issues contributed to the delay in issuing the state notes, especially the higher denominations. The February 14, 1861, enabling legislation stated "said circulating notes shall be ... legal tender in payment of all entries of land, taxes, fines, duties, debts, demands and sums payable of whatsoever character...." However, the Florida Constitutional Convention on April 29, 1861, passed an ordinance "that the Register of Public Lands is hereby instructed to receive in payment for any lands sold nothing but gold or silver coin or the bills of solvent banks." Since land was the only real backing for the state paper money, this ordinance limited the acceptability of the paper. The remedy came on January 23, 1862, when, at the Governor's request, the convention passed an ordinance that stated "...in payment for these lands, the Treasury Notes of the State of Florida shall be receivable."

First Printings (Handwritten dates September — December 1861)

Undated $1, 2, and 3 notes were printed first, "in payment of taxes and other public dues" instead of the proper obligation "in payment of all dues and demands." The wording was corrected when the higher denominations with engraved dates were printed. The same design, based on the Hawes $1 essay, was used on all three denominations.

Madison Starke Perry was governor until October 7, 1861, and personally signed low denomination notes. Robert Ares estimated that about 3,000 $1s, 1,000 $2s, and 1,000 $3s, all bearing the handwritten date September 16, 1861, were signed by Perry. Although all the notes signed by Perry were of the plate variety with the denomination spelled out at the top right, Governor Milton signed both plate varieties, with handwritten date October 9 or 10, 1861. Charles H. Austin "signed" as Treasurer on these notes and all other Florida Civil war currency issues.

$1: 288,000 notes ($288,000) with Plate letter A

3. Washington, Tellus. "ONE" spelled out in upper right corner (Cr. 9)
   A. Signed by Milton R5/6
   B. Signed for Milton and countersigned R4

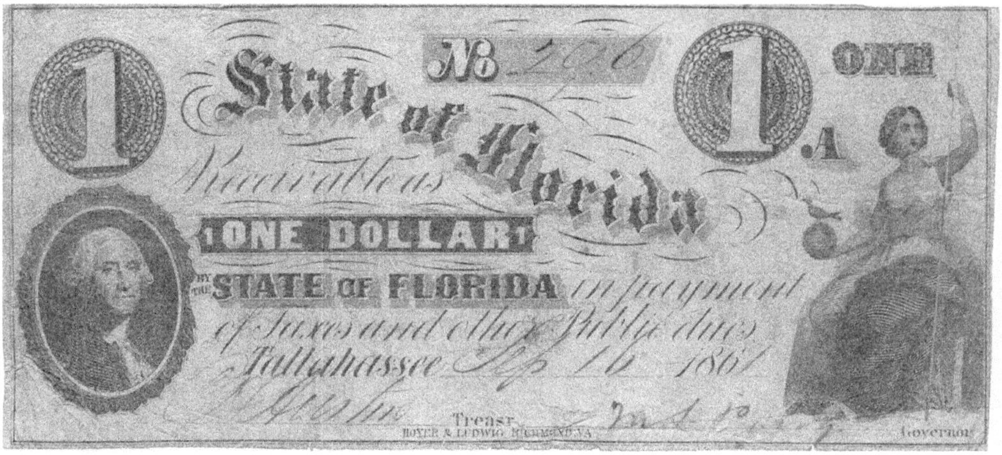

   C. *(Shown above)* Signed by Perry R6

4. Without "One" spelled out in upper right corner. (Cr. 9A)
   A. *(Shown above)* Signed by Milton R5
   B. Signed for Milton and countersigned R3

$2: 11,879 notes ($23,758) with Plate letter B

5. "TWO" spelled out in upper right corner (Cr. 8)
   A. Signed by Milton R5/6

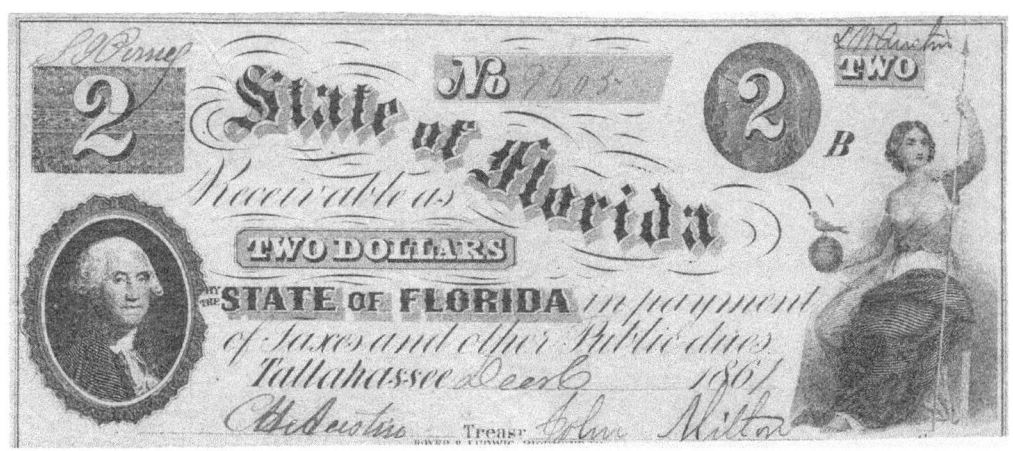

B. *(Shown above)* Signed for Milton and Countersigned R5
C. Signed by Perry R6

6. Without "Two" spelled out in upper right corner (Cr. 8A)
A. Signed by Milton R5

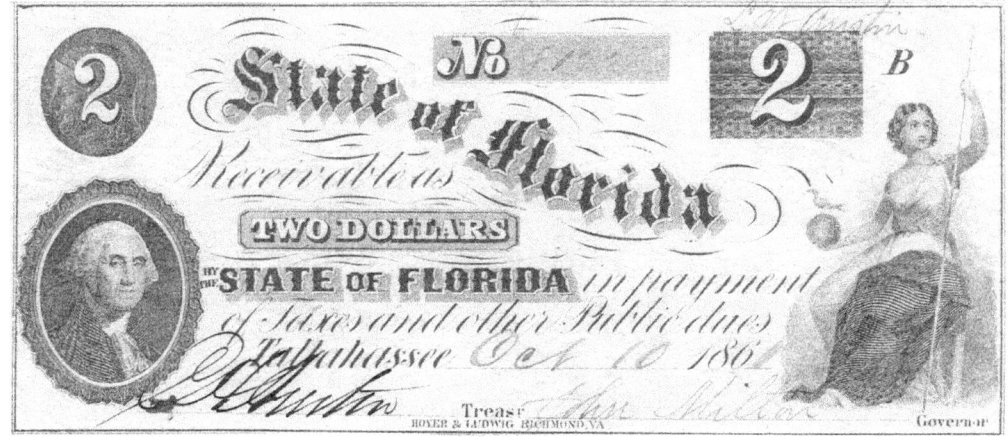

B. *(Shown above)* Signed for Milton and Countersigned R3

$3: 4454 notes ($13,362) with Plate letter C

7. "THREE" spelled out in upper right corner (Cr. 7)
A. Signed by Milton R5/6
B. Signed for Milton and countersigned R4

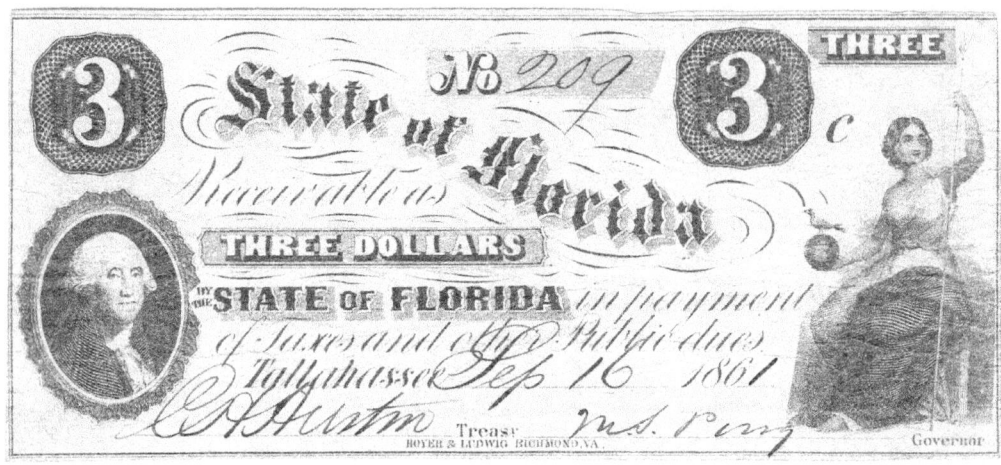

C. Signed by Perry R6

8. Without "Three" spelled out in upper right corner (Cr. 7A)
 A. Signed by Milton R5

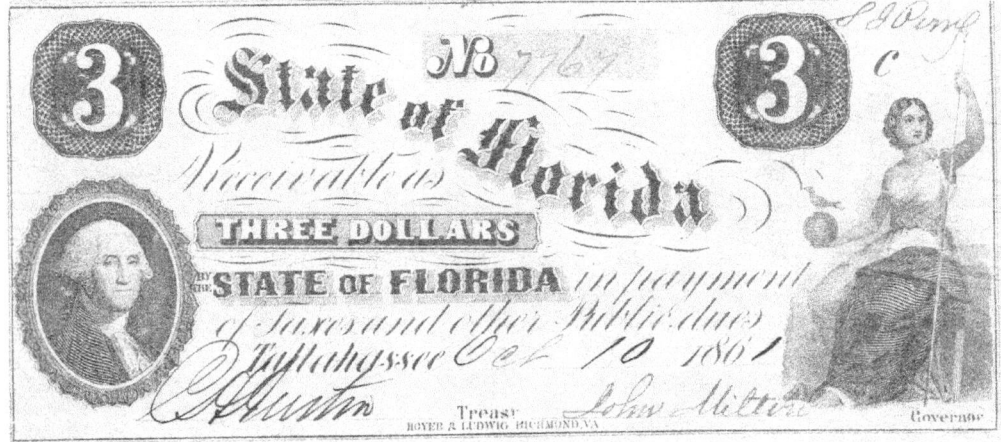

 B. *(Shown above)* Signed for Milton and countersigned R3

The countersigned "B" varieties are the most common. Most of these are dated December 6, 1861, because Resolution 21, providing for five alternate signers in the presence of the Governor, passed the House and Senate on December 5, 1861. Some notes signed by these alternate signers had apparently been dated earlier. The earlier-dated A and C varieties are generally not found above Fine condition.

The notes with the denomination spelled out were printed from different plates from those without the spelled-out denomination, and not from reworked versions of the same plates. The most notable other differences in the plates are in the positioning of the words "BY THE" and the curved calligraphic ornament near the bird in the vignette.

Second Printings (Engraved date October 10, 1861)

A total of $174,880 higher denomination notes were issued between November 1, 1861, and November 1, 1862. This completed the $500,000 issue authorized by the legislature on February 14, 1861. However, on December 11, 1862, the Treasurer reported that he had an additional $340,000 in blank 1861-dated notes from this issue which could be issued to aid families of soldiers in accordance with Chapter 1337 passed on December 6, 1862. These were issued in 1863.

A breakdown by denomination is not available. It cannot usually be determined which 1861-dated notes were issued in 1861–1862 and which were issued in 1863, except for those actually signed by Milton or Perry in 1861. It is not clear that the numbering of each denomination began with 1 nor is it clear whether there were any gaps or overlaps when the 1863 release of 1861-dated notes was numbered.

All five higher denominations use the same design loosely modeled after the Hawes $20 essay.

9. $5, Ceres. Plate letter D (Cr. 6)
 A. Signed by Milton R7

 B. *(Shown above)* Signed for Milton and countersigned R3

10. $10, Plate letter E (Cr. 5)
 A. Signed by Milton R7

B. *(Shown above)* Signed for Milton and countersigned R3

11. $20, Plate letter F (Cr. 4)
    A. Signed by Milton R7

B. *(Shown above)* Signed for Milton and countersigned R3

3. Civil War Currency

12. $50 "50" top left, Plate letter G (Cr. 3B)
    A. *(Shown above)* Signed by Milton R5
    B. Signed for Milton and countersigned R4

13. $50 "L" top left, Plate letter G (Cr. 3)
    A. Signed by Milton R4

B. *(Shown above)* Signed for Milton and countersigned R3

14. $50 "L" top left, "Fifty" under "Florida" inverted, Plate letter G (Cr. 3A)
    A. Signed by Milton R5

B. *(Shown above)* Signed for Milton and countersigned R4

15. $100, Plate letter H (Cr. 2)
   A. *(Shown above)* Signed by Milton R4
   B. Signed for Milton and countersigned R3

No $500 notes were included in the 1861 legislation nor were any mentioned in detailed reports by the treasurer and comptroller. A survey of auction catalogs, dealers, and collectors including Grover Criswell found no one who had ever seen such a note. I conclude that no 1861 $500 notes (Cr. 1) were printed.

1862 Dated Issues

$500,000 Authorized
$233,000 issued in 1862; $159,605 issued in 1863

Chapter 1279, "An Act to Provide for the Payment of the War Tax" was signed by the Governor on December 16, 1861. It authorized the issue of notes, not to exceed $500,000, of denominations not less than five nor more than one hundred dollars. Unlike the previous issue that the Governor was too busy to sign, these were to be signed by the Comptroller and Treasurer. The obligation printed on the notes was changed to "will pay to bearer on demand." These notes would be used to pay a tax levied on Florida by the Confederate States of America. Hoyer and Ludwig of Richmond prepared a new design which was used for all denominations in this issue. Walter Gwynn, who assumed the position when Robert C. Williams went off to war early in 1862, signed as Controller.

16. **$5, Slaves, Prosperity, Commerce & Navigation
    engraved date January 1, 1862 (Cr. 14)** R3
    7000 notes A1–7000 issued in 1862
    3025 notes A7001–10025 issued in 1863

17. **$10, engraved date January 1, 1862**
    4600 notes E1–4600 issued in 1862
    18 notes E4601–4618 issued in 1863
    A. *(Shown above)* **Plain E plate letter (Cr. 13)** R4

B. *(Shown above)* Fancy E plate letter (Cr. 13A) R3

Comptroller Walter Gwynn

18. **$20, engraved date January 1, 1862**
   2600 notes F1–2600 issued in 1862
   15 notes F2601–2615 issued in 1863
 A. *(Shown above)* Plain F plate letter (Cr. 12) R5

B. *(Shown above)* Fancy F plate letter (Cr. 12A) R3

19. $50, engraved date January 1, 1862 (Cr. 11) R4
    2000 notes G1–2000 issued in 1862
    440 notes G2001–2440 issued in 1863

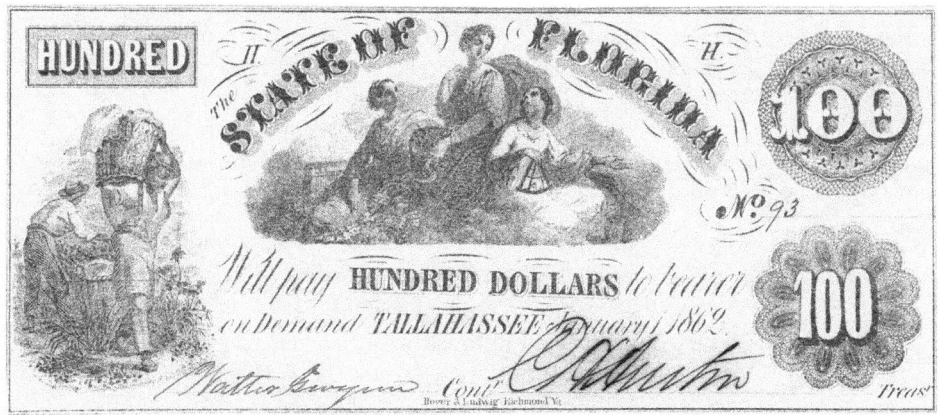

20. $100, engraved date January 1, 1862
    1220 notes H1–1220 issued in 1863
    A. *(Shown above)* Plain H plate letter (Cr. 10) R4

B. *(Shown above)* Horizontal bar missing in plate letter H (Cr. 10A) R5

The total value of notes issued under this act was only $392,605. This included $159,605 released in 1863 under the December 6, 1862, act to aid families of soldiers. As the Governor said in a November 16, 1863, speech, "the amount authorized to be issued for the purposes of the government far exceeded the necessities of the state."

1863 Dated Issues

Chapter 1372, enacted on December 13, 1862, called for the issue of $300,000 in Treasury Notes with signatures of the Governor and Treasurer as on the 1861 notes. It specified the eight denominations and quantities shown below, plus $25,000 in $20s, $25,000 in $50s and $50,000 in $100s that were never issued.

However, on November 16, 1863, the Governor reported to the legislature:

> It was early discovered that there were too many large bills in circulation, and that there was a great demand for notes of a small denomination, particularly for fractional parts of a dollar. No blanks have been prepared for the twenty, fifty and one hundred dollar bills authorized.... In lieu, therefore, of the blanks for $50,000 in bills of the denomination of one hundred dollars, I had that amount of blanks in fractional parts of a dollar engraved, but ... they were not prepared and issued. It is for your honorable body to determine whether they shall be used or not.

Chapter 1398, which became law on November 30, 1863, amended the previous act to substitute $50,000 of fractionals for hundred dollar bills.

Fractional Issues, Engraved date February 2, 1863
$50,000 authorized 12/13/62 and issued in 1863
$50,000 authorized 11/30/63; $51,084 issued in 1864
No Engraver's Imprint

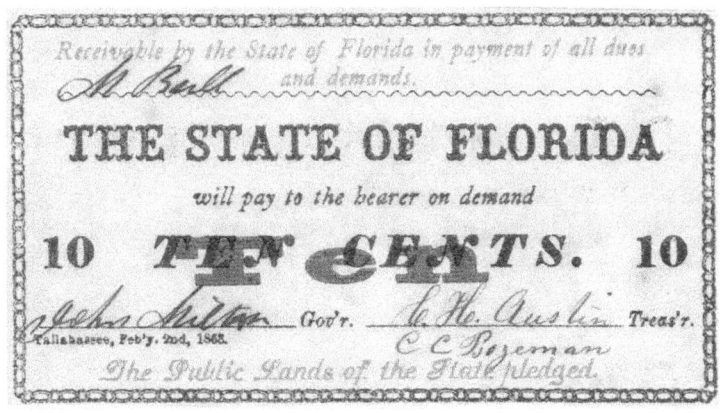

21. 10¢, two signature spaces — governor and treasurer — plain paper (Cr. 28) . R2

22. 10¢, one signature space — for treasurer R2
    A. Plain back, no watermark (Cr. 30) R3
    B. Plain back, watermarked paper (Cr. 31A) R7

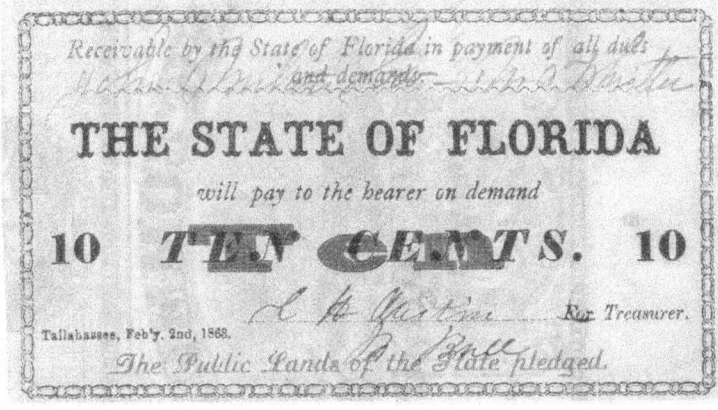

C. *(Shown above, face [TOP] and back)* Portion of unissued Florida note on back (Cr. 30A) R3
D. Portion of unissued Florida bond on back (Cr. 30B) R3
E. Error — red overprint on back instead of face R8

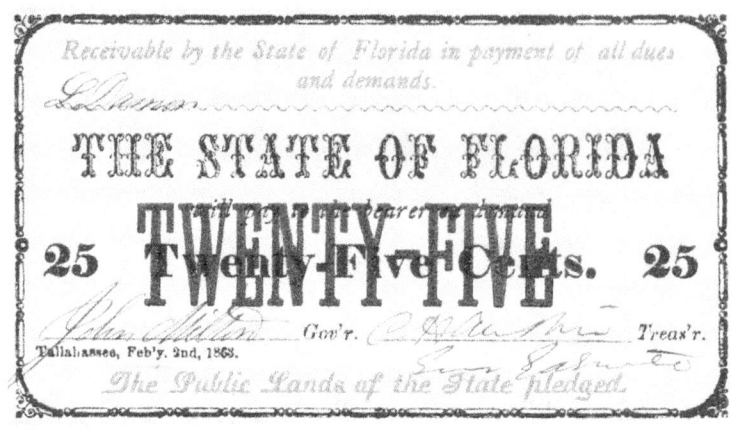

23. 25¢, two signature spaces (Cr. 24) R2

24. 25¢, one signature space R2
   A. Plain back, no watermark (Cr. 26) R3
   B. Plain back, watermarked paper (Cr. 27, 27A) .... not confirmed
   C. Note back (Cr. 26A) R3

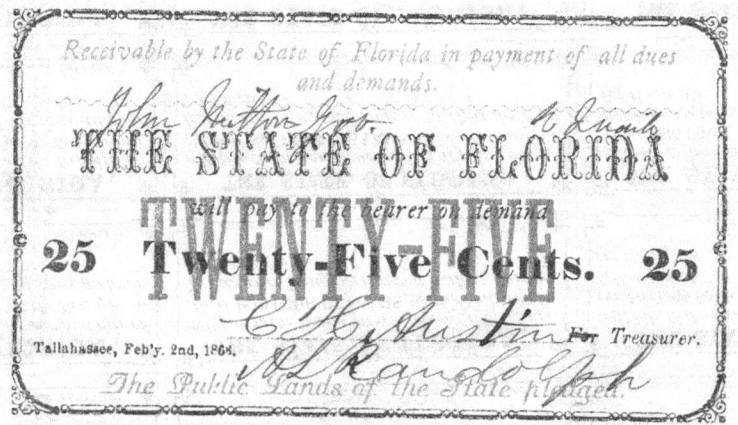

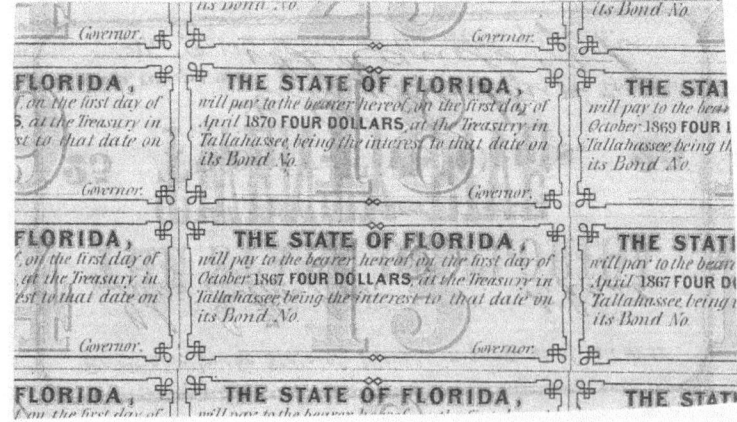

D. *(Shown above, face [TOP] and back)* Bond back (Cr. 26B) R3

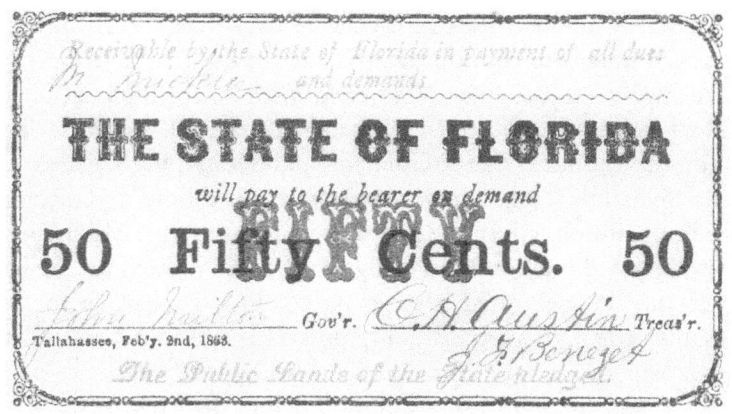

25. 50¢, two signature spaces (Cr. 20) R2
26. 50¢, one signature space R2

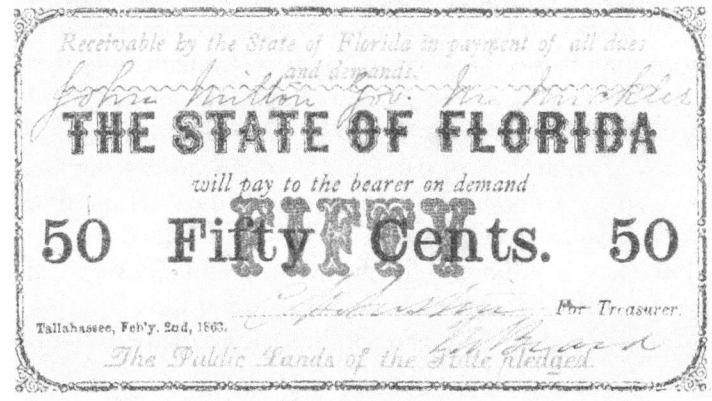

A. *(Shown above)* Plain back, no watermark (Cr. 22) R3
B. Plain back, watermarked paper (Cr. 23, 23A) .... not confirmed
C. Note back (Cr. 22A) R3
D. Bond back (Cr. 22B) R3

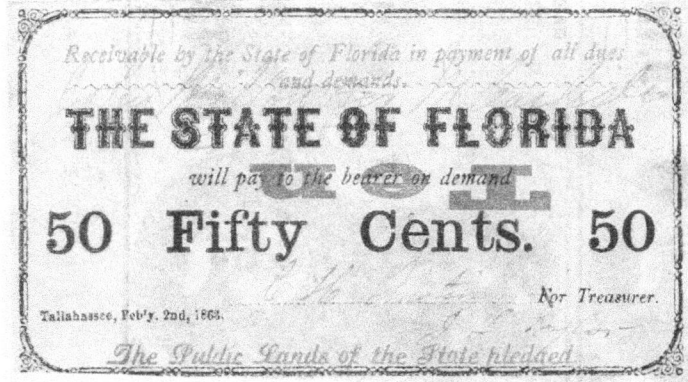

E. Note back, inverted overprint "Ten" R8

I believe Criswell numbers 20A, 20B, 21, 24A, 24B, 25, 28A, 28B and 29 never existed; I have been unable to confirm the existence of 23, 23A, 27, 27A, 31 and 31B.

I believe the two-signature-line notes were printed for the 1863 release in accordance with the enabling legislation (Chapter 1372), and that the one-signature-line notes were from the unauthorized printing by the Governor and released in 1864 after being authorized by Chapter 1398. The single signature was more expeditious and distinguished these notes from the first printing. Given the increasing paper shortage, this hypothesis is reinforced by the widespread presence of one-signature notes printed on the backs of other notes or bonds, and the lack of such recycling of older fiscal paper for two-signature notes. Indeed, this issue marks a transition point. The 1861, 1862, and early 1863 issues were all on plain paper. The late 1863 and 1864 issues were mostly on paper produced for other purposes, and the 1865 issues were printed on the backs of 1864 issues.

The watermarked notes are rare. The nature of the watermarks is not completely resolved. Bradbeer listed the watermarks as "W. T. & Co.," the same as the common watermarks on the 1864 issues. I believe that Bradbeer made an unwarranted assumption — at most one letter or two partial letters of the 1864 "W.T. & Co." watermark would fit on these small notes. No such notes have been seen by any of the collectors or dealers I surveyed, nor have there been any appearances in auctions. Similarly, I cannot confirm the existence of any notes watermarked "FIVE" as listed in Criswell. On the positive side, I have seen 10¢ notes watermarked "TEN." These have also appeared in auctions and collector inventories. However, I cannot confirm the existence of any 25¢ or 50¢ notes watermarked "TEN."

On some notes, incorrect or defective type was used; the date appears as 1866 or 1868.

Dollar Issues, Engraved date March 1, 1863
$150,000 was authorized for the five denominations printed
$114,635 issued in 1863; balance in 1864
$100,000 authorized for $20, $50 and $100 denominations not printed

Engraved by Keatinge and Ball, Columbia S.C.
All have plate letter J and denominations overprinted in red
Signed by Governor and Treasurer

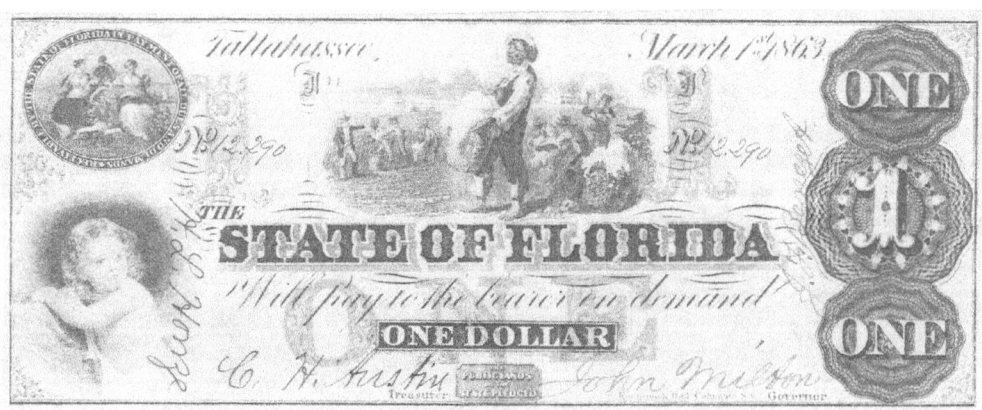

27. $1 Rev. L. Elwyn as a child, slaves (Cr. 19)
30,000 notes authorized. Approximately 24,000 issued R3

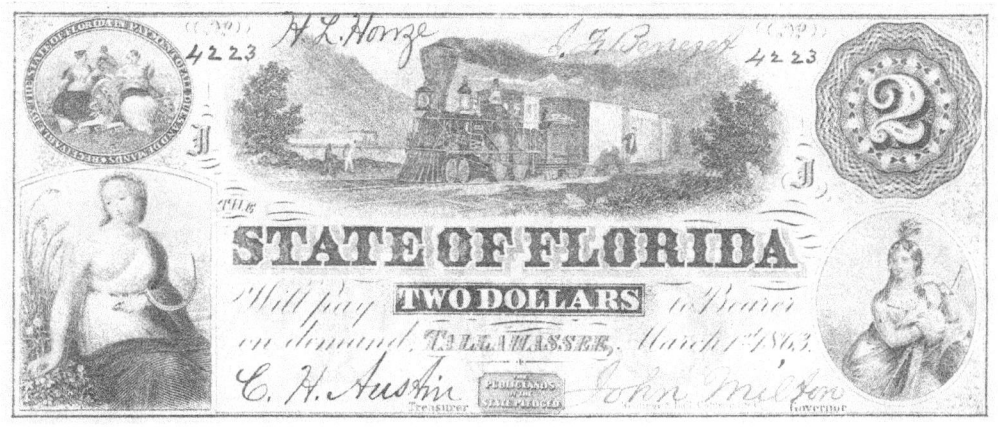

28. $2 Ceres, train, Indian maiden (Cr. 18)
 15,000 notes authorized. Approximately 12,600 issued R3

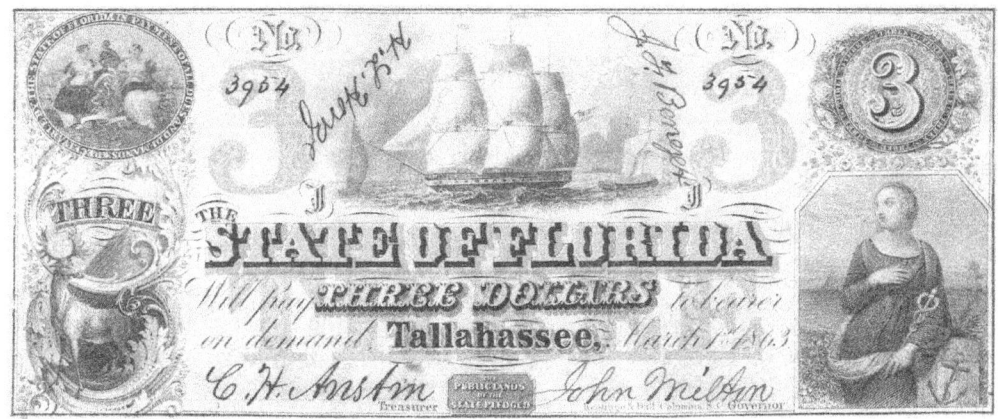

29. $3 Elk, ship, St. Catherine of Alexandria (Cr. 17)
 10,000 notes authorized. Approximately 12,600 issued R3

30. $5 Indian, Moneta (Cr. 16)
 6,000 notes authorized. Approximately 4,200 issued R3

31. $10 Ship, Ceres, Slave (Cr. 15)
  3,000 notes authorized. Approximately 4,200 issued R4

1864 Dated Issues

$300,000 authorized December 3, 1863 and issued in 1864
Engraved by Keatinge and Ball, Columbia, S.C.

Chapter 1420, enacted December 3, 1863, authorized the issue of $300,000 in treasury notes to help fund a $500,000 appropriation for relief of families of soldiers. Denominations were not specified in the legislation nor in the Comptroller and Treasurer reports that confirmed that all were issued. Designs are the same as March 1, 1863, issues. Notes were signed by the Governor and Treasurer. All bear plate letter J.

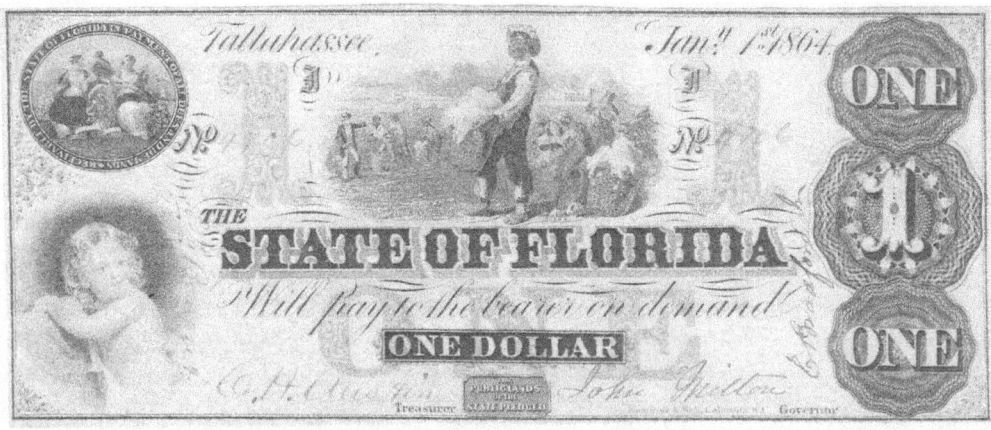

32. $1 dated January 1, 1864 .... R3
  A. Watermarked W. T. & Co. (Cr. 41) R3
  B. Plain paper (Cr. 40) R7

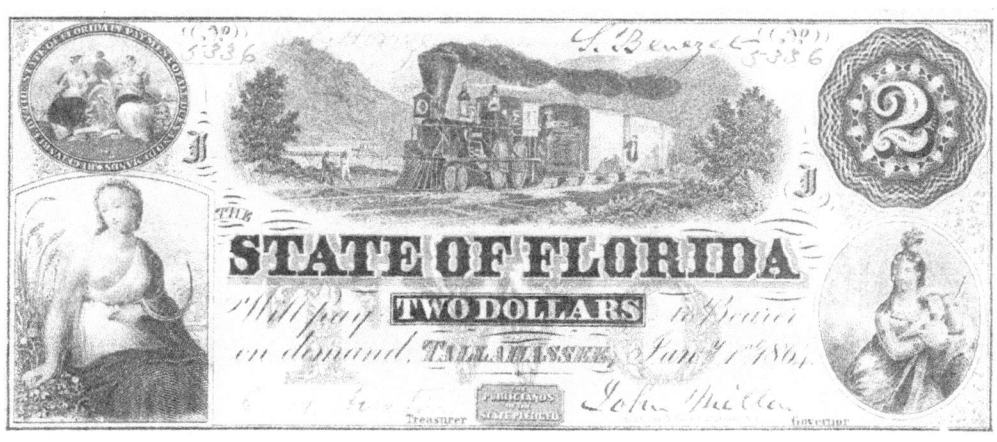

33. $2 dated January 1, 1864 .... R3
  A. Watermarked W. T. & Co. (Cr. 39) R3
  B. Plain paper (Cr. 38) R7

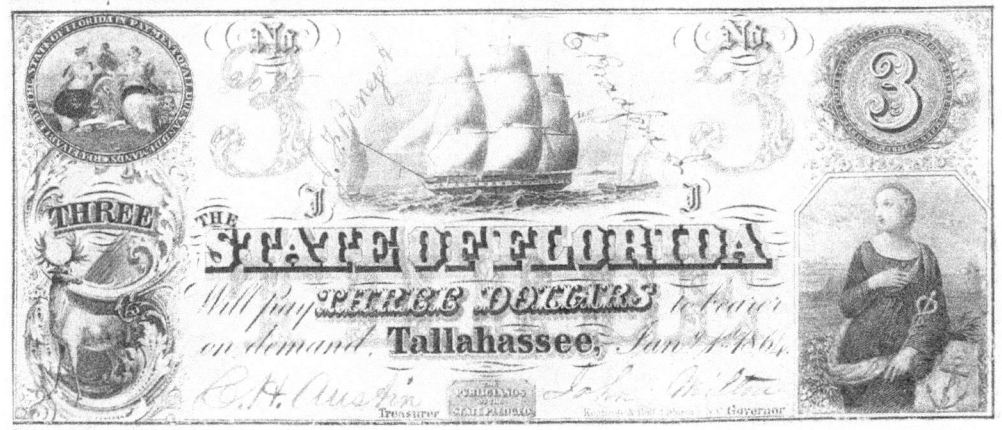

34. $3 dated January 1, 1864 .... R3
  A. Watermarked W. T. & Co. (Cr. 37) R3
  B. Plain paper (Cr. 36) R7

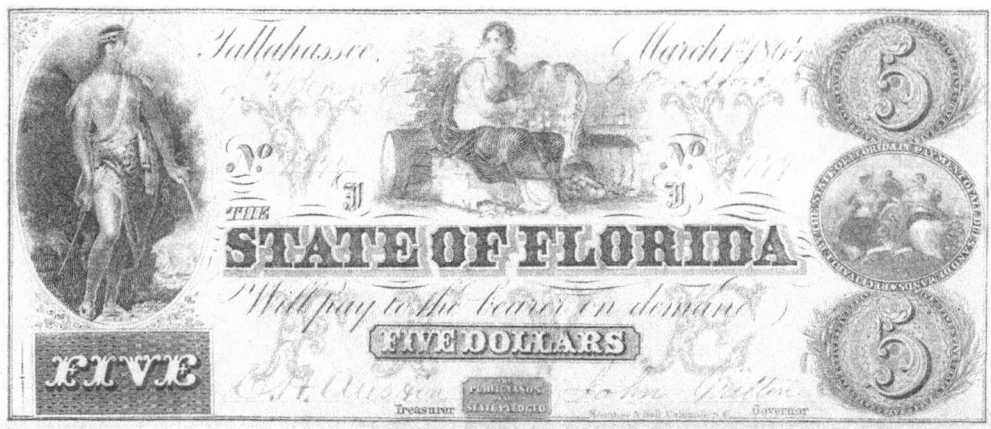

35. $5 dated March 1, 1864 .... R3
  A. Watermarked W. T. & Co. (Cr. 35) R4
  B. Plain paper (Cr. 34) R4

36. $10 dated March 1, 1864 .... R3
  A. Watermarked W. T. & Co. (Cr. 33) R4
  B. Plain paper (Cr. 32) R4

According to Dr. Douglas Ball, W.T. & Co. is Wiggins, Teape & Co. of London, a firm that supplied paper to the Confederacy, also. This watermark didn't always span all notes on a sheet.

1865 Dated Issues

Chapter 1463, passed December 7, 1864, authorized an issue of $350,000 in Treasury notes "to meet the wants of the government." Denomination selections were left to the Governor. All notes are dated January 1, 1865, and have no printer's imprint. Notes were printed on the backs of 1864 Florida state notes, with spaces for the signatures of the Governor and Treasurer. All have plate letter K in Gothic type similar to Cloister Black and Hanover Bold type fonts.

3. Civil War Currency

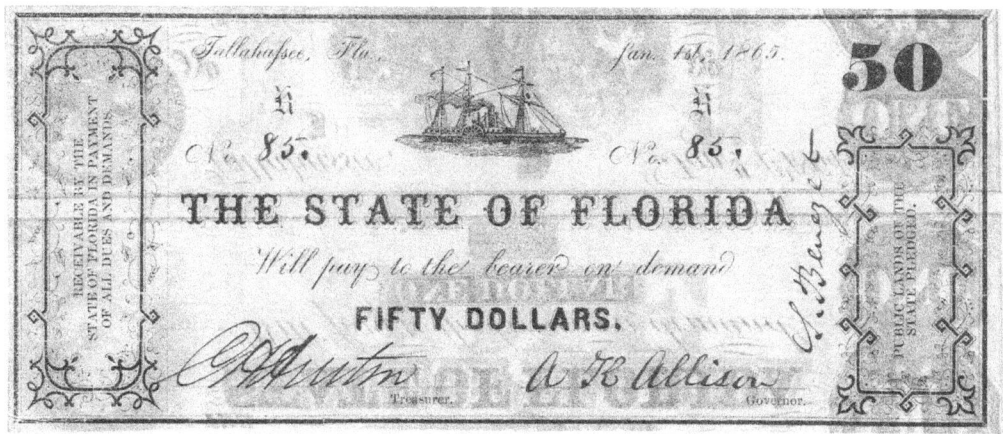

37. $50 Ship (Cr. 42) $40,000 (800 notes) printed R6

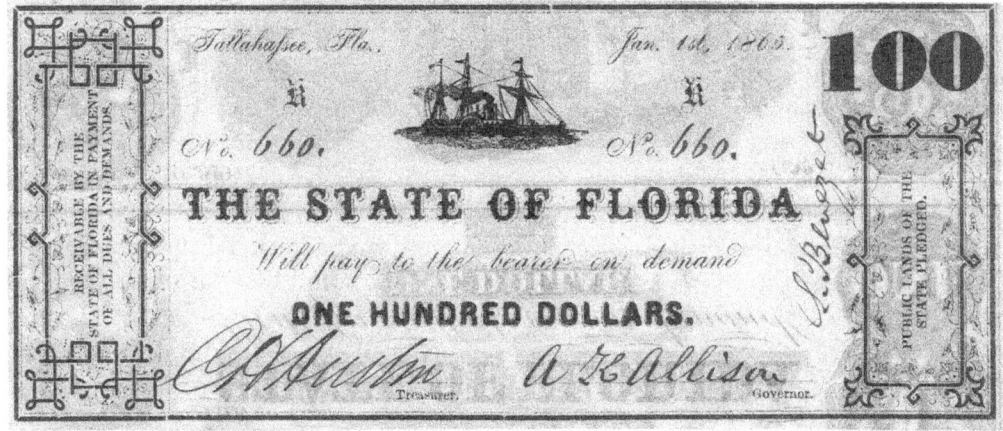

38. $100 (Cr. 43) $120,000 (1200 notes) printed R5

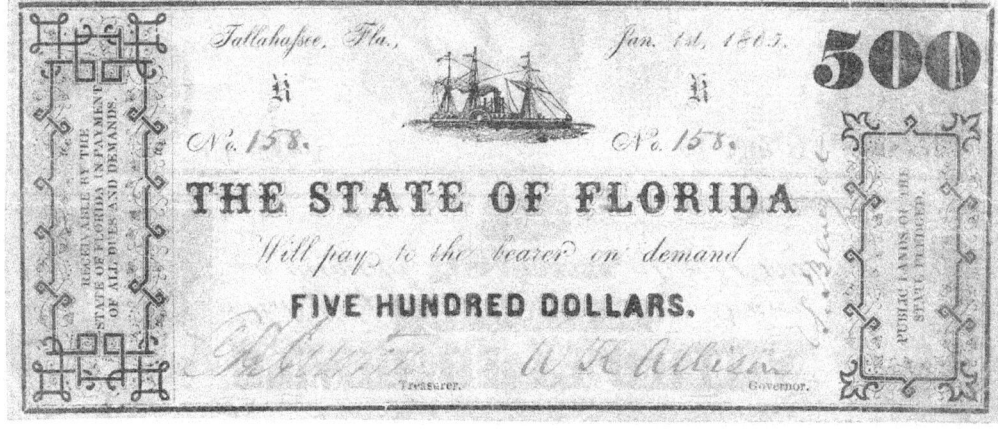

39. $500 (Cr. 44) $190,000 (380 notes) printed R7

Left: Governor Abraham K. Allison. *Right:* Charles H. Austin, Treasurer on all notes.

Although these notes were printed and sent to Governor Milton in January 1865, all surviving copies were signed for Abraham K. Allison who became Governor on April 1, 1865. Since the Allison notes bear low serial numbers, it is unlikely that Milton signed any 1865 notes. Analysis of serial numbers indicates approximately half of those printed were actually issued. There is evidence of an additional unauthorized printing of $363,500 of $50s in April 1865, but no evidence that any of these were signed nor issued.

Although the Civil War and the Confederacy itself officially ended with General Robert E. Lee's surrender at Appomattox Court House on April 9, 1865, it is possible some of these notes were signed later. Union troops did not reach Tallahassee, the only Confederate States capital never captured during the war, until May 10, 1865.

4
Florida Currency During Reconstruction

Florida was in financial ruin after the Civil War and resorted to several issues of circulating scrip to pay its employees and creditors. Most of this scrip had not been described in numismatic literature prior to my article in the January/February 1999 issue of *Paper Money*. An extensive search of archival and legislative records and contemporary writings yielded considerable information about this little-known currency.

INTERIM CURRENCY 1865–1870

Florida fell under military rule when the war ended in 1865. Specie had long since vanished. Both Florida's wartime currency and Confederate currency had become worthless in the marketplace, and ultimately irredeemable by passage of the 14th Amendment to the U.S. Constitution which barred redemption of any obligation incurred in aid of the Southern rebellion. Most residents were destitute. The state had no money to pay anybody for anything. And rampant corruption was on the way.

In the absence of "real money," a system of Comptroller's warrants and Treasury certificates provided some circulating scrip. This system was conceptually simple. The Comptroller would receive requests for payment for services or goods provided to the state, verify them and issue a warrant, directing the Treasurer to pay the claimant and indicating which account to debit. Before the war, the Treasurer would redeem the warrant or any bank would cash it. After the war, the Treasurer had no specie and would merely exchange warrants for Treasury certificates. The warrants and certificates circulated, but generally below face value. They had value as speculative IOUs of Florida and could be used to pay taxes. In some instances they could be used to purchase government land or bonds.

Over the years, there were many printings of Comptroller's warrants that varied in size, style and format. Some were printed on blue paper and were known as "blue scrip." Large, elaborately engraved treasury certificates evolved to smaller certificates preprinted in denominations of $25, $50, and $100 plus blank certificates enabling other amounts.

A Comptroller's Warrant for $30 issued in 1868 signed by Comptroller R. H. Gamble and countersigned vertically by Governor Harrison Reed as required by an 1868 law. The counterstamp shows it was redeemed in 1870 (for a new scrip issue).

Fifty dollar treasury certificate with engraved issue date of 1869 in text and 1870 cancellation stamp.

1870 Currency Issue

The large, high denomination certificates did not meet the needs of the citizens for currency for daily commerce. Accordingly, Chapter 1737 of the Laws of Florida, approved

February 18, 1870, provided for an issue of paper money called Comptroller's Warrants to replace all circulating Comptroller's Warrants and Treasury Certificates issued since the end of the Civil War. It prohibited the Comptroller and Treasurer from issuing any more of the previous forms except for paying salary and expenses of the current legislature.

The amount of currency to be issued was dependent on the amount of outstanding paper to be redeemed, subject to a maximum: "Comptroller shall have engraven without delay warrants ... equal in amount to the whole amount of comptroller's warrants and treasury certificates which have been issued ... within five years next preceding the passage of this act and which are now outstanding.... Provided however, that the whole amount of warrants so engraved shall not exceed two hundred and fifty thousand dollars."

The appearance and denominations were specified: "The said warrants shall be engraved in a neat and careful manner and shall consist of the following denominations: ones, threes, fives and twenties in equal proportions."

"The said warrants shall read upon their face as follows: 'State of Florida, Comptroller's Office, March 1st 1870. To the Treasurer of the State of Florida: Pay to the bearer the sum of ___ dollars, due for outstanding State indebtedness, in accordance with an act approved February 18, 1870' and shall be signed by the Comptroller and countersigned by the Governor. Upon the reverse shall be engraved the following words: 'This warrant is receivable by the State of Florida, or by any officer or agent thereof, for State taxes, for public lands sold by the Trustees of the Internal Improvement Fund, or by any other officer or agent of the State, and for all other State dues, and for any fines or penalties imposed.'"

Additionally the law required the Comptroller to give public notice to all holders that they should bring their notes in for exchange. It also required a register of redemptions and notes issued. The 1870 stamps on the certificate illustrated above show that they were redeemed under this new law for the new notes.

An editorial in *The Weekly Floridian* published in Tallahassee on March 1, 1870, referring to the pre–1870 scrip as consisting of high denominations on oversize paper observed: "The new warrants are to be of such small denominations and of such shape as to render them more convenient as a circulating medium, easily used in everyday transactions."

The Comptroller, Robert H. Gamble, sought proposals to produce the new currency. The proposal from National Bank Note Company was accepted. Because the expense of engraving the plates was the major part of the cost, Gamble decided to print the full $250,000 authorized even though it was not needed immediately. The notes were produced, and $187,845 of them were shipped to the Comptroller along with an invoice for $4,376. Since there was no money in the Treasury to pay the bill, a Comptroller's warrant for the amount was issued on September 21, 1870. The printer refused to accept the warrant as payment and refused to send the remaining notes.

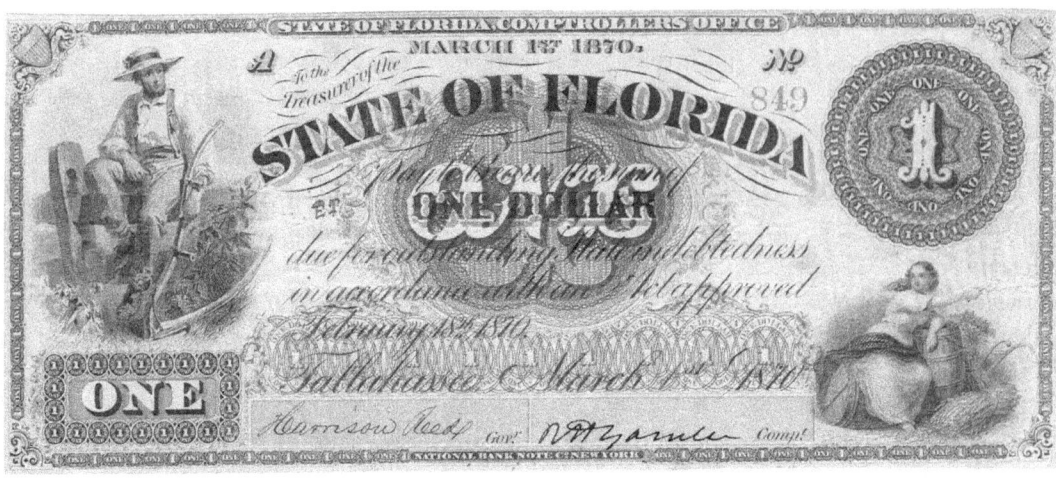

40. $1 (Cr. 45) R6
40A. Signed by R. H. Gamble, Comptroller R7

Back of $1 note of the 1870 issue with engraved signature of Governor Harrison Reed and handwritten signature of Comptroller R. H. Gamble. Similarities with back designs on U.S. notes of the 1860s produced by the National Bank Note Company are evident.

40B. Signed by Clayton A. Cowgill, Comptroller R7

Note from the group withheld by National Banknote Company for nonpayment. It was signed in late 1873 or 1874 by Clayton Cowgill, who became comptroller on January 15, 1873. Although Harrison Reed's term as governor ended on January 7, 1873, his engraved signature appears on these previously printed notes.

Of the $187,845 in notes available, $150,557 were issued and $22 were destroyed as defective in 1870. An additional $31,175 were issued in 1871; the remaining $6,091 in 1872.

The National Bank Note Company went unpaid and the remaining notes undelivered until the new comptroller, Clayton A. Cowgill convinced the legislature to approve Chapter 1958 of the Laws of Florida on February 20, 1873, "An act authorizing the Comptroller to settle with the National Bank Note Company and to authorize the Comptroller to sign the greenback scrip." Negotiations over interest and discounts ensued, and the debt was settled for $4,780.57 on October 1, 1873. Unsigned notes amounting to $83,004 were received from NBN Co. Cowgill signed $62,177, which brought the total issued up to the $250,000 authorized. Of these, $22,874 were released in 1873 and $39,303 in 1874.

There remained unsigned $20,827, all in one dollar notes, serials A, B, C 13893-20834 plus A13892, for which the Comptroller requested authorization to sign and issue. The legislature did not authorize their release. Serial numbers on $1s imply $62,502 printed which is one fourth of the $250,000 authorized. Assuming a standard four-note sheet and the legislative requirement for "equal proportions," there were $62,502 in $3 bills with serial numbers D1 through D20834. Similarly, if the higher denomination sheet format was 5-5-5-

Governor Harrison Reed

20, then 4,167 sheets would yield $62,505 in $5 bills and $83,340 in $20 bills for a total printing $21,081 above the $250,000 authorized. A modest allowance for destruction of defective notes beyond the $22 reported for 1870 suggests the $20,827 left over in 1874. The $5 bills had serial numbers 1-4167 with plate letters either A, B and C or E, F and G while the $20 bills had serial numbers 1-4167 with plate letter D or H. I am unaware of any surviving examples of the $3, $5, or $20 denominations.

REDEMPTION AND DESTRUCTION OF NOTES

R. H. Gamble delivered his Comptroller's Report to the Governor and General Assembly on January 2, 1871. He began by quoting from his previous year's report, "the finances of the State are in very unsatisfactory condition. There is no money in the Treasury and the scrip is far below par." He then added, "I consider our financial condition now as even worse than at the end of the last fiscal year." He went on to state that the paper issued under the February 18, 1870, Act did not provide relief and the value of state scrip had dropped to 40 cents on the dollar.

On January 26, 1871, the legislature authorized the issuance of $100, 30-year, 7% bonds equal to the amount of comptroller's warrants and treasurer's certificates currently outstanding, but not to exceed $350,000. The interest coupons could be used to pay state taxes. These bonds could be purchased using comptroller's warrants and treasury certificates at par. Since the warrants and certificates circulated below face value, there was an incentive to convert them to the more valuable bonds. The legislation required the warrants that were redeemed to be marked "cancelled" immediately.

An 1873 Act authorized $1 million of 8% 30-year bonds. Scrip was variously reported as selling in the range of 35 to 62 cents on the dollar, depending on type. A ring was formed to buy up scrip and convert it to bonds.

The legislative audit committee reported in January 1872 that the books of redemptions and cancelled notes were in order, and that they had destroyed the "large amount" of engraved warrants as well as the older comptroller and treasurer certificates that had been redeemed that year. The total destroyed was $1,175,935 including $101,319 of greenback scrip.

Subsequent audits indicated that the redemption and cancellation system was less than perfect. In 1872 a Senate committee reported that $30,000 in cancelled blue scrip was redeemed a second time. Government officials, including tax collectors, substituted cheaply obtained scrip for money they collected. An 1876 audit showed that some exchanges of the engraved 1870 scrip had not been recorded. Also, some warrants were issued and redeemed more than once.

In his January 1, 1877, report to the governor and legislature, Comptroller Cowgill sarcastically wrote about the 1872 audit: "Notwithstanding this report, it is apparent that all the warrants and certificates paid by Treasurer Conover were not found cancelled, and that all were not burned by the committee." Cowgill concluded that it was impossible to ascertain the exact amount of engraved 1870 Comptroller's warrants outstanding at the end of 1876. A sufficient number had been redeemed to account for the entire issue.

More information and examples of treasury certificates as well as biographies of the signers of the 1870 notes can be found in my article in the January/February 1999 issue of *Paper Money*.

5

Obsolete Notes and Scrip

ALAFIA

Fort Alafia, in eastern Hillsborough County, was built in 1849 near the Alafia River on the government road (originally a Seminole Trail) between Fort Brooke and Fort Meade. Antoine Wordehoff was one of four Prussian mercenary soldiers (out of 42) stationed there for the Seminole War. After the war, the 120-acre site was sold in 1854 to Thomas P. Kennedy. Wordehoff built a log cabin on the site, opened a general store and became the first postmaster of Alafia on September 4, 1855. The store became a stagecoach stop on the Tampa–Ft. Meade route. He purchased the 120 acres in 1859, and lived there until his death on November 22, 1887.

An historical marker on the east side of State Road 39, about a half-mile north of State Road 676, indicates the location. Nothing remains of the fort nor the house, which was torn down after Antoine's son Henry sold it in 1906. The post office was discontinued in 1920.

Antoine Wordehoff

Small, hand-signed scrip notes on low quality brown paper. Engraved date 1862. Handwritten dates in August. Payable in current bank bills.

1A. 10¢ train vignette heavy 10, large date R7
1B. 10¢ train vignette, heavy 10, small date R7

2. 10¢ two masted schooner, heavy 10 ....R7
3A. 25¢ small gunboat, solid 25 ....R7
3B. 25¢ small gunboat, shaded 25 ....R7
4. 25¢ horse and wagon, shaded 25 ....R7

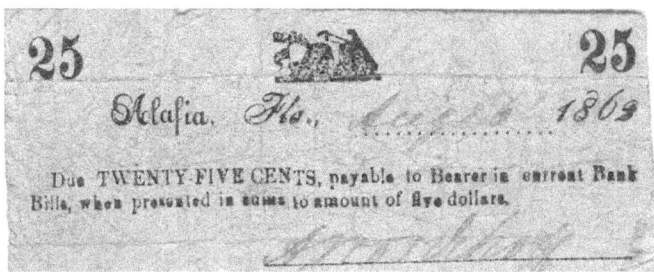

5. 25¢ two masted steamship, solid 25 ....R7
6. 25¢ three masted schooner, elongated 25 ....R7
7. 50¢ side wheeler, solid 50 ....R7
8. 50¢ three masted steamship, heavy 5, thin 0 ....R7
9. 75¢ two masted schooner, small 75 ....R7

Illustrations of other vignettes can be found under Bay Port, Brooksville, Hernando County, Manatee, Orange Springs and Tampa.

Apalachicola

In the 1830s Apalachicola was Florida's largest city. Strategically located on the Gulf of Mexico at the mouth of the Apalachicola River, it was the major shipping point for cotton and other agricultural products from the Florida Panhandle, and Georgia and Alabama which could send their products via the Chattahoochee and Flint Rivers into the Apalachicola.

Bank of West Florida

The Bank of West Florida was approved by the Territorial Legislature over the veto of Governor Duval on November 17, 1829. The bank was to be located in Marianna and capitalized at $100,000. On February 12, 1831, the Legislative Council approved an increase of the capital stock to $500,000 and authorized a branch location in Apalachicola. On February 12, 1832, the bank was authorized to move to Apalachicola and keep an agency in Marianna. On January 29, 1833, capital was increased to $1,000,000. The bank failed to issue financial reports in 1834 and was completely gone by 1837. However, on April 28, 1838, The *Niles Register* reported "The Bank of West Florida has been reorganized and is about to re-commence operations in Apalachicola. Old bills have been called in and will be paid off on sight." But *The Pensacola Gazette* reported on August 4, 1838, that

Bank of West Florida money was selling at five cents on the dollar. The bank's failure became final in 1842.

1832 Issue, Appalachicola spelled with double "PP," engraved by Rawdon, Wright, Hatch & Co., New York. Signed by Thomas Bertram and Martin Brooks.

1. $1 Commerce seated holding scales at dock R5

2. $3 Hebe pouring drink for eagle R5

3. $5 Justice with eagle, design same as number 12 ....R4
4. $10 Liberty seated with staff and liberty cap, design same as 13 ....R4

1832 Issue, Appalachicola spelled with double "PP," engraved by Draper Underwood Bald & Spencer. Signed by Thomas Bertram and Martin Brooks. (There is evidence these were printed in 1833 and backdated 1832.)

5. $10 Agriculture and Commerce R5

6. $20 Commerce with eagle R5

1833 Issue, Apalachicola spelled with single "P," engraved by Rawdon, Wright, Hatch & Co.

Signatures other than Bertram and Brooks are questionable.

7. $1 Hope with anchor, Providence, Ceres R6

8. $2 Archimedes, Washington, Hebe or Commerce R6

9. $3 Justice, cherub, Indian and sailor R6

1838 Issue, Apalachicola spelled with single "P," engraved by Rawdon, Wright, Hatch & Co. Signatures other than J.C. Wiggins, Cashier are highly questionable.
10. $1 Design same as 1 ....R7
11. $3 Design same as 2 ....R7

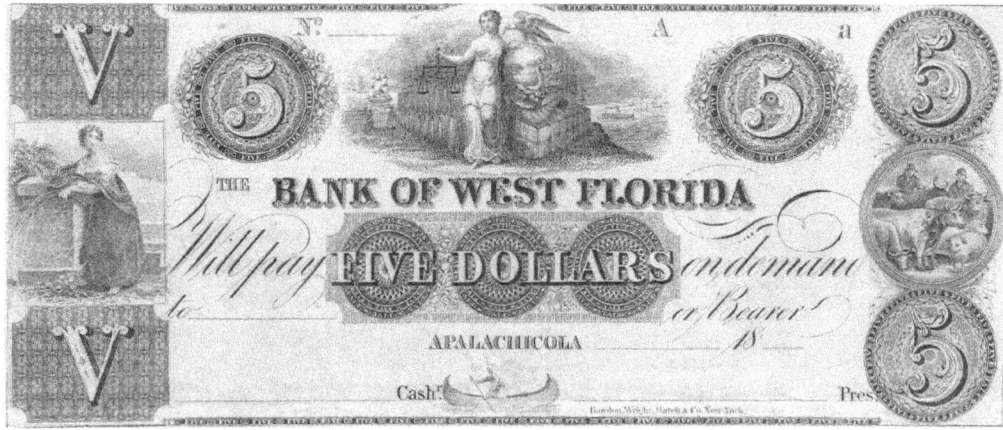

12. $5 Justice with eagle R7

13. $10 Washington, Liberty seated with staff and liberty cap R7

Commercial Bank of Florida

The Legislative Council of the Territory of Florida approved the incorporation of the Commercial Bank of Florida on February 7, 1833, over the governor's veto. Capitalization was $500,000. Banknotes up to $1,500,000 were authorized. In 1837 circulation was reported at $49,003 in regular notes and $33,255 in post notes. John C. Maclay was president from incorporation until June 4, 1837, when Hugh Stephenson bought control and became president. On June 20, 1837, Stephenson left town with the bank's assets. He was arrested, and the banknotes recovered. The August 4, 1838, *Pensacola Gazette* reported that a five dollar note was only good for three drinks. The bank also operated an unauthorized branch in St. Joseph that also issued notes.

Demand notes were engraved by Chas. Toppan & Co. Phila. Only the signatures of M. Clark or William Patrick, Cashier, and J. C. Maclay, President, are authentic.

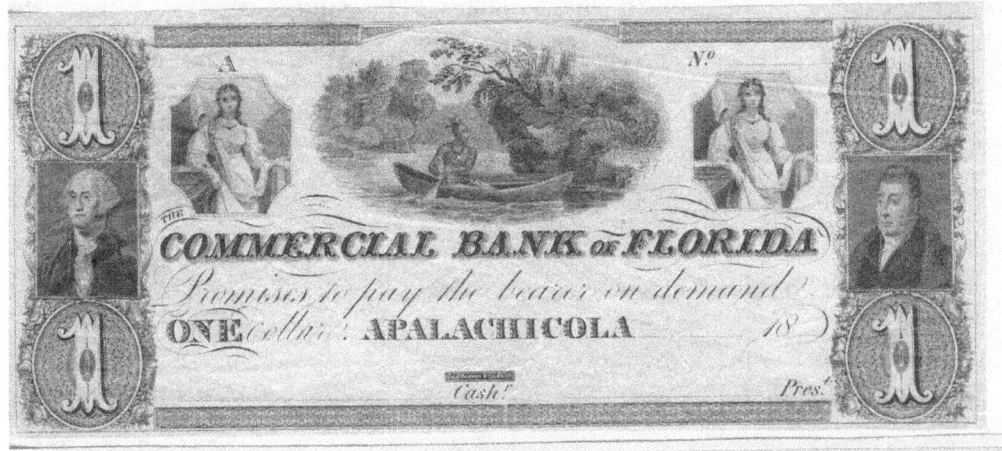

14. $1 Washington, Liberty, Indian in Canoe, Liberty, Lafayette R5

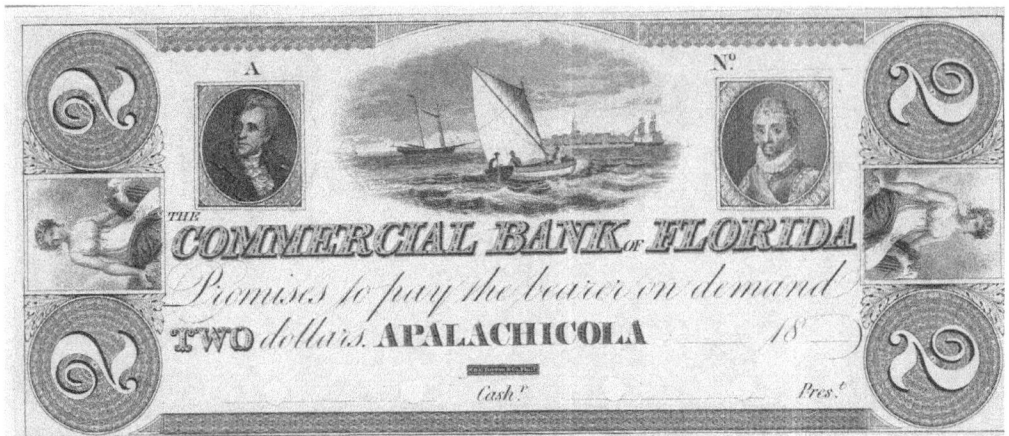

15. $2 Jackson, Sailboats, De Soto R6

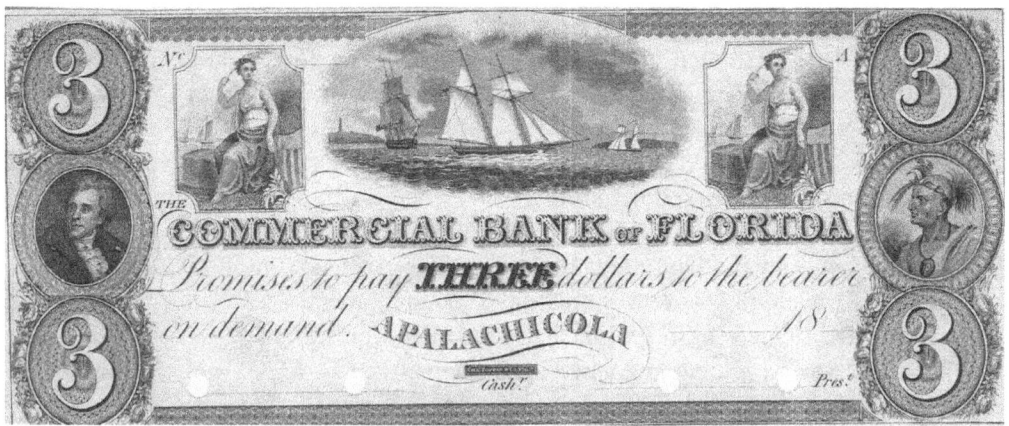

16. $3 Jackson, Commerce, Sailboats, Commerce, Tahcoloquiot R6

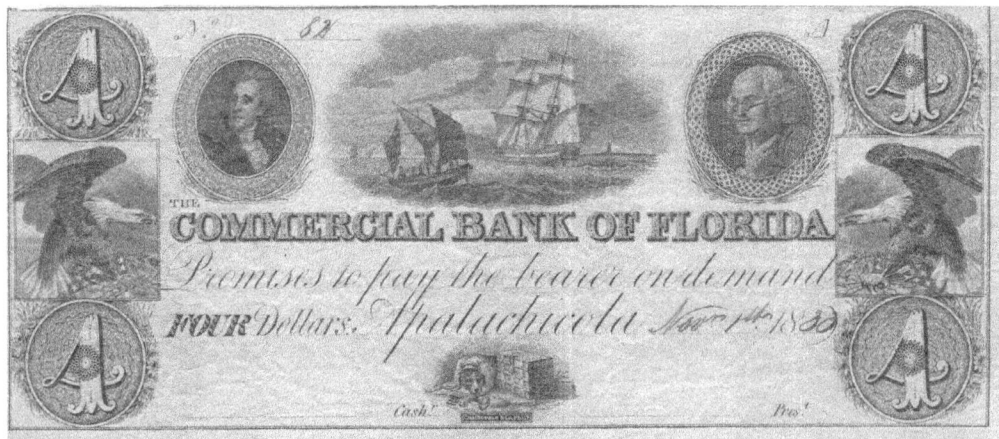

17. $4 Jackson, Sailboats, Franklin R6

5. Obsolete Notes and Scrip — Apalachicola

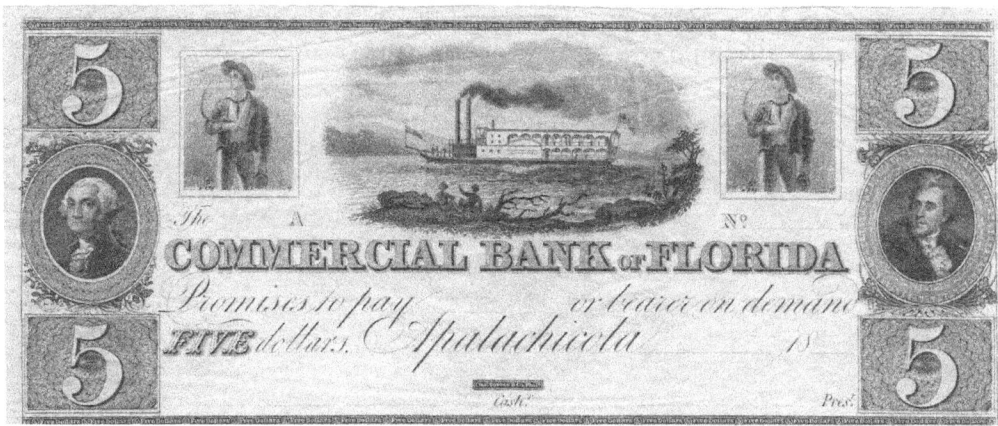

18. $5 Washington; boy with sickle, steamboat, boy; Jackson R5

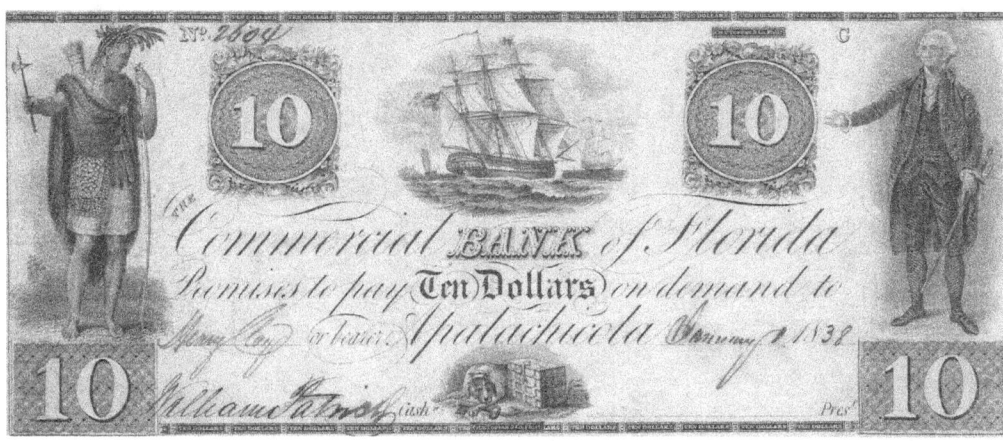

19. $10 Standing Indian, Sailboat, Standing Washington R5

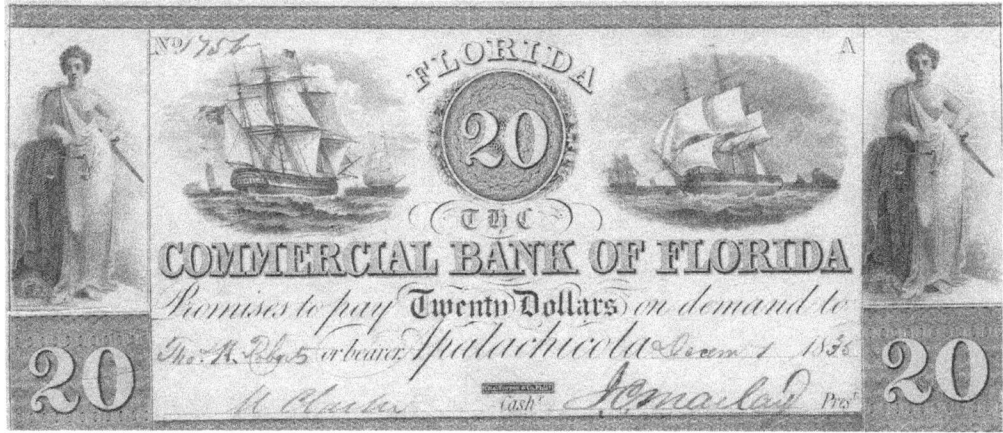

20. $20 Justice, Sailboat, Sailboat, Justice R5

Post notes engraved by Draper, Toppan, Longacre & Co. Phila. & NY. Date and place payable to be filled in by hand. Authentic signatures same as preceding issue.

21. $5 Washington, Marshall, Fulton, Franklin, Sailboats R6

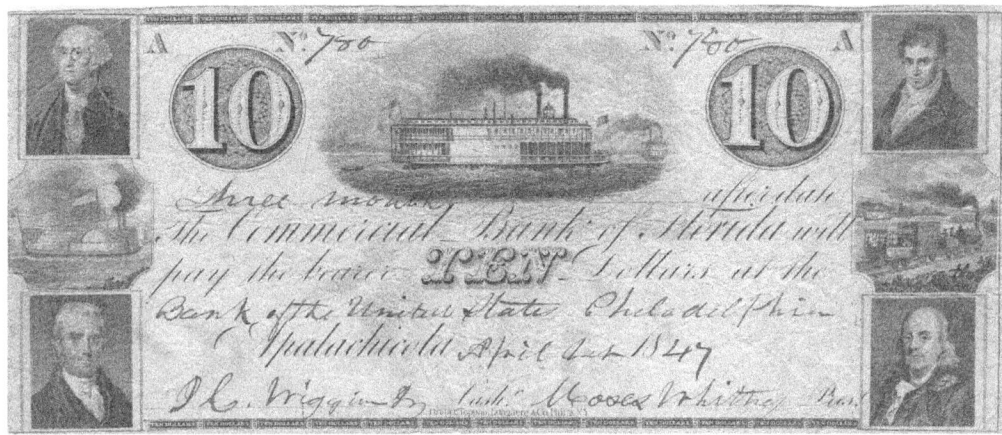

22. $10 same portraits, Steamboat R6

23. $20 same portraits, different sailboats R5

Post notes engraved by Rawdon, Wright & Hatch, New York. Date and place payable to be filled in by hand. Authentic signatures same as preceding issue.

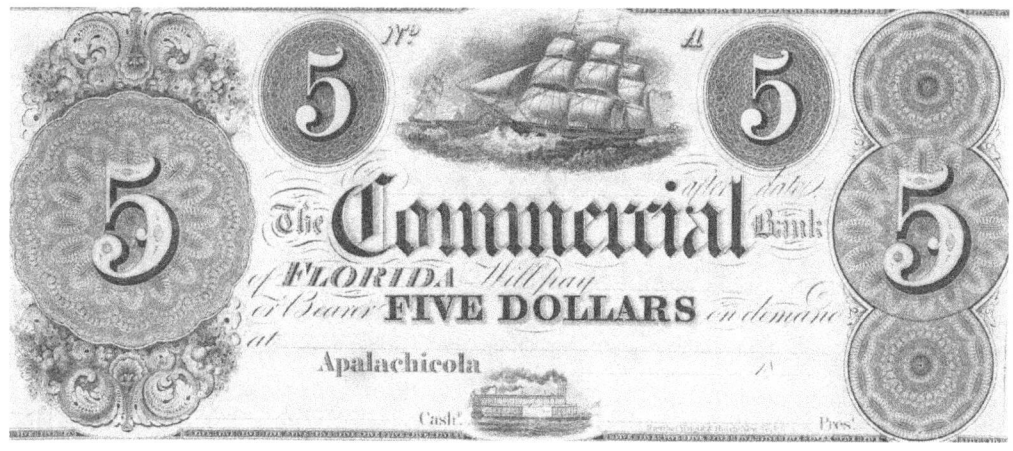

24. $5 Sailboat R6

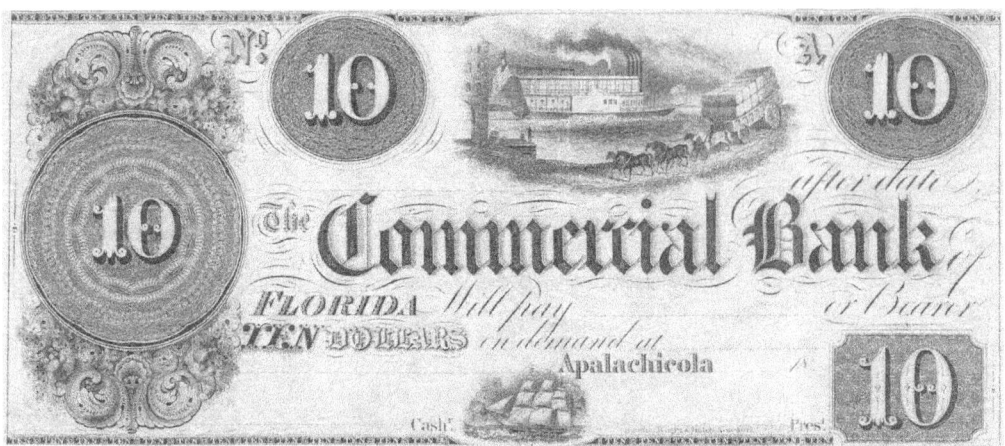

25. $10 Steamship and horse-drawn wagon R6

26. $20 Griffin, Providence and Mercury R7

Exchange & Banking Company of Apalachicola

Fictitious bank. Engraved by Durand & Compy. New York with December 20, 1841, date. Presumably created to fill the void left by the failure of Apalachicola's legal banks.

5. Obsolete Notes and Scrip — Apalachicola

27. $1 Hope, Ceres, Bull's head R5

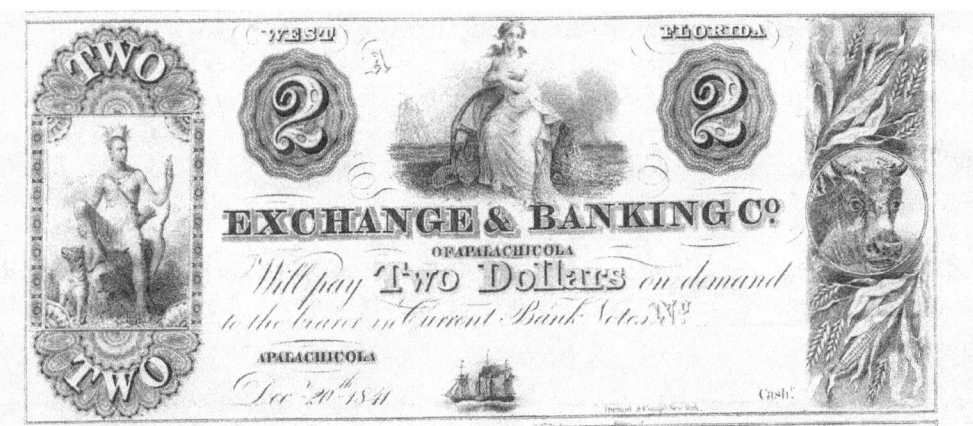

28. $2 Indian, Hope, Bull's head R6

29. $3 Art, Train, Bull's head R6

Appalachicola Lands

Engraved by Rollinson & Comp. Issuer, date of issue and place of issue unknown. Dates and signatures, if any, on known notes are fictitious.

These notes are problematic. The most likely issuer was the Appalachicola Land and Development Company, formed on November 28, 1835, by the Spanish company in Cuba that acquired the Forbes Purchase lands from John Forbes & Company in 1817. The style of the notes suggests that William Rollinson engraved them around 1818–1822. At that time, Spanish influence was dwindling and squatters were ignoring the claims of land ownership. However, in 1819 the sale of East and West Florida to the United States was negotiated for transfer in 1821. Presumably, the notes were printed after 1821, with the then-current spelling of Appalachicola with a double "PP." However, the validity of the trade with the Indians and confirming Spanish grant to Forbes was questioned and the land was not sellable. The issue was resolved in a pair of decisions by the United States Supreme Court in March 1835. First, it declared the Spanish grant to Forbes invalid. Second, it declared the Appalachicola Land and Development Company's title valid since they had bought it in good faith. Marketing of the land, some already occupied, began in April 1836. Sales were slow due to claims from the heirs of Forbes, Leslie and Panton that the land wasn't completely paid for, the Second Seminole War, and the 1837 financial panic. The notes, if used at all, would have been used in 1836 and the years following. Those that chose not to buy started the town of St. Joseph 28 miles to the west along the Gulf of Mexico.

30. $1 Allegorical seated female combining Agriculture, Commerce and Hope . . R8
31. $2 same vignette R8
32. $3 same vignette R8

33. $5 same vignette R8

The Bank of St. Marys, Office at Columbus, Georgia

Engraved by Danforth, Underwood & Co. New York and Underwood, Bald, Spencer & Huffy, Philada.

John G. Winter was a prominent capitalist in Columbus, Georgia. He created the Bank of St. Marys as a vehicle for issuing change bills that would rarely be redeemed. Because such privately-issued bills were illegal in Georgia, they were printed as Apalachicola bills. To avoid having to redeem many of them, they were redeemable in Charleston or New York. After the Columbus newspaper complained, Mr. Winter replied that he would redeem them in Columbus "provided my teller is not annoyed by their presentment too often and in sums too small." On April 23, 1852, with $350,000 outstanding, the bank suspended specie payments.

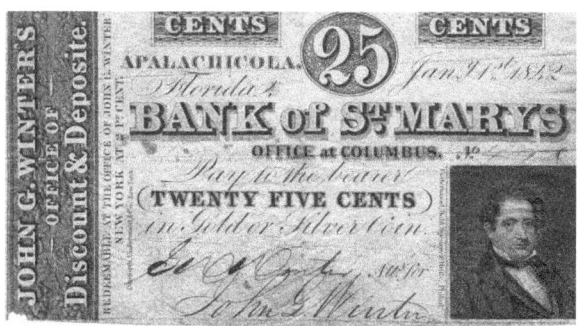

34. 25¢ Portrait of John G. Winter, engraved date January 1, 1842 . . . . .R7

35. 50¢ same, January 1, 1842 . . . . .R7
36. $2 Female seated in numeral 2, engraved date September 15, 1843 . . . . .R7

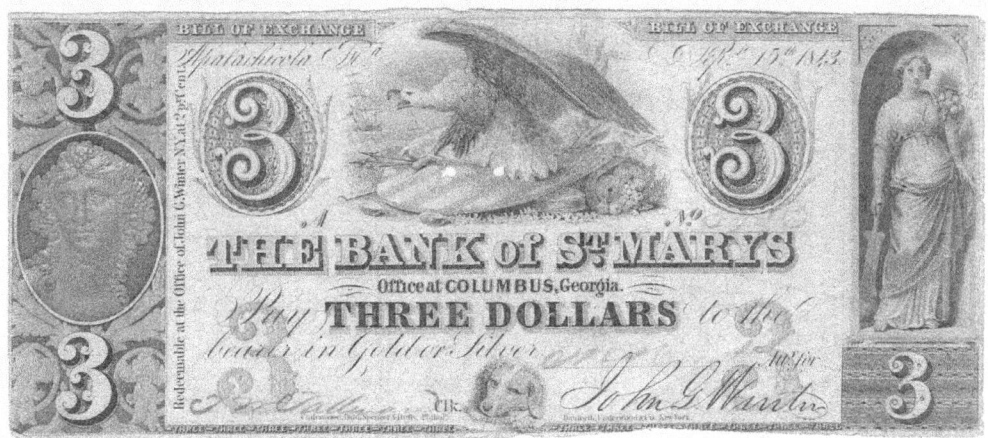

37. $3 Eagle on shield, September 15, 1843 . . . . .R6

Eight plate letters A–H were used to print 25¢ notes. No $1 notes were printed. Notes with $5, $10 and $20 denominations do not say Apalachicola and are considered Georgia notes only.

Bank of St. Marys, Office at Savannah

Engravers same as Columbus office.
38. 25¢ Portrait of John G. Winter, engraved date January 1, 1842 . . . . R6

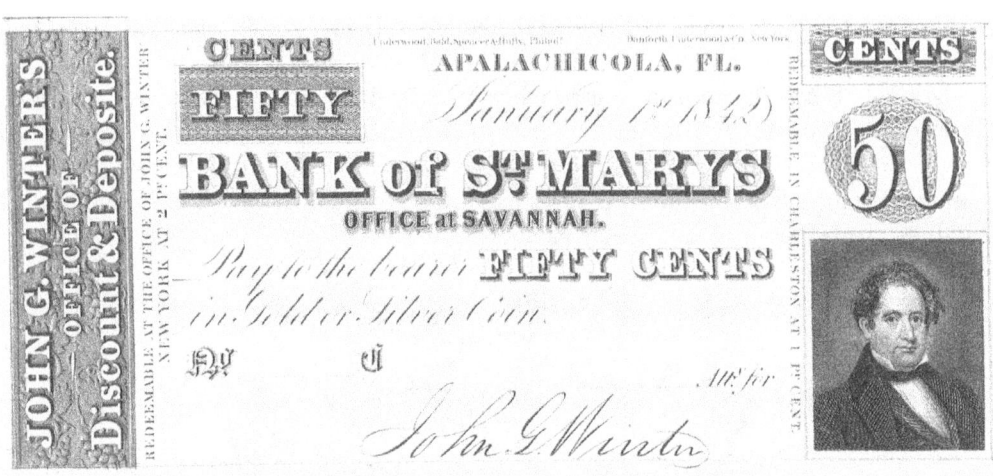

39. 50¢ same, January 1, 1842 . . . . R6

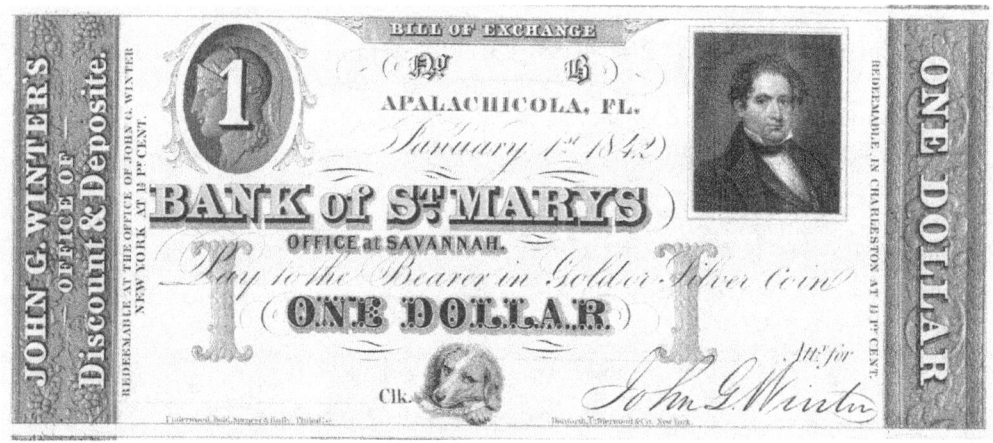

40. $1 same, January 1, 1842 . . . . R6

41. $2 Female seated in numeral 2, engraved date September 15, 1842 ....R6
42. $3 Eagle on shield, September 15, 1842 ....R7

The lower denominations were printed on sheets of seven notes with plate letters A-B-C-D for the 25¢ notes and A-B-C for the 50¢ notes. The $1 notes were printed in sheets of four A-B-C-D. The $2 and $3 appeared together on sheets of four with plate letters A-B and A-B.

City Council of Apalachicola

Engraved by Rawdon, Wright & Hatch New York. Handwritten dates in 1840–1844.

43. 6¼¢ Running deer R7
44. 12½¢ (wider format) eagle, cherub, steamship R8

City of Columbus, Georgia

Engraved by Rawdon, Wright & Hatch New York.

These notes were issued by John D. Howell, a drygoods merchant and cotton dealer between 1838 and 1842. The payment clause reads "in the City of Columbus, I promise to pay...." In 1843 he advertised "to retire his change bills from circulation, there now being a sufficient amount of specie." Partial specimens are known from the backs of 1862 Columbus notes.

45. 6¼¢ fragments seen R8
46. 12½¢ standing female, seated male R8
47. 25¢ Allegorical literature, steamship R7
48. 50¢ man striking anvil, center vignette not seen R7

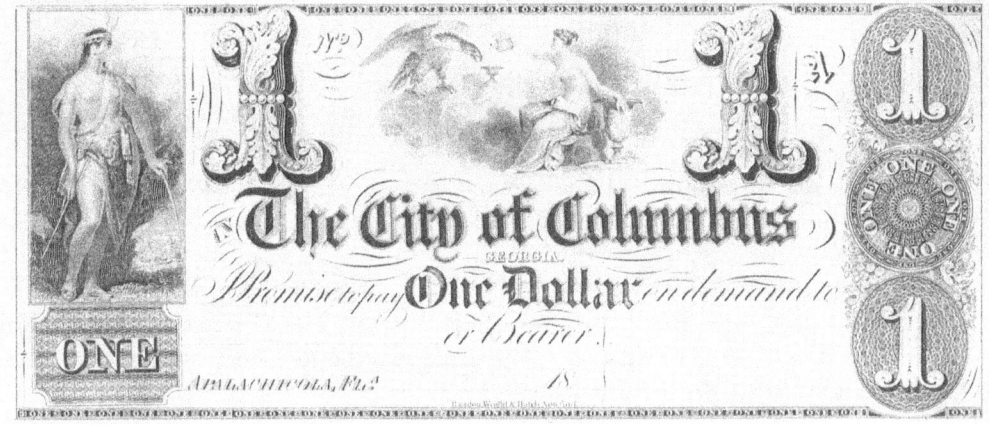

49. $1 standing Indian, Hebe pouring drink for eagle R7
50. $2 Mercury, sailing ship, two silver dollars R8
51. $3 three, Archimedes with lever and globe, portrait R8

Coweta Falls Manufacturing Company

In 1827, the Georgia Legislature recognized the establishment of a trading town near the Coweta Falls of the Chattahoochee. The town became Columbus, with strong economic ties to Apalachicola. Farish Carter, a wealthy planter, land speculator, investor and entrepreneur co-founded this, the first cotton textile mill in Columbus, in 1844. Notes have engraved date of January 1, 1855. Notes say Apalachicola to evade Georgia laws.

52. 25¢ Liberty, Reverse of 1831–1838 quarter dollar R8

5. Obsolete Notes and Scrip—Apalachicola

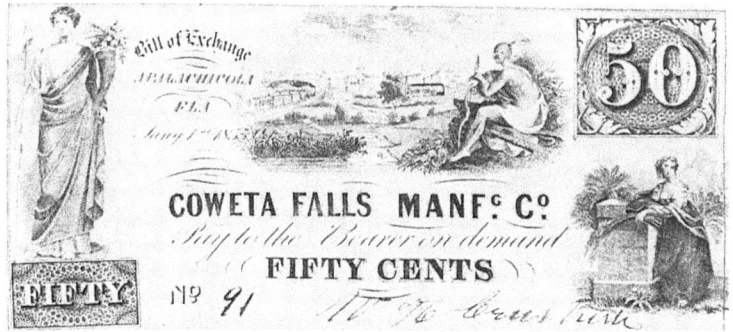

53. 50¢ Liberty, Progress (Indian overlooking city), Ceres R8

RULES AND REGULATIONS

To be observed by all persons in the employment of the

COWETA FALLS MANUFACTURING COMPANY.

The Overseers are to be punctually in their rooms at the starting of the Mill, and not to be absent unnecessarily during working hours. They are to see that all those employed in their rooms are in their places in due season—and they must be the last to leave the room at night, to see that the lights are all properly extinguished—that there is no fire in the room—that the Buckets, &c. are in proper order—and they may grant leave of absence to those employed under them, when there are spare hands in their rooms to supply their places—otherwise they are not to grant leave of absence, except in cases of absolute necessity.

All persons in the employ of the Company, are required to observe the regulations of the room where they are employed. They are not to be absent from their work without consent, except in case of sickness, and then they are to send the Overseer word of the cause of their absence.

All persons entering into the employment of the Company, are considered as engaged to work *Twelve Months*.

All persons intending to leave the employment of the Company, are to give two weeks notice of their intention to their Overseer—and their engagement with the Company is not considered as fulfilled, unless they comply with this regulation.

Settlements will be made up to the last Saturday in every month.

Any hand will be considered answerable for improper conduct out of the Mill, and forthwith discharged.

These regulations are considered part of the contract with all persons entering into the employment of the Company.

COLUMBUS, March 5, 1845.

Eagle Manufacturing Company

Engraved by Doty & Bergen, N.Y. Engraved date May 5, 1852. Signed by William H. Young.

William H. Young was born in New York City on January 22, 1807, and settled in Apalachicola as a commission merchant in 1839. In 1852 he founded the Eagle Manufacturing Co. in Columbus, and in 1855 became the first president of the Bank of Columbus. The Eagle mill was famous for making the best osnaburgs in the world. (Osnaburg is a plain, heavy, coarse cotton weave used for grain sacks or finished and printed for draperies and slip covers.)

54. 25¢ Hebe seated serving drink to eagle. "Q" overprinted in blue R8
55. 50¢ Hebe standing serving drink to eagle, Commerce.
    "50" overprinted in blue R8
56. $1 Hebe standing serving eagle, eagle on shield. No overprint R8

Bay Port

Major John D. Parsons received land at the mouth of the Weeki Wachee River in place of money for his service in the Second Seminole War, which concluded on May 10, 1842. Other settlers arrived in the area as early as March 1842 in anticipation of free land under the Armed Occupation Act which Congress finally passed on August 4, 1842. Parsons built a house in 1842, and soon expanded to a hotel for fishermen, vacationers, and tradesmen involved in the export of cotton, produce and timber. Although originally from New Hampshire, Parsons raised a company of Hernando County men in 1861 to defend the Gulf coast from Federal gunboats. Bay Port succeeded as a haven for blockade runners even after a Union attack in April 1863.

John Parsons

Years 1862 and 1863 printed, dates written in. Bay Port in script letters, Florida abbreviated unless otherwise indicated. Payable in State or Confederate notes.

1. 5¢   1863, small three-masted schooner, small type R8
2A. 50¢   1862, three-masted schooner, denomination medium type R8
2B. 50¢   same, narrow type R8
3. 50¢   1863, gunboat, Bay Port in hollow block letters R8

4.	50¢	1863, gunboat, Florida spelled out	R8
5.	75¢	1862, two-masted schooner, medium type	R8
6.	75¢	1862, gunboat, narrow type	R8

7.	75¢	1863, three-masted schooner, narrow type	R8
8.	75¢	1863, gunboat, narrow type	R8
9.	$1	1862, railroad, heavy type	R8
10A.	$1	1863, railroad, heavy type, Bay Port in block letters	R8
10B.	$1	same, medium type	R8

BROOKSVILLE

The town of Brooksville was created in 1856 on land donated by residents of inland Hernando County who objected to the county seat being in Bay Port on the county's western edge.

C.L. Friebele

Christopher L. Friebele was born in Karlsruhe, Germany, in 1815, and came to Tampa in 1848. He operated a general store there until February 1862 when Union bombardment forced a move inland to Brooksville. Later that year he became a blockade runner, was captured in July 1864, and imprisoned for the remainder of the war. He was married to a daughter of Perry G. Wall, who issued Hernando County scrip. In November 1866 he reopened in Tampa with his brother-in-law Edward A. Clark, whose store is mentioned on similar scrip in Cork. He died in 1886.

All notes have printed year 1862.

1.	25¢	Horse and wagon, hollow 25	R8
2.	25¢	medium 3-mast schooner, heavy 25	R8
3.	25¢	small 3-mast schooner, medium 25	R8
4.	25¢	medium 2-mast schooner	R8

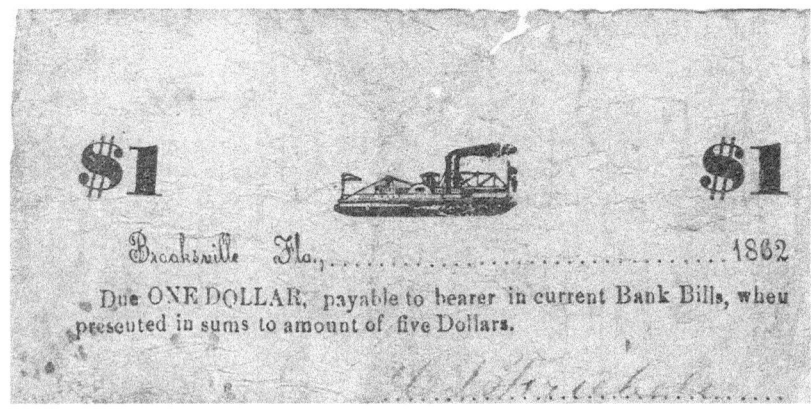

5.	50¢	large 3-mast schooner, heavy 50	R7
6.	50¢	small 3-mast schooner, medium 50	R8
7.	75¢	small 2-mast schooner, thin 75	R8

8.	$1	gunboat, heavy 1	R7

BRUNSWICK & FLORIDA STEAM BOAT & STAGE LINE

The first six notes show Baltimore as the place of issue but indicate that they can be "redeemed in current bank notes at our offices in Charleston, Brunswick, Tallahassee, St. Josephs, Mobile & New Orleans."

The last two notes cannot be attributed to any specific place. They qualify only marginally as currency. Each note declares itself to be a ticket for a seat on a specific trip between Charleston and Mobile (or between Mobile & Charleston) via Apalachicola, St. Josephs, St. Marks, Tallahassee and Pensacola. But it is also good for $65 at any company office. The signature lines are for Proprietor and Ticket Agent.

Engravers' imprints are Underwood, Bald, Spencer & Hufty, Philadelphia and Danforth, Underwood & Co. New York. Late 1830s.

1. 12½¢   Hebe pouring drink for eagle R8
2. 25¢   Woman with sheaf of grain, man with rod R8
3. 50¢   Justice and Washington, Ceres, allegorical plenty R8
4. $1   Agriculture holding numeral 1 ....R8
5. $2   Agriculture and Commerce R8
6. $3   Liberty, Justice and American eagle R8

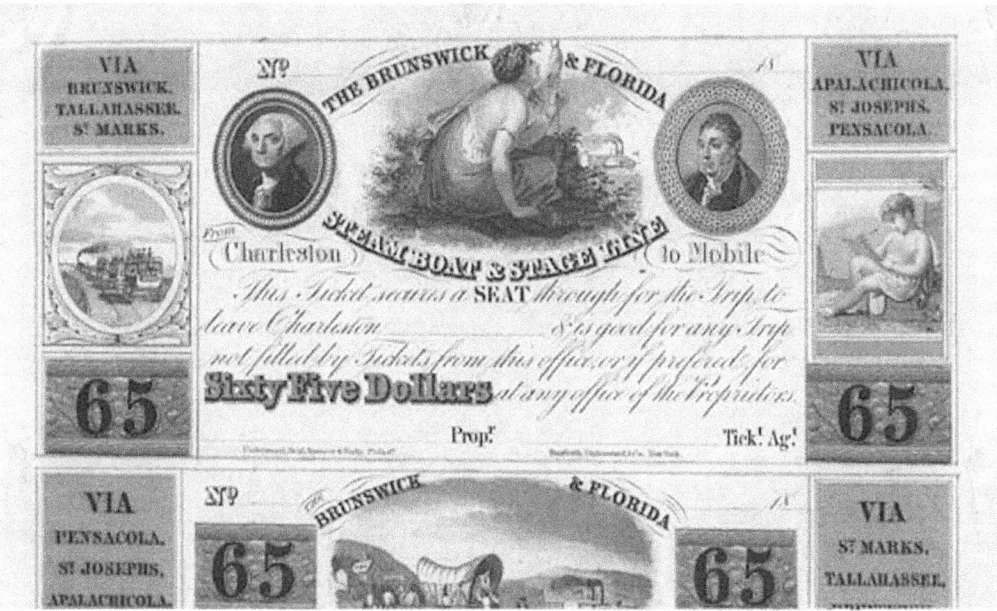

7. Charleston to Mobile or $65 Washington, seated woman and steamboat, Lafayette R7
8. Mobile to Charleston or $65 Covered wagon and steamboat R7

Cedar Keys

The Cedar Keys were a group of islands off the Florida peninsula in the Gulf of Mexico. The town's early growth was fueled by Eberhard Faber who acquired extensive land in the area in 1855 for 50¢ an acre, and proceeded to remove all the cedars for pencils. The Florida Railroad connecting Cedar Key and Fernadina, which had been cut off early in the Civil War, was restored in 1868. The town of Cedar Key incorporated in 1869.

Tucker, Gaston & Co.

James Tucker managed this enterprise that supplied ships and area residents with a variety of goods and services.

Scrip also redeemable at N.S. Gaston & Co., Fernandina. Engraved date of June 1, 1869, on 10¢ and 25¢ scrip; May 1, 1869, on 50¢. Imprint of Verelst & Co. Lith 44 Cedar St. N.Y. on 25¢ and 50¢; same without N.Y. on 10¢. The remarkable coincidence of the Cedar Keys lithographer being on Cedar Street has been verified. All have the same design in green on back. Higher denominations are progressively larger.

1. **10¢ sidewheel steamship** R7

2. **25¢ railroad train** R8
3. **50¢ cotton boll (back illustrated)** R7

Historical records indicate that Levy County and other merchants also issued scrip in the 1869–1871 period, but no surviving examples have been seen.

Cork

Cork was founded as Ichepucksassa by cattle baron Jacob Summerlin in 1849. When Irishman Daniel Hughes became postmaster in 1860, he changed the name to Cork. In 1884 the town adopted its present name, Plant City.

William C. Brown

William Charles Brown was a civil engineer who worked for railroads in Ohio until his health forced him to move to a warmer climate. He was a clerk in Edward A. Clark's general store in Tampa in 1860. In 1862, the store moved inland to Cork for safety. Brown managed the store while Clark was running the blockade and imprisoned. Brown became postmaster in 1863. After the war he returned to Tampa where he became city clerk, county surveyor, court clerk, and delegate to the 1884 Democratic national convention.

Scrip is numbered, Cork may be printed or written, Clark's store may be mentioned. May be dated or undated.

1. 10¢ gunboat, undated, Cork written in text R8

2. 25¢ 3-mast schooner, undated, Cork printed in text R7
3. 25¢ 3-mast schooner, 1862 printed, Cork printed in text R8
4. 50¢ 3-mast schooner, 1862 printed, Cork printed above text R8
5. 50¢ gunboat, undated, Cork written in text R8

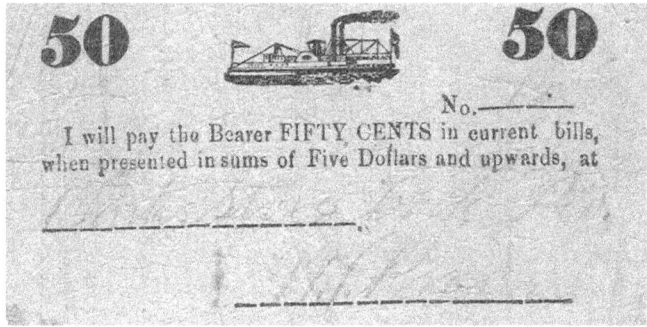

6. 50¢ gunboat, undated, Clark's Store Cork Fla. written in text R8

DUTTON

Charles K. Dutton and George Rixford founded the town of Dutton along the Florida Railroad route for turpentine and resin distilleries in the early 1870s. The town expanded to include orange groves, a sawmill, and a mule-driven tram road to the St. Marys River. The town declined as the timber dwindled. In 1898 it was renamed Verdie.

C.K. Dutton

Engraved date January 1875. Engraver's imprint: The Major & Knapp Eng. Mfg. & Lith. Co. 56 Park Place N.Y.

1. $1 Face: officer and cannon, Paul Revere's ride R8
   Back: factory scene

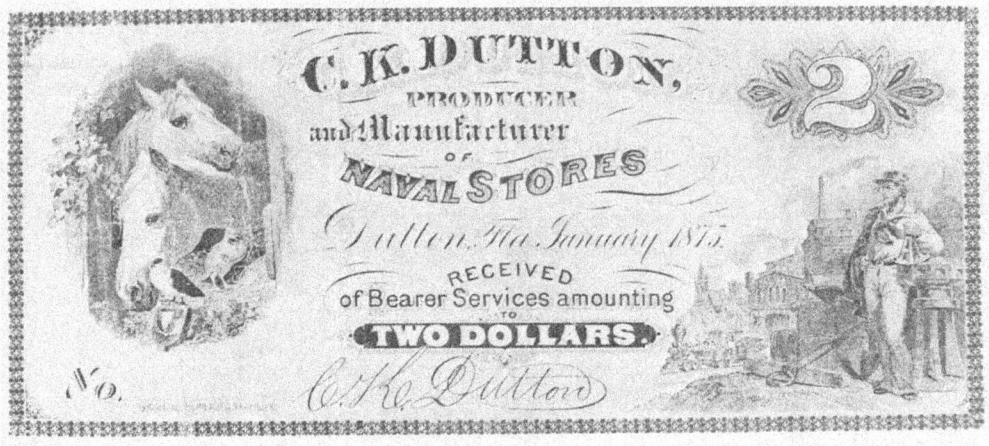

2. $2 Face: horse heads, sailor standing R8
   Back: George Washington
3. $5 Face: woman, steamship; Back: not seen R8

ELLAVILLE

George F. Drew was born in New Hampshire in 1827, learned the machinist's trade, and worked in New York, where he met John G. Winter who encouraged him to move to Columbus, Georgia. From 1865 to 1869, backed by New York financier Louis Bucki, he purchased thousands of acres of timberland and a mill on the Suwannee River in Florida. The workers were paid in scrip redeemable in the company store. Drew was elected governor of Florida from 1877 to 1881. As governor he restored Florida's finances after Reconstruction. After serving as governor he moved to Jacksonville and sold his interests in Ellaville to Bucki.

Drew & Bucki

1. 5¢ Nov. 1, 1870. Eagle, "in merchandise or currency first of every month," . . R8
   plain back, no engraver imprint
2. 5¢ May 1871. Head of bull. "Received of bearer services amounting to," . . . R8
   elaborate green back, no imprint. Issued notes also have serial number stamped top center

3. 5¢ May 1871. Larger head of bull. "Received of bearer services amounting ..R8
to," elaborate green back. Engraver's imprint: Pelletreau & Raynor,
New York. Serial number stamped top center

4. 10¢ May 1871. Eagle facing left, green back, no imprint R8
5. 10¢ May 1871. Eagle facing right, serial number stamped top left, ...R8
    engraver imprint: Pelletreau & Raynor, New York
6. 25¢ May 1871. Head of dog, green back, no imprint. R8
7. 50¢ May 1871. Beehive, green back, no imprint R8

Suwannee Steam Saw Mills, Drew & Bucki

The mill is illustrated at the bottom of page 67. Printed date March 1874. Engraver's imprint: The Major & Knapp Eng. Mfg. & Lith. Co. 56 Park Place N.Y. Elaborate green backs. (Note: "Suwannee" is spelled wrong in drawing but right on scrip.)

8. 5¢ **George Washington, serial number stamped bottom left** R8
9. 25¢ **Man carrying basket of cotton, place for serial number top right** R8

Contemporary accounts describe widespread use of payroll scrip in Dutton, Ellaville, and other north Florida lumber camps. Additional note discoveries are expected.

Fernandina

Fernandina, in northeasternmost Florida, got its start as a land grant to Don Domingo Fernandez in 1785. It soon became a busy seaport. Its importance was further enhanced by the completion in March 1861 of the Florida Railroad connecting it with Cedar Key on the Gulf of Mexico, and serving many inland farm areas. Restoration of the rail route after the Civil War was completed in 1868.

Bank of Commerce

The bank was approved on February 14, 1861, but apparently never opened due to the outbreak of the Civil War. Engraved by Danforth, Wright & Co. New York & Philada. Elaborate brown overprints. Serial numbers in blue. Backs of notes are plain or show portions of Florida 1863 notes.

1. $5 sailboat, comptroller seal, Calhoun R6

2. $10 locomotive, comptroller seal, palm trees, ... R7
   Most surviving specimens have been pieced together.
   Illustration is a modern proof.

3. $20 comptroller seal, sailboats, woodsman with axe R6

Bank of Fernandina

The charter was approved on January 15, 1859, under the general incorporation laws rather than under the banking laws. Circulation in 1861 was $33,100. The bank moved to Starke (and issued scrip there) in March 1862 when Union forces captured Fernandina.

Engraved by American Bank Note Company. Side panels overprinted in red. "Stockholders personally responsible" along bottom border. Genuine signatures are George S. Roux and A. H. Cole.

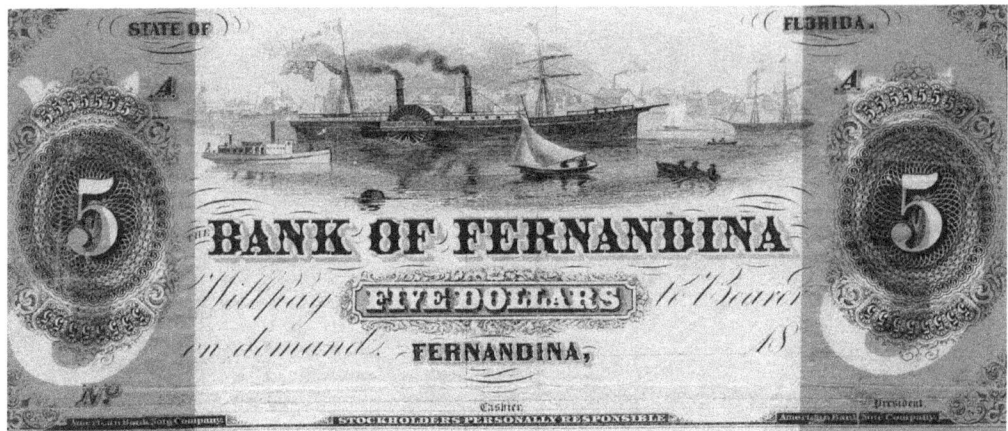

4. $5 sidewheel steamboat in harbor scene R6

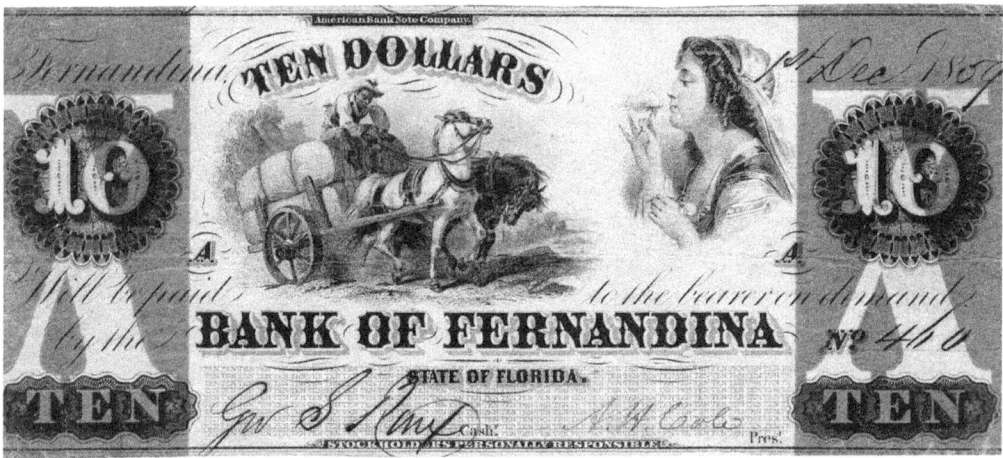

5. $10 horsecart and driver, woman with cotton boll R7

5. Obsolete Notes and Scrip — Fernandina

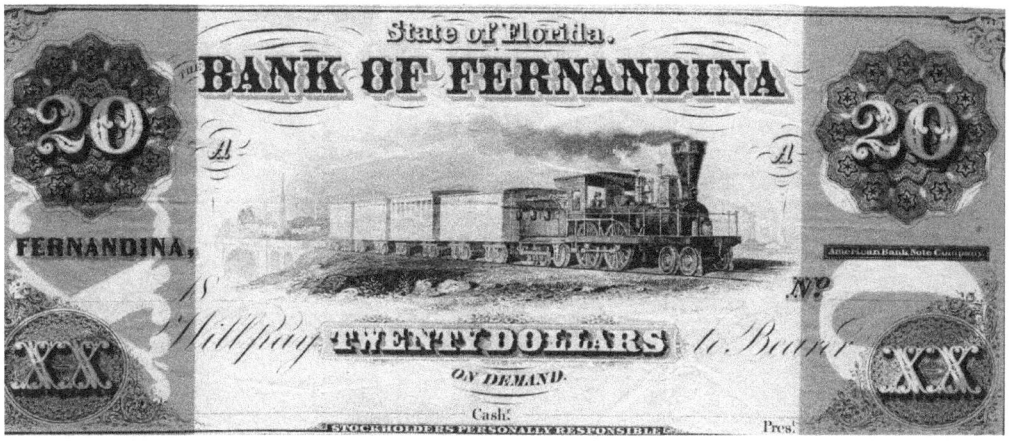

6. $20 locomotive and four railroad cars R6

The Florida Railroad Company

The Florida Railroad was incorporated in 1853 with David Levy Yulee, Florida's first U.S. Senator, as president. Construction began in 1855 on the tracks that would connect Cedar Key on the Gulf coast with Fernandina on the Atlantic coast, thereby opening the interior's agricultural and lumber resources to development. Florida gave the railroad a wide right of way and other lands, and Federal land grants gave the railroad 500,000 acres. The road was officially completed on March 1, 1861, between Secession on January 11th and the outbreak of war on April 12th. In March 1862, Union forces occupied Fernandina, and the railroad's operations were centered in Gainesville. After the war new owners took over the bankrupt railroad. By late 1868 the tracks had been restored, and the railroad was fully operational. The fare was $11 for the 12-hour 155-mile journey across Florida.

Small scrip dated 1st August 1861. No engraver imprint.

7. 5¢ Will pay the bearer in transportation R7
8. 10¢ same R7
9. 25¢ same R8
10. 50¢ same R7

Notes engraved by American Bank Note Company. Signature spaces for Treasurer and Superintendent. Plain back. Handwritten dates in 1861. George Call signed as treasurer, Archibald H. Cole, J.E. Larkin and Alex MacRae, as superintendents.

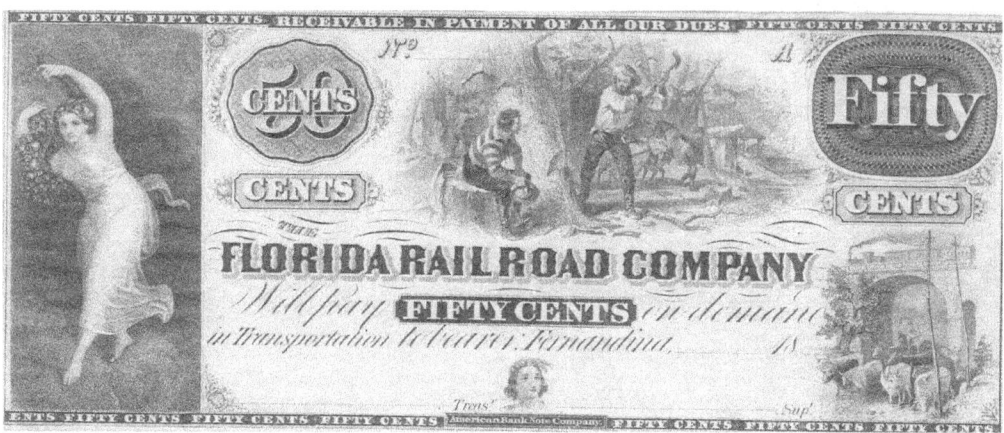

11. 50¢ Phoebe, loggers, cattle under viaduct R6

12A. $1 railroad train at station, woman with rose R7
12B. $1 same, signature spaces for Secretary and President R7
13. $2 sidewheel steamer, two children R7
14. $3 same vignettes as on 11 ....R7

Notes engraved by American Bank Note Company, engraved signature of Wm. S. Roberts, Treasurer, green overprint "1867" on face, and reversed in register on back, printed serial numbers in red.

15. $1 young girl, other vignettes as on 12 ....R7

16. $2 same vignettes as on 13 ....R7
17A. $3 same vignettes as on 11 and 14 ....R7
17B. $3 same, overprint is blue, minor differences in plate R7

Fort Blount

R. R. Blount

The issuer is Riley Redding Blount (1824–1887). He led one of the seven families that moved from Columbia County to the area that is now Bartow in what was then Hillsborough County in 1851. The log blockhouse he built to protect the settlers from the

Indians led to the community being named Fort Blount in 1856. The fort was used in the Third Seminole War and the Civil War. In 1858 he opened a general store and carriage shop. He sold this property in 1862, but operated other businesses in the area until he died. In 1867 Fort Blount was renamed Bartow.

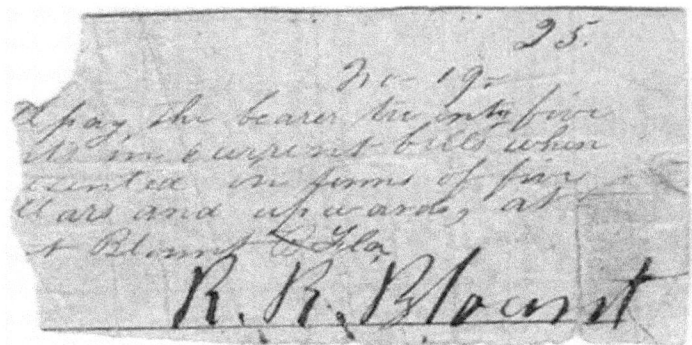

1. Entirely handwritten note: "25, No. 19, pay the bearer twenty five cents . . . .R8 in current bills when presented in sums of five dollars and upwards at Fort Blount, Fla." Signed R. R. Blount. No date.

Handwritten notes are not usually included in collections of obsolete paper money. Freeman considered this note worth listing; Cassidy did not. RARCOA listed it separately from the other banknotes and scrip. I choose to follow Freeman because the note is numbered, and the legend is more typical of scrip than a promissory note.

Hernando County

In addition to the privately issued scrip from the Hernando County towns of Bayport and Brooksville, the county treasurer issued similar small scrip. The notes have serial numbers, handwritten dates in 1862, and are signed by Anderson Mayo, Treasurer and Perry Green Wall, Judge of Probate. Mayo was a wealthy plantation owner, who moved to the county from South Carolina in 1851. Wall served in the Second Seminole War and settled west of Brooksville in 1845. He owned 1860 acres before the war. Interestingly, his daughter Julia Ann married Christopher L. Friebele who issued scrip in Brooksville, and his daughter Sarah married Edward A. Clark, whose store is mentioned on Cork scrip. After the war, Wall became a judge and postmaster in Tampa.

1. 25¢ small sailing ship, heavy type R8

2A. 25¢ gunboat, heavy type R8
2B. 25¢ gunboat, heavy 2, medium 5 . . . . .R8
3A. 50¢ gunboat, heavy type R8

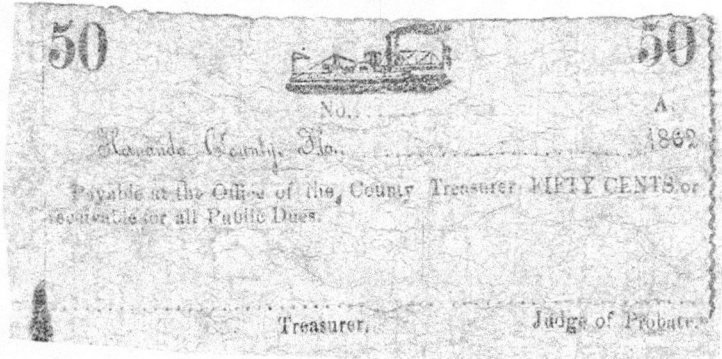

3B. 50¢ gunboat, medium type R8
4. $1 gunboat, heavy type R8

HIGHLAND

Highland, a whistle stop on the Florida Railroad before the war, was the nearest village to the sawmill operating in the 1880s at an area known as Keystone Heights. The site was converted into a state park in the 1930s.

Keystone Mills

Engraver's imprint: Corlies, Macy & Co. Stationers, 39 Nassau St. N.Y. Elaborate blue-green lathework on face and back.

1. 1¢ beehive R8

2. 5¢ Columbus R7
3. 50¢ Washington R8

Other denominations (10¢ and 25¢) were probably issued.

Iola

Iola was a short-lived boom town that owed its creation to the 1835 Supreme Court decision regarding Apalachicola lands and the founding of St. Joseph as part of a plan to bypass Apalachicola. The original bypass plan was a canal connecting Lake Wimico and St. Joseph, but the lake proved to be too shallow. So, in April 1837 a new plan was developed involving a railroad and a new town, Iola, on the west bank of the Apalachicola River north of the mouth of the Chipola River. The 30-mile St. Joseph and Iola Railroad was completed in November 1839. Unfortunately, the rail route was more expensive than the river route to Apalachicola. In 1841, a yellow fever epidemic caused most people to leave St. Joseph, and then in September a hurricane leveled the town. The *Niles Register* reported on February 27, 1842, "A gone city — The city of Apalachicola has bought out the city of St. Joseph...." Iola continued as a river port and recreational town, but not as the commercial and banking center originally envisioned.

The presidents of the Union Bank, Commercial Bank of Apalachicola, Bank of Columbus, and Bank of West Florida had financial interests in the new town. No banks were approved for Iola by the Florida Territorial Legislature. Columbus, Georgia, banks were responsible. Most surviving specimens of Iola currency are proofs from the American Bank Note Company. All bear the imprint of Rawdon, Wright & Hatch New York.

Bank of Columbus

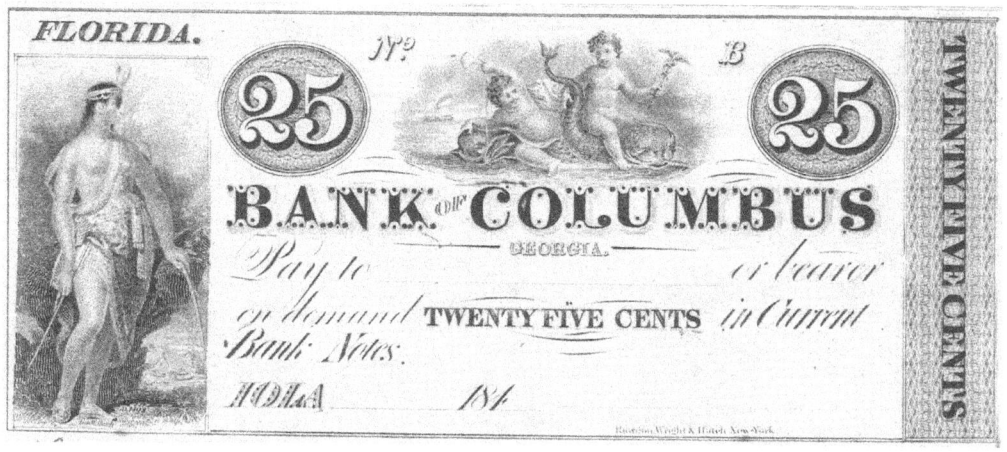

1. 25¢ Indian observing Columbus' arrival, children on dolphins R7
2. 50¢ same Indian, sailboat R7

3. $1 commerce and prosperity R7

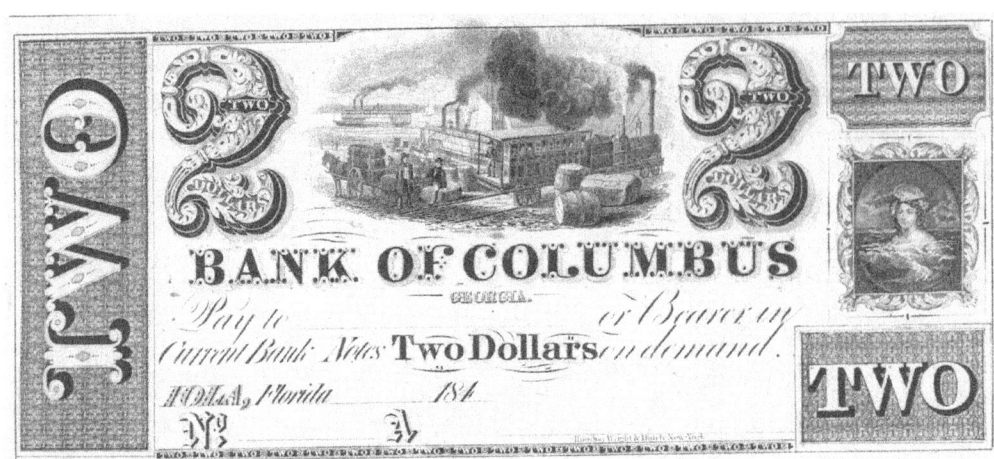

4. $2 train, cart and steamboats R7

Phoenix Bank of Columbus

5. $1 Amphitrite and Neptune R8

Planters & Mechanics Bank of Columbus, Geo.

6. 25¢ Indian observing Columbus' arrival, children on dolphins R7

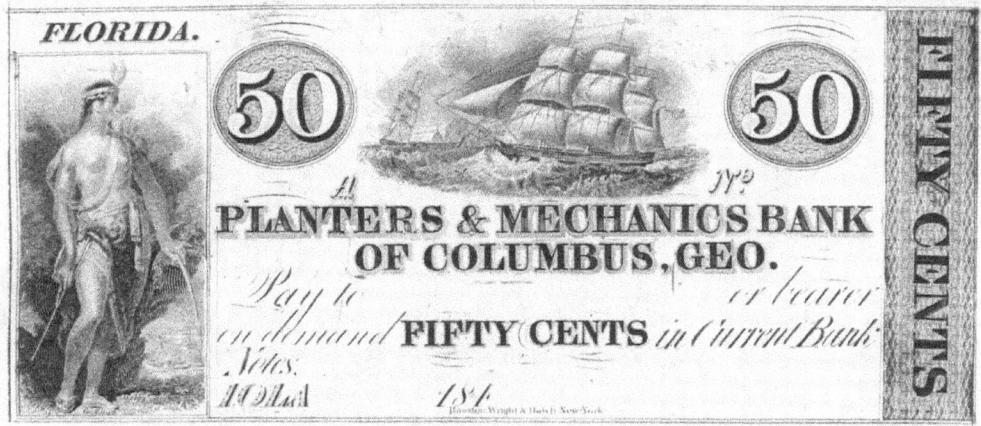

7. 50¢ same Indian, sailboat R7
8. $1   commerce and prosperity R7
9. $2   train, cart and steamboats R7

JACKSONVILLE

Bank of Jacksonville

The Legislative Council of the Territory of Florida voted to incorporate the bank on February 10, 1835, and the Governor approved on February 14. Initial capital was $75,000. The legislation required that 25% be paid in specie before any bills could be issued, and that the amount of bills issued not exceed three times the amount of specie in the vault. Sales of stock in the bank did not start until 1837. Bills amounting to $7,000 were circulated in 1837. On January 30, 1838, the capitalization was increased to $100,000. Later in 1838 the bank suspended specie payments, and failed to file required reports to the Governor. Early in 1839 the bills were selling for ten cents on the dollar. The St. Augustine Herald reported on April 4, 1839, that J. B. Morgan, the bank's president, had vanished and only $132 remained in the vault. On February 24, 1841, the Legislative Council passed a resolution demanding the Governor revoke the bank's charter.

In October 1841 a fraudulent scheme appeared to bring the bank back to life. A confederation of bankers from New York, Maine, and Maryland bought up the remaining supply of notes and then advertised to redeem outstanding notes with 1½ % interest. After thus reestablishing the reputation of the bank, they proceeded to float a fresh supply of notes with fraudulent signatures. The fraud was quickly exposed and the bank "failed" again.

Notes engraved by New England Bank Note Co. Boston. Legitimately issued notes have handwritten dates in August 1837 and signatures of J. Gutterson and J. B. Morgan. Fraudulently issued notes have signature of L. M. Alverson and a fake J. B. Morgan signature. Some notes may bear a redemption stamp. Some remainder notes have been filled in with a variety of fictitious dates and signatures.

1A. $1 sailboats and steamship, shepherd on horseback .R4

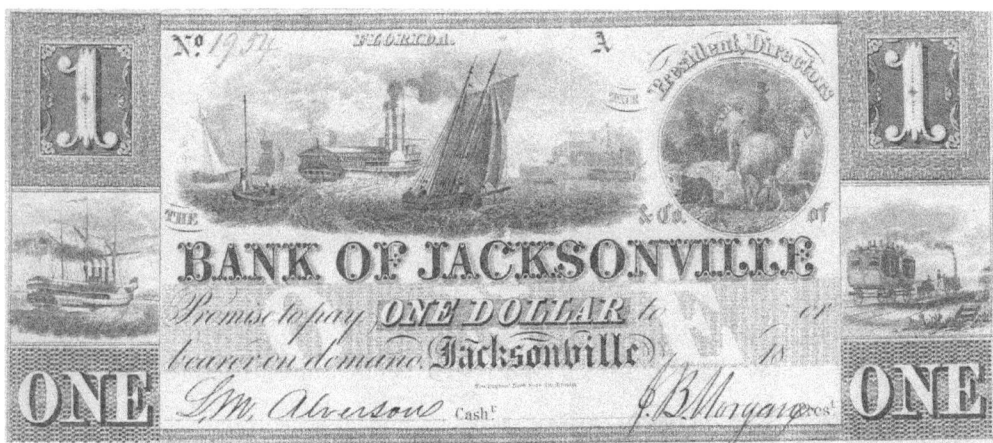

1B. $1 same, fake signatures R4

1C. $1 same as 1A, stamped "Redeemed by M.Y. Beach, New York, ...R7
at 1½ per cent" . . . .

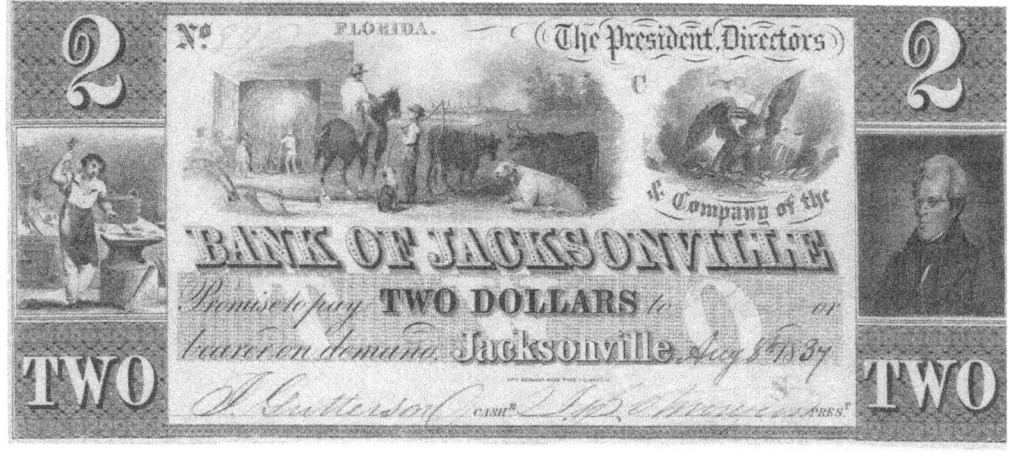

2A. $2 farm workers and cattle, eagle with shield, Jackson R4
2B. $2 same, fake signatures R4

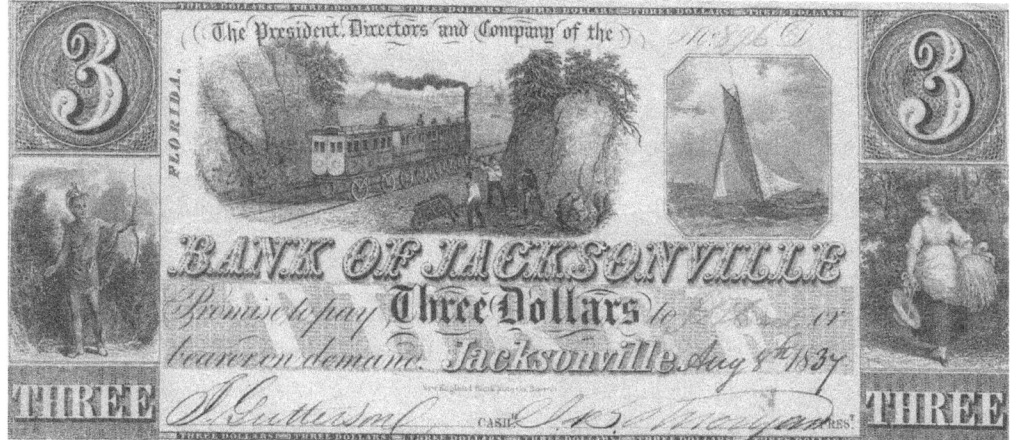

3A. $3 early train and workers, sailboat R4
3B. $3 same, fake signatures R4

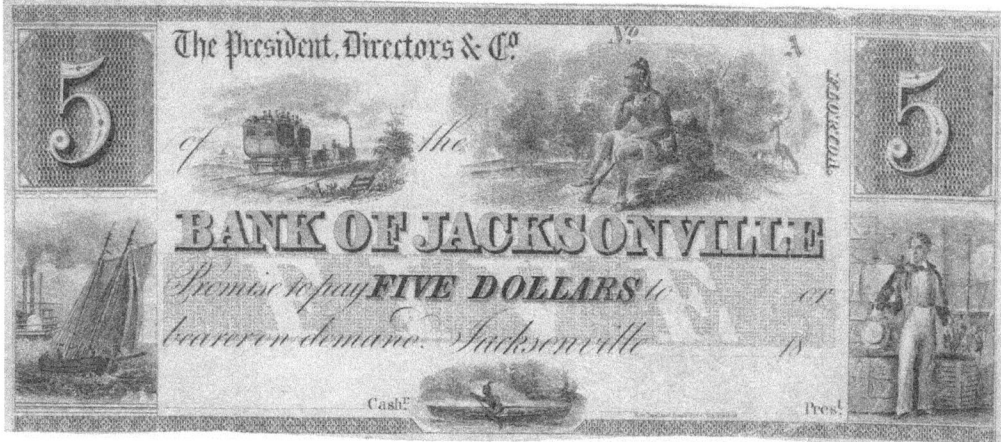

4. $5 steam engine pulling stagecoach, seated Indian R5

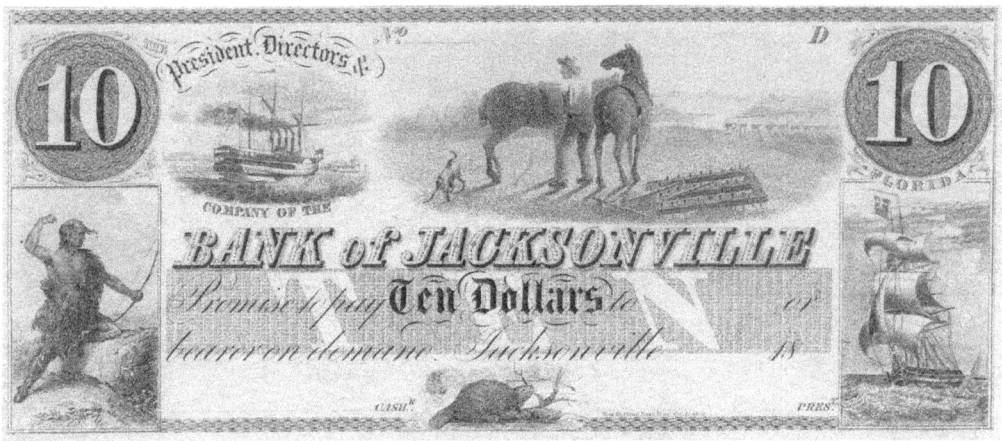

5. $10 steamship, man with two horses R5

Bank of St. Johns

The bank was founded in 1858 by Arthur M. Reed, who had been operating an agency of the Bank of Charleston in his grocery and dry goods store since 1849. In 1858, the legislature passed laws severely limiting out-of-state banks, so Reed converted his bank to The Bank of St. Johns. Although it was never granted a state charter, it complied with the state banking laws and deposited $125,000 in bonds with the State Comptroller, who then authorized the state seal on the notes and countersigned each note. Circulation in 1861 was $51,510. In March 1862 the bank retreated to Lake City and functioned until 1865. Among the bonds deposited were $30,000 of the Florida Atlantic & Gulf Central Railroad.

Notes engraved by Danforth, Wright & Co. New York & Philada. On April 29, 1858, Danforth Wright merged with six other firms to form the American Bank Note Company and their logo was added to the plates. Signed by A. M. Reed and George L. Bryant and countersigned by Theodore W. Brevard, Comptroller. (It is interesting to note that, earlier in his career, Reed signed notes issued by the Southern Life Insurance and Trust Company in St Augustine.) Handwritten dates May 2 or October 1, 1859, known. Elaborate reddish brown security printing.

6A. $5 train, cotton boll, comptroller seal R2

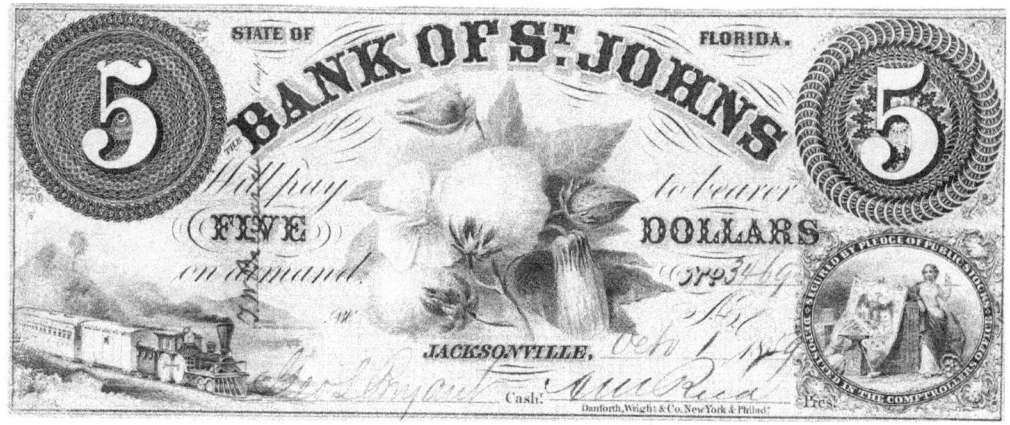

6B. $5 same, with ABCo. logo below last "d" in demand R3

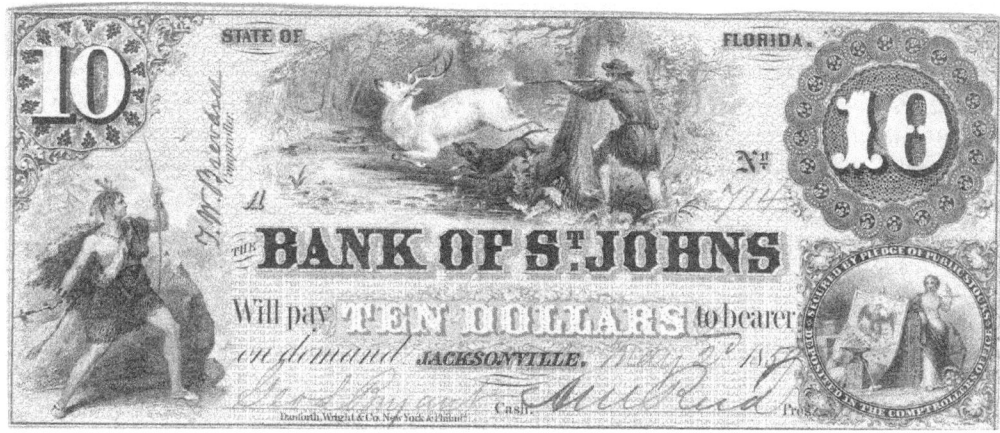

7. $10 Indian, hunter shooting deer, comptroller seal R5

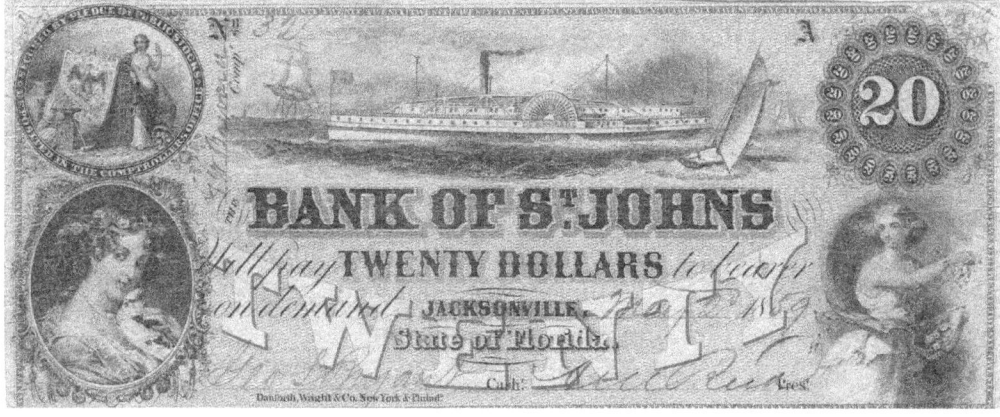

8. $20 female portrait, seal, steamboat Everglade, woman with flowers R6

Bearer certificates of deposit with printed date March 1, 1862, numbered and signed by J. H. H. Bours, Cashier. Some are printed on backs of Florida Atlantic and Gulf Central Railroad bonds.

9. 5¢ similar to 25¢ R6
10. 10¢ similar, but border like $1 . . . . .R6
11. 15¢ similar, but border like $1 . . . . .R6
12. 20¢ similar, border not seen R7

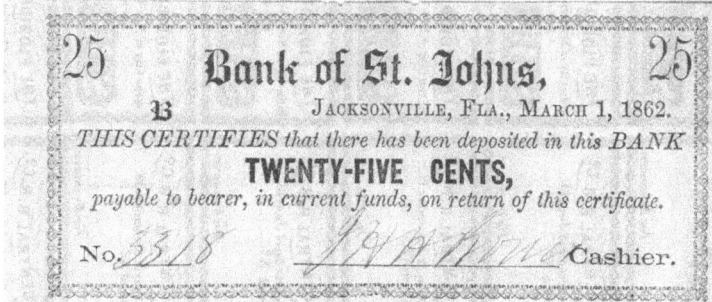

13. 25¢ illustrated R6
14. 50¢ similar, but border like $1 . . . . .R6

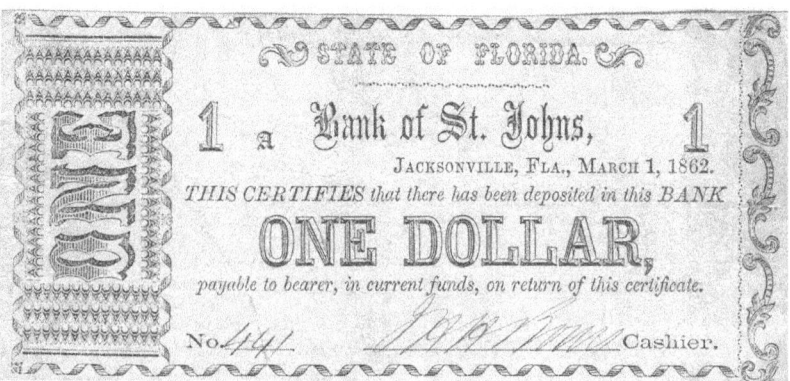

15. $1 illustrated R6
16. $2 similar to $1 . . . . .R6

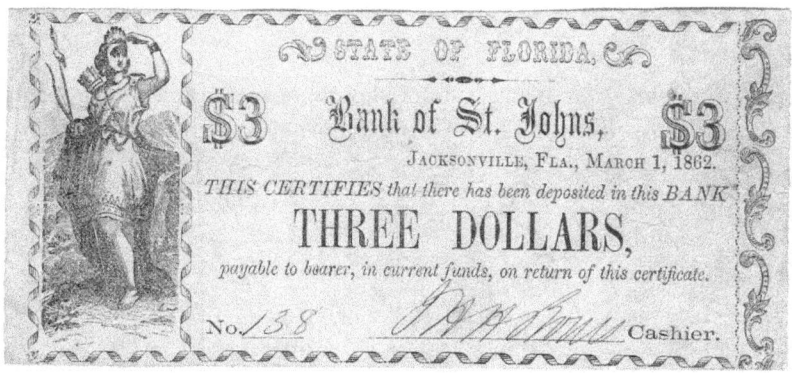

17. $3 Indian, illustrated R6

Another series of bearer certificates of deposit was issued with names of specific merchants and printed dates in February 1862. Scrip has serial numbers and signatures of J. H. H. Bours or I. B. Smith.

Bisbee & Canova

Cyrus Bisbee and Lawrence Canova owned a grocery store on the south side of Bay Street between Ocean and Newnan.

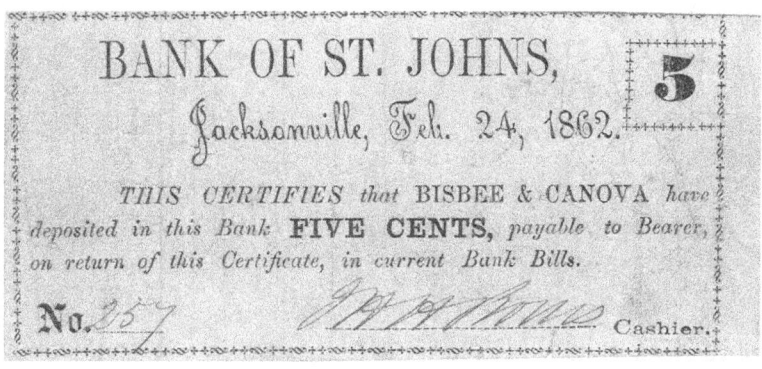

18. 5¢ illustrated R7
19. 10¢ same as 5¢ except denomination R8

S. Fairbanks

Samuel Fairbanks operated a sawmill and store at the west end of town.

20. 15¢ design similar to Bisbee and Canova R8

Wm. Grothe

William Grothe was a Prussian watchmaker who operated a jewelry store. He was also postmaster from April 19, 1854, to April 8, 1862.

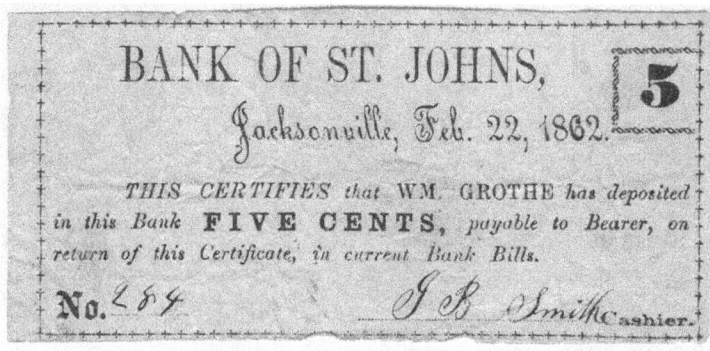

21. 5¢ design similar to Bisbee and Canova R8

T. Hartridge

Theodore Hartridge was a physician from Georgia who became a dry goods retailer on Bay Street.

22. 10¢ design similar to Bisbee and Canova R7
23. 25¢ same R7

24A. 50¢ same, fifty cents in large type R7
24B. 50¢ same, fifty cents in small type R7

Confederate Gun Boat

This is the first of two related issues of payroll scrip payable to bearer at the Bank of St. Johns. George Mooney, an Irish machinist, signed these notes as contractor. Handwritten dates in November and December 1861. Printed on the back of Bank of Jacksonville notes.

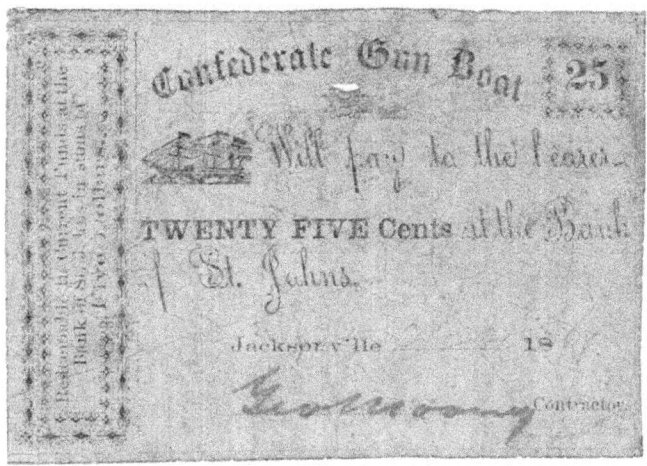

25. 25¢ small ship R6
26. 50¢ same R7

Confederate Packing-House

Issued notes signed by J. Remington with handwritten dates around July 1862.

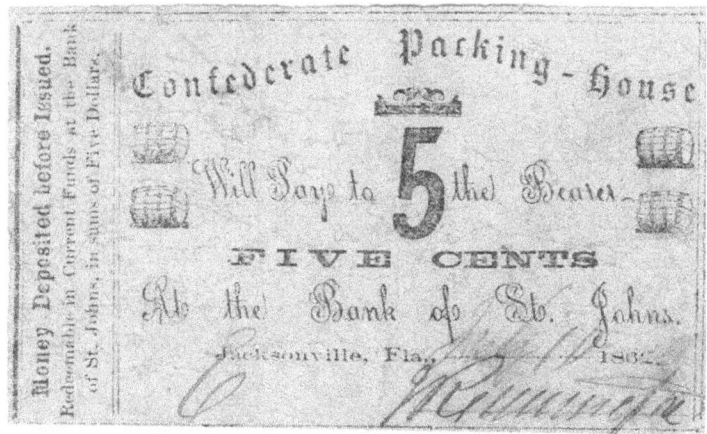

27. 5¢ four barrels, "money deposited before issued" R7
28. 10¢ same R7
29. 15¢ same R7

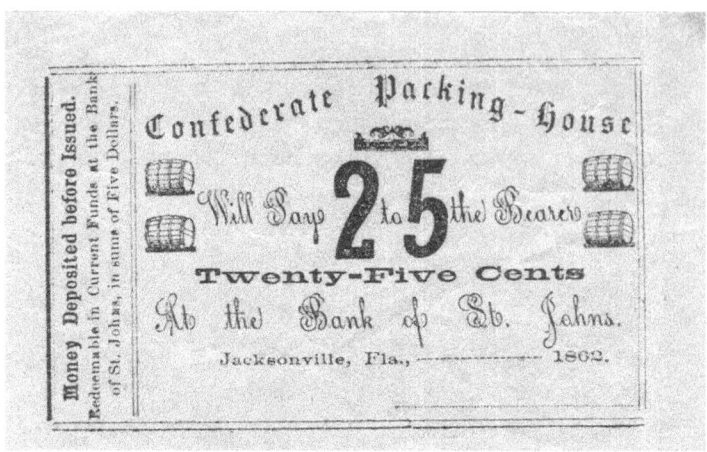

30. 25¢ same R7

C.W. Denny, Banker

C. W. Denny was a partner in Denny and Brown, a private bank established in 1870. It failed in September 1874.

Certificate of deposit engraved by Florida Union Printing. Counterstamped vertically "I certify that the resolutions of the public meeting of Sept. 30, 1873 have been complied with in this certificate of deposit" and signed by the chairman of the supervising committee. Elaborate green design on back with Liberty center. Hand dated October 4, 1873. This bank note was printed to cope with the financial panic that began on September 18, 1873.

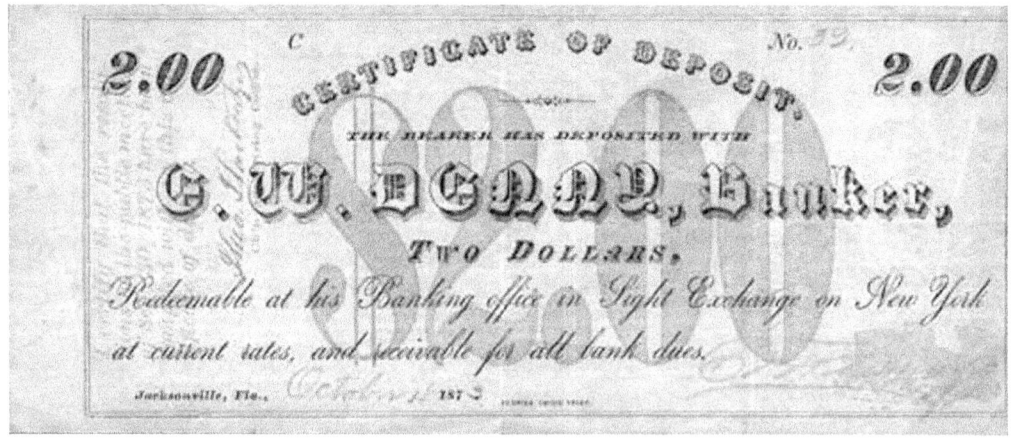

31. $2 $2.00 overprinted in green R8

It is very likely other denominations were issued, but none are known to have survived.

Florida Atlantic & Gulf Central Railroad Co.

The railroad was organized in 1851 under leadership of Dr. Abel Seymour Baldwin to go from Jacksonville to Alligator Town (renamed Lake City in 1859). The Florida Internal Improvement Commission granted extensive land around the right-of-way from Federal lands received under the Swamp Land Act. Jacksonville issued $50,000 in bonds to help finance. Track was completed March 13, 1860. Service was disrupted intermittently during the Civil War. This company remained the only railroad serving Jacksonville until 1881.

Notes engraved by North, Sherman & Co. 96 Chambers St. N.Y. Handwritten dates between 1856 and 1859. Various signers.

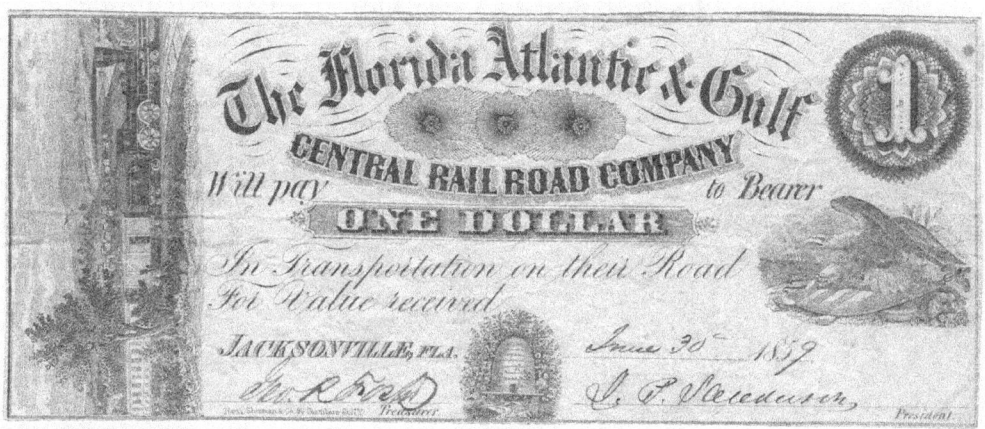

32. $1 railroad, beehive, eagle R6

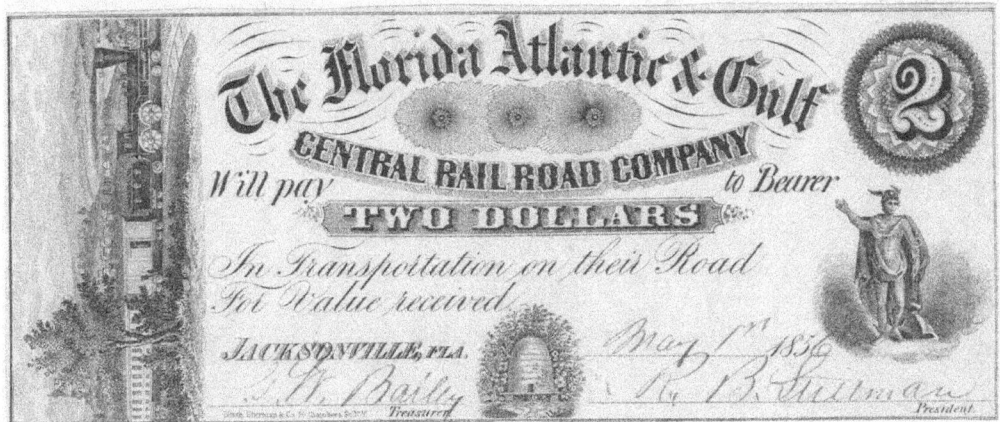

33. $2 railroad, beehive, Mercury R7

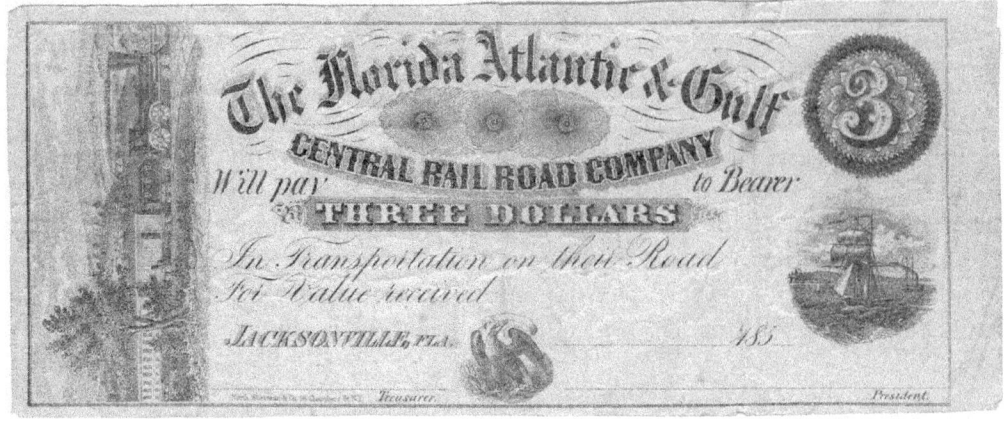

34. $3 railroad, eagle, sailboat R7

Notes engraved by American Bank Note Company, New York. Handwritten dates between 1859 and 1861 on uniface issue; later dates on green back issue.

35. $1 plain back; train under viaduct, two horses, portrait in oval R5
36. $1 green back; same vignettes R5

37. $2 plain back; two Indians, train heading right, cotton and palms R7
38. $2 green back; same vignettes R6

39. $3 plain back; cattle, train heading left, Indian mother and child R7

40. $5 green back; same vignettes as $3 ....R6

E. P. Webster & Co. Druggists

Dr. Edward P. Webster was a druggist from New York. His store stayed open during the 1857 yellow fever epidemic and gave away medicine to those who couldn't pay. His scrip has handwritten dates in 1861 and the legend "These are issued merely as a mutual convenience during the scarcity of silver change." They further promise "On demand, we promise to redeem this bill, either in goods from our store, to its value, or in current funds, when presented to the amount of one dollar, or upwards." Surviving notes are torn and stained.

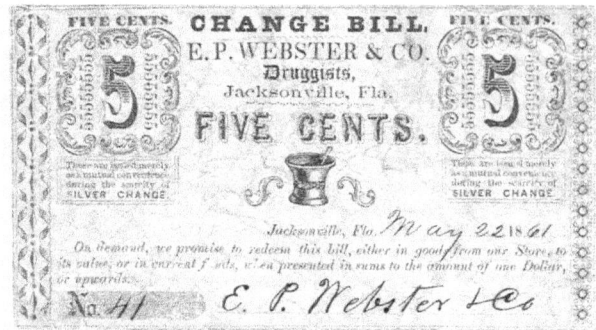

41. 5¢ small mortar and pestle in center R8
42. 10¢ same R8
43. 25¢ same R8
44. 50¢ same R8

Key West

A. Del Pino & Brothers

Antonio Del Pino and brothers Rafael and Luis were cigar makers from Cuba. The company started in the early 1880s. By 1890 there were 12,000 workers making cigars in Key West. The notes were probably used to pay workers who could redeem them at the firm's grocery store or to make change at the store. Notes are mechanically numbered in blue with IOU overprint in red.

1. 5¢ factory, IOU overprint R8
2. 10¢ same R8
3. 25¢ same R8
4. 50¢ same R8

Madison

The town name was shortened from Madison Court House after the Civil War.

Pensacola and Georgia Railroad

The railroad was chartered in 1851. By 1860 tracks were complete between Tallahassee and Lake City. Madison C.H. was midway between the endpoints. In 1869 a merger first with the Tallahassee Railroad and then the Florida Atlantic and Gulf Central Railroad led to the formation of the Jacksonville, Pensacola and Mobile Railroad.

Scrip note with the legend "The subscriber will pay twenty-five cents to bearer on demand in current bank notes when the sum of five dollars is presented. Station 5 P.&G.R.R. Madison Co. Florida." No vignette.

1A. 25¢ Received for all Dues to the Subscriber R8
1B. Same, with Co. instead of CH. R8

Magnolia

Merchants' and Planters' Bank at Magnolia

The first notes printed for this bank in 1832 had the corporate name slightly different from the name in the enabling legislation. The correct name — without apostrophes and with "of" instead of "at" — appears on the second series of notes, printed in 1833.

Notes engraved by Rawdon, Wright, Hatch & Co. New York. Legitimate signatures are Jeremiah Powell as president and Thomas G. Gordon as cashier prior to November 13, 1833, and Gordon as President with E. Seixas as cashier afterwards. Gordon signed many notes and left Florida on November 27, 1833.

1. $1 Indian sitting, female holding American eagle, Washington R4

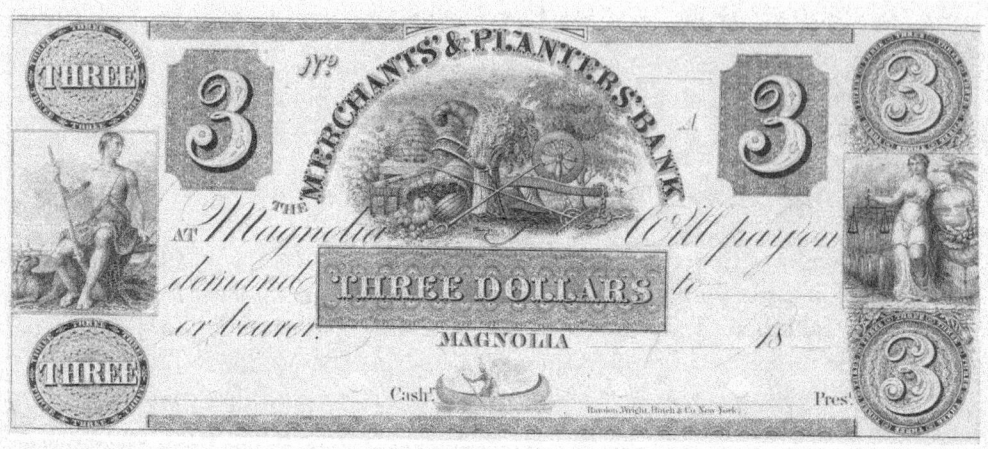

2. $3 Indian with rifle, farm implements and produce, Justice R4

3. $5 Mercury R4

4. $10 Franklin, Archimedes, Ceres R4

Merchants and Planters Bank of Magnolia

The bank's charter was approved by the territorial legislature on February 8, 1832, over the governor's veto. Capitalization was $200,000. Issuance of bank notes was limited to three times the actual amount of specie or United States obligations actually in the vault.

The bank suspended specie payments on January 25, 1834, with $65,618 of notes outstanding. On February 15, 1834, again over the governor's veto, the legislature offered the stockholders an incentive to redeem the outstanding notes: If they redeemed all of the notes within 95 days, they could reopen in Tallahassee as The Merchant's and Planter's Bank of Florida.

Notes engraved by Draper Underwood Bald & Spencer. Signatures same as preceding issue. The Powell signatures on notes dated November 14, 1832, are suspect since, according to Rice, Robert Bald and Asa Spencer did not join Draper, Underwood & Co. until 1833.

5. $10 farm scene with woman carrying sheaf of grain R6

6. $20 allegorical representation of commerce or Ceres R6

Manatee

The town of Manatee became the county seat of Manatee County when it was created from the southern portion of Hillsborough County in 1855. In 1944 it was absorbed by Bradenton.

James Williams

Small scrip of the type issued in Alafia, Orange Springs and other towns in this part of Florida. Handwritten date in 1862.
1. $1 railroad train vignette. "Due to bearer one dollar payable in state . . . . . .R8 or Confederate notes when presented in sums of five dollars"

Marianna

Bank of West Florida

The Bank of West Florida was approved by the Territorial Legislative Council on November 17, 1829, over-riding the rejection by Governor Duval. Initial capital was authorized up to $100,000 and approval was granted to issue bills of credit up to three times the actual paid in capital. The directors were personally liable if excess bills were issued. On February 12, 1831, an increase in capital to $500,000 and the opening of a branch at Apalachicola were approved. On February 12, 1832, removal to Apalachicola with an agency in Marianna was approved. The bank reorganized in 1838 and failed again in 1842.

Notes engraved by Balch, Stiles & Co. N. York. Handwritten dates in 1830 and 1831. Signatures of Eleazar Early, Cashier and Robert Beveridge, President, and of Thomas Bertram as Cashier with J. W. Campbell are authentic. Other (similar) signatures or issue dates after 1831 are not.

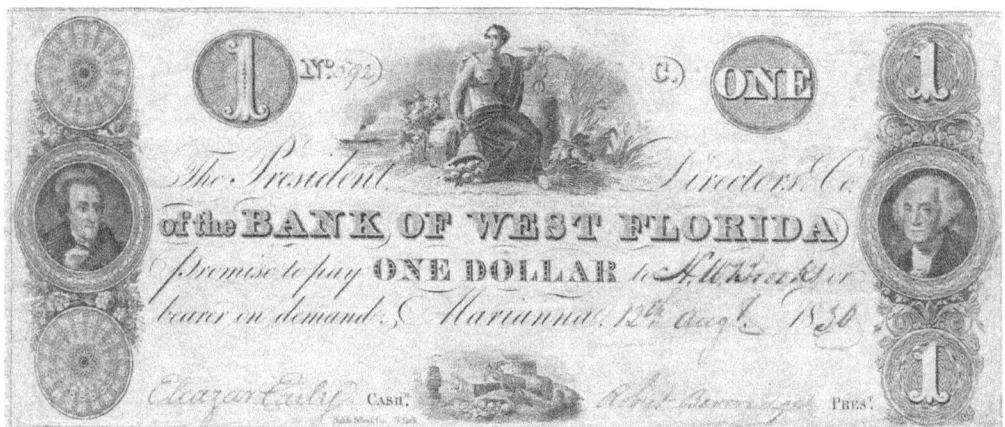

1. $1 Jackson, Ceres, Washington R5

5. Obsolete Notes and Scrip — Marianna

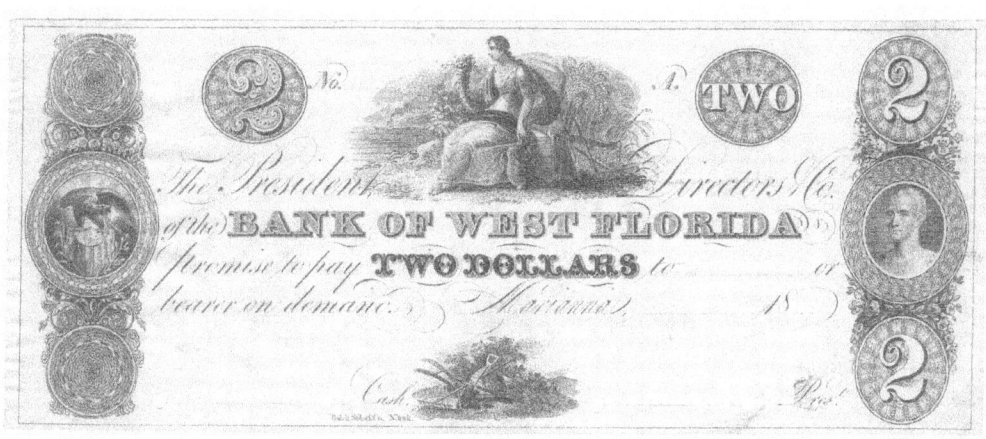

2. $2 eagle, Ceres, Roman head R7
3. $3 description not available R8
4. $5 description not available R8
5. $10 Juno, Commerce, Hebe giving drink to eagle R7
6. $20 description not available R8

Notes engraved by Draper Underwood Bald & Spencer. Handwritten dates in 1838. Signatures of J. C. Wiggins and H. Stevenson are authentic.

7. $50 allegorical female combining liberty, hope and commerce R8

8. $100 Ceres, Liberty and youth R6

Farmers Bank of Florida

On February 10, 1834, the Territorial Legislative Council overrode the governor's veto and approved the bank with initial capitalization of $75,000. Issuance of banknotes was limited to three times the specie in the vault. In 1837, the officers of the bank fled to Perry, Georgia, leaving $25,938 in notes in circulation. They continued operating and issuing currency in Georgia. On February 10, 1838, the governor approved legislation that allowed the bank to increase its capitalization to $200,000 provided it closed its agency in Georgia and redeemed all outstanding bills. The charter was revoked in 1842.

Notes printed for Marianna. Engraver's imprint Casilear, Durand, Burton & Edwards. N. York. Thomas M. White or Carlton Wellborn as cashier and Elijah E. Crocker or James J. Pittman as president are believed to be the only authentic signers.

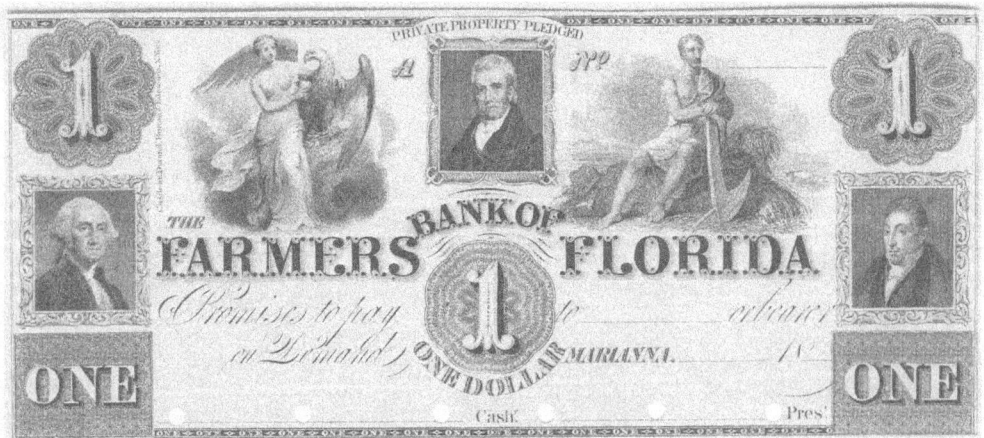

9. $1 Washington, Hebe, Marshall, Agriculture, Lafayette R7
10. $2 Ceres, Washington, Water God R7

11. $3 Commerce R7
12. $5 Ceres? Note not confirmed.

Freeman reported the preceding series being re-engraved with a blank line above the signatures to be filled in by hand "at its agency in Perry Georgia." Freeman conceded he had not seen the $1, $2 or $3, but assumed they were the same as above. Cassidy followed Freeman, listing all four denominations with matching descriptions, but with no photographs of actual notes. Haxby lists only the $5 with a blank line to be filled in. Since I cannot locate an example, photo, nor auction listing of the three low denomination notes and since their design does not lend itself to relocating the word "Marianna," I believe these notes do not exist. Furthermore, since the $5 plate appears again with Perry engraved and since neither Haxby nor I could locate any description of the Marianna $5, I suspect the latter may not exist. I have included them in this catalog to maintain continuity with Freeman and Cassidy (but not Haxby) and to benefit any collector who finds my conclusions to be in error.

Notes with blank line to be filled in with redemption information. Engraver and signers as above.

13. $1 probably same as 9, if this note exists
14. $2 probably same as 10, if this note exists
15. $3 probably same as 11, if this note exists

16A. $5 Ceres and cattle. "bearer" engraved before blank line R7
16B. $5 same. "bearer at" engraved before blank line R7

Notes with "bearer at its agency in Perry, Georgia" engraved. Engraver and signers as above.

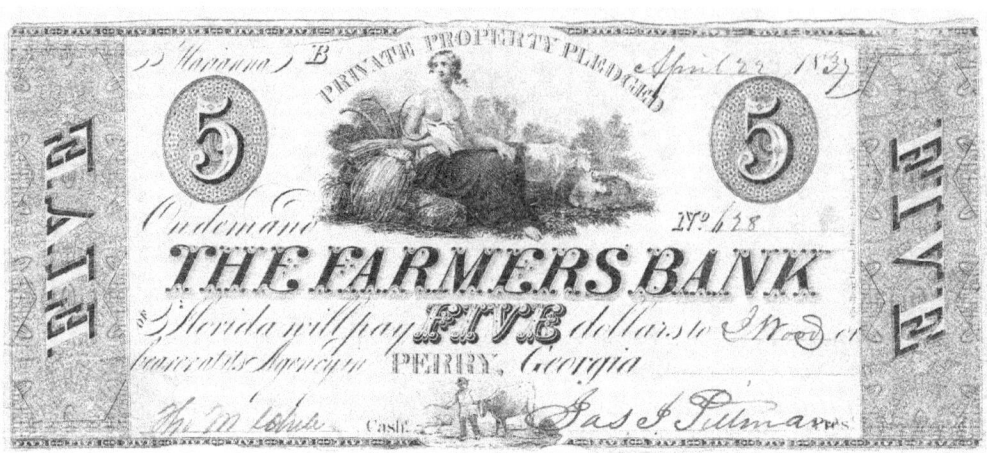

17. $5 Ceres and cattle R7

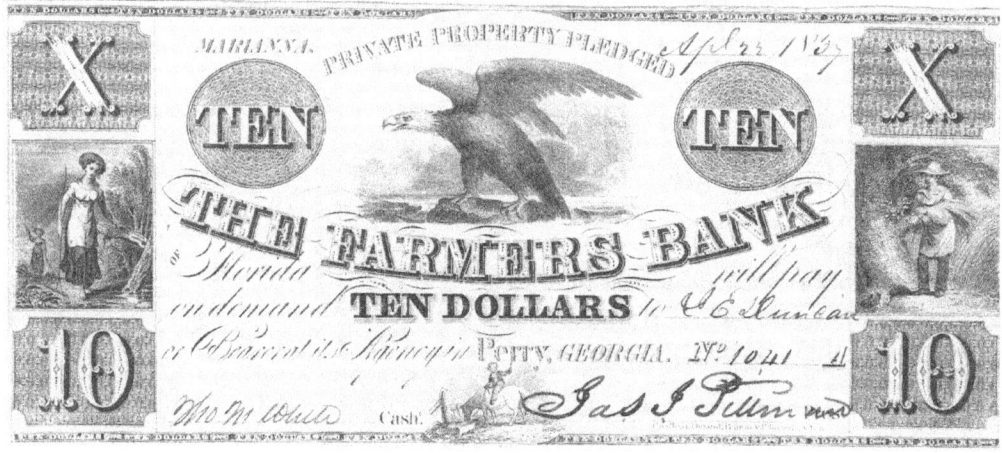

18. $10 Eagle R7
19. $20 Lafayette, Hebe and eagle, Washington R7

MICANOPY

R. E. Johnston

Johnston was a 43-year-old merchant from North Carolina; Stevenson, a 29-year-old farmer. The Alachua County town of Micanopy is Florida's oldest inland town.

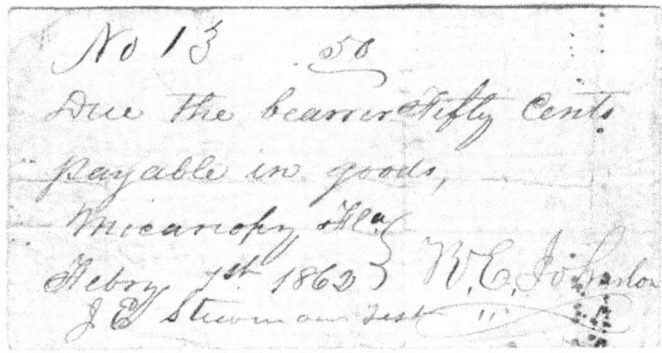

1. Entirely handwritten note on blue ruled white paper: "No. 13, 50, Due the bearer fifty cents payable in goods. Micanopy Fla., Febry 1st 1862." Signed R. E. Johnston and J. E. Stevenson Test.

Handwritten notes are not usually included in collections of obsolete paper money. Freeman considered this note worth listing; Cassidy did not. Rarcoa listed it separately from the other banknotes and scrip. I chose to follow Freeman because the note is numbered and the legend is more typical of scrip than a promissory note.

MILLVIEW

Millview was in Escambia, Florida's westernmost county. The lumber industry thrived there from the early 1870s to the early 1890s.

J. B. Johnson

James B. Johnson was a lumber merchant. Notes are undated and unsigned with imprint J. Douglas, Engraver, New Orleans on 1 and 2, Douglas Engravers & Lithographers on 3.

1. 25¢ Liberty symbolizing America; Lumbermen working logs R8
   in river on back of note

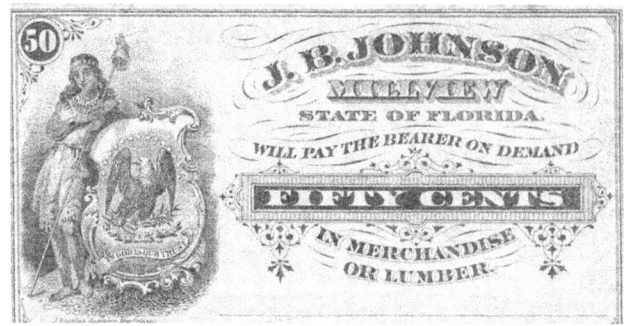

2. 50¢ same R8
3. $1 lumbermen cutting trees; female and eagle on back R8

Geo. W. Robinson

George W. Robinson was a millwright. Notes are undated, signed by a member of the Robinson family with imprint Milwaukee Lithographing Co. "Will pay the bearer on demand ten [twenty five] cents in merchandise or lumber."

4. 10¢ Liberty head, green back R8

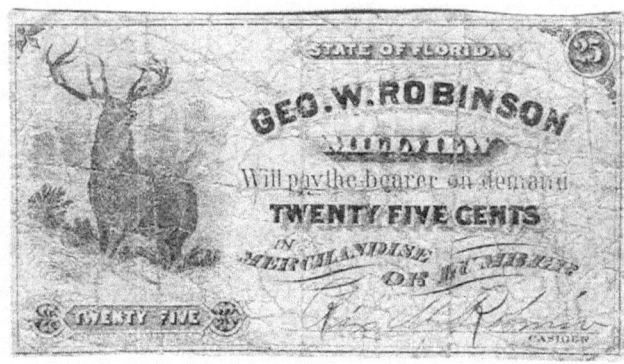

5. 25¢ elk, green back R8

MILTON

A. & G. Forcheimer

Abraham and Gershon Forcheimer came to Florida from Bavaria as children. Subsequently, they operated a grocery and general store in this western Florida town near the Alabama border. After the war, Gershon, the younger brother, opened his own general store in Pensacola while Abraham remained with the Milton store.

Scrip payable in Georgia, South Carolina, Alabama and Confederate notes (but no mention of Florida notes!). Imprinted Keefe & Bro. Printers, 57 Gravier Street, N.O.

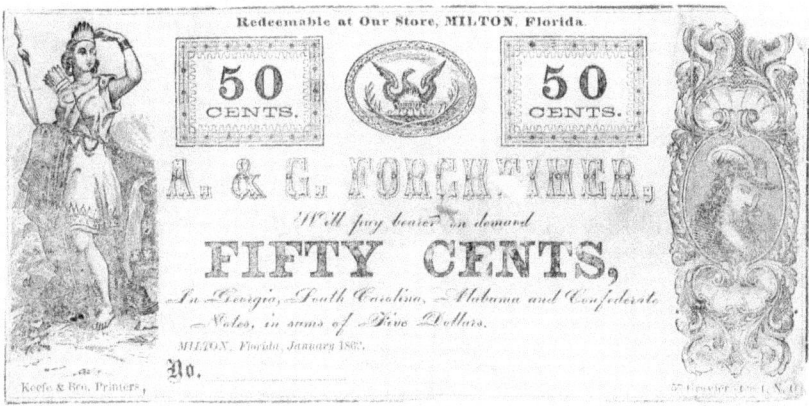

1. 50¢ Indian maiden standing R8

MONTGOMERY, ALABAMA

There were two issues of "crossover" notes from Montgomery, Alabama, that were valid in Florida and other states. J. R. Powell was responsible for both issues.

James Robert Powell was born December 7, 1814, in Powellton, Virginia. In 1836 he moved to the Montgomery area. Starting with a contract as a mail rider on the Pony Express route between Nashville and Montgomery, he competed fiercely for stage routes and mail contracts. He merged with competitors, bought them out, or drove them out of business with price cutting. Powell and his competitor-partner Robert Jemison, Jr. are credited with developing the extensive stage system in the southeast in the 1850s.

By 1860 he had interests in stage lines that owned more than 4,500 horses and mules. When the southern states seceded, Powell outfitted an entire cavalry troop with horses and mules. When the end of the Confederacy was near, he arranged to surrender the city of Montgomery and spare it any damage by Union troops. In 1870, he co-founded the city of Birmingham, Alabama, and became mayor in 1873. Unfortunately, he was shot to death by a drunken former employee on December 9, 1883. (For additional information, see my article "J.R. Powell's Multi-State Notes," *Paper Money*, March/April 2004, pp. 85–91.)

J. R. Powell

Scrip dated January 15, 1862, payable to bearer in current funds and receivable for stage fare in Georgia, Florida, Alabama, Mississippi and Louisiana. The notes are signed Powell and Taylor. William Taylor (a former partner of John G. Winter — see Apalachicola, Bank of St. Marys) was Powell's junior partner for a few months.

1. 5¢ eagle vignette, same size and format as 10¢ R8

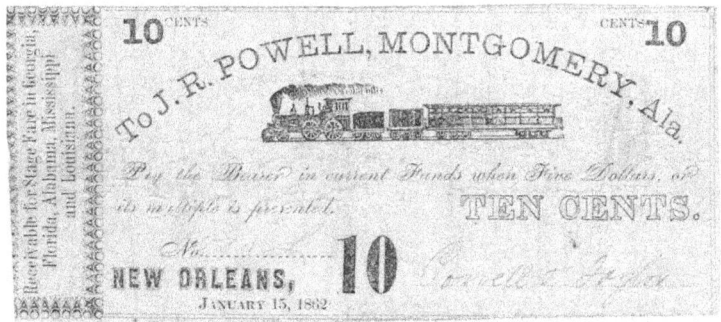

2. 10¢ face printed in blue, railroad train heading left; 10 cents in red on back .R5

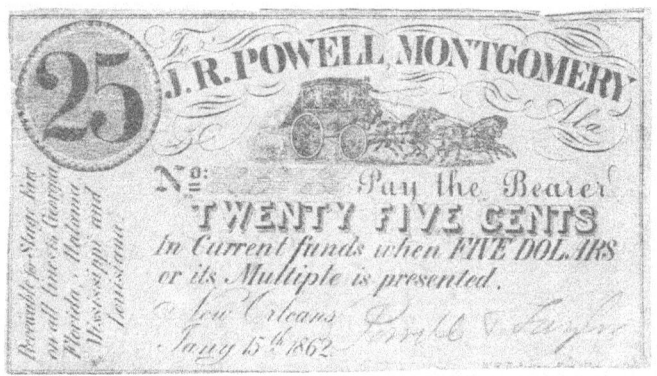

3. 25¢ stage coach R5

4. 50¢ railroad train heading right R5

Powell issued a $3 note, but it was only good in Alabama. On March 18, 1862, Powell moved into the Montgomery Insurance Building and advertised to redeem the notes.

The multi-state capabilities alluded to on the scrip were real. Powell owned the stage lines from Montgomery to Huntsville in Alabama; from Decatur, Alabama, to Rome, Georgia; from Montgomery to Columbus and Aberdeen, Mississippi; and a large share in lines in Florida, Louisiana and Texas. He had a monopoly on mail routes connecting New York with New Orleans, Texas, and beyond.

Montgomery Insurance Company

Notes signed by J. R. Powell alone. Dated April 7, 1862. With the addition of Texas, valid in six states. With Powell's mail route contracts, they were good for postage as well as stage fares. Notes vary in colors of overprints, secondary vignettes in lower right, and positions of pointing fingers before or after the receivable legend.

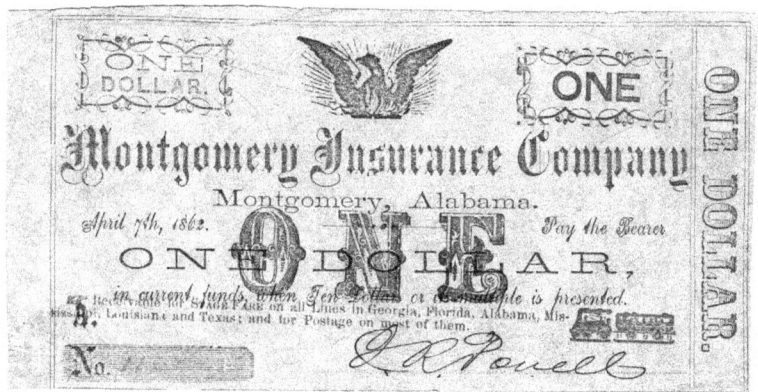

5. $1 eagle vignette, brown ink, denomination overprint green R5
5A. train lower right and one finger before "receivable" in red
5B. stagecoach, additional pointing finger after "them"

6. $2 steamboat vignette, blue ink, red overprint R5
6A. train, two fingers in red

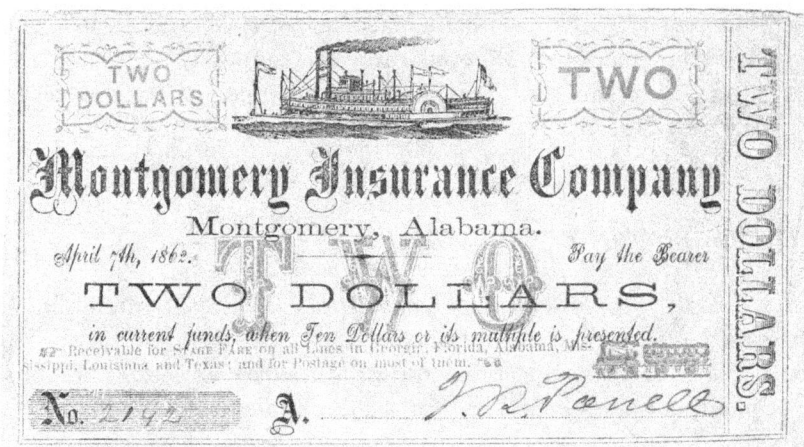

6B. train, two fingers in green
6C. stagecoach, one finger in red
6D. stagecoach, two fingers in red
6E. stagecoach, one finger in green
6F. stagecoach, two fingers in green
6G. Larger size, green overprint, dated May 8, 1862
7. $2.50 steamboat vignette, blue ink, red overprint R7
7A. train, one finger in red
8. $3 railroad vignette, green ink, brown overprint R5
8A. stagecoach, one finger in red

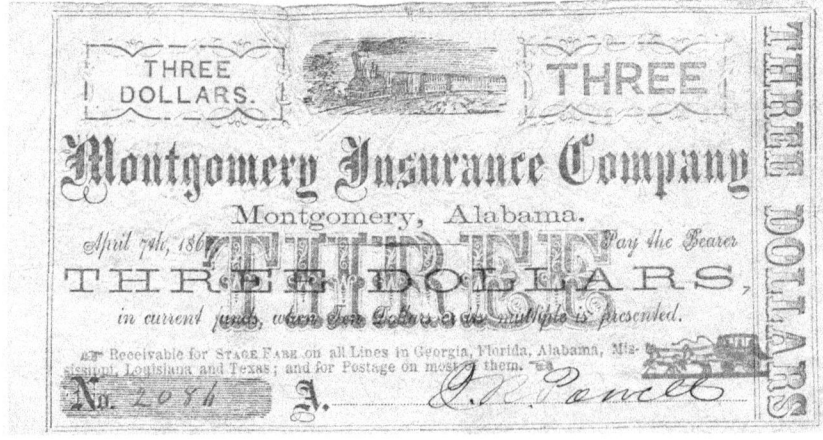

8B. stagecoach, two fingers in red
8C. train, two fingers in red

9. $4 safe and dog, black ink, green overprint R6
9A. stagecoach, one finger in red

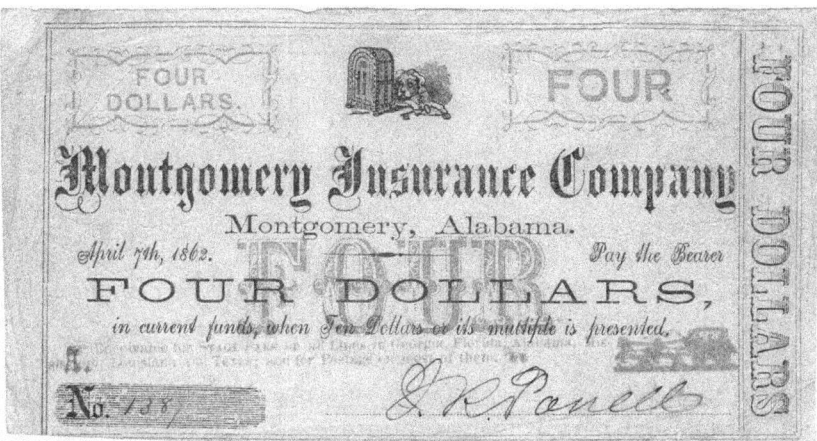

9B. stagecoach, two fingers in red
Other combinations undoubtedly exist, but have not been seen by the author.

MONTICELLO

When Jefferson County was established in 1827, the county seat was, appropriately, named Monticello.

County Treasurer

Notes dated April 18, 1864 redeemable in the new issue of Confederate treasury notes.
1. $1 New York State shield vignette R8

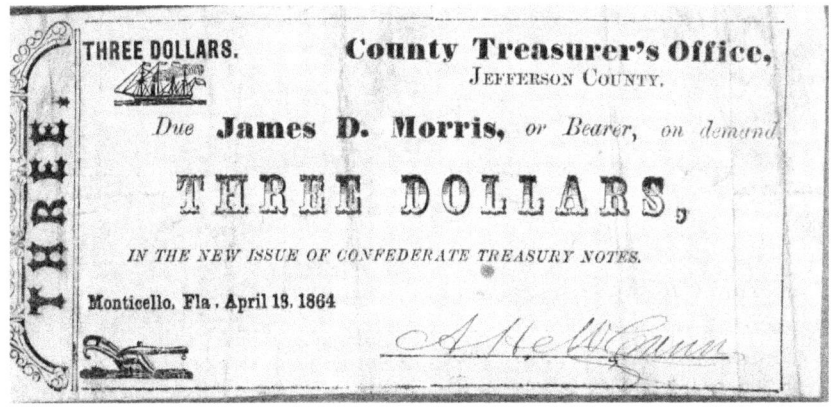

2. **$3 ship and plow vignettes** R8
It is likely that other denominations were issued, but none are known to have survived.

> **MONTICELLO.**
> FRESH GOODS.—Just received by Brig Thacher consisting of superfine Broad Cloths, Cassimers Cassinetts, Hats, Boots, Shoes, &c. Coffee, Whiskey Rum, Cogniac Brandy, and good wines, Mackerel Herring—and many other articles which we wish the public to call and examine for themselves. Fresh Drugs and Medicine.   D. WILLIAMS, & Co.
> Monticello, September 4th 1832.   4tf

D. Williams

Darius Williams opened a general store in Monticello in 1832 and served as postmaster from October 16, 1835 to December 1, 1853. The fractional scrip is undated but appears to be the type issued during the financial panic of 1837. The scrip was payable in postage at the post office. On some specimens the references to postage and post office are overwritten with "in Union Bank Bills;" on others the overwrite is simply "Currency." The $1 scrip is payable in current bank bills. The apparent date of 1818 on the $1 note is impossibly early and presumably was supposed to be 1838. On some specimens the signature is Denham and Palmer. William Denham and Joseph Palmer were partners with Darius Williams from 1838 or 1839 to 1850.

3. 6¼¢ horse R8
4. 12½¢ reported but not seen R8
5. 25¢ stagecoach R8
6. 50¢ lyre and horn R8

5. Obsolete Notes and Scrip — Monticello, Ocala, Orange Springs

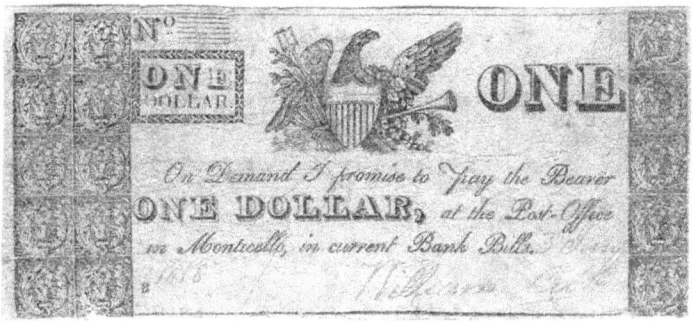

7. $1 eagle R8

OCALA

Commercial Store

Scrip dated March 1858, imprinted T. E. Sutton, Pr. 142 Fulton St. N.Y. No trace of Mr. Dean, the apparent signer, was found in census records, county records, or a search at the local historical society.

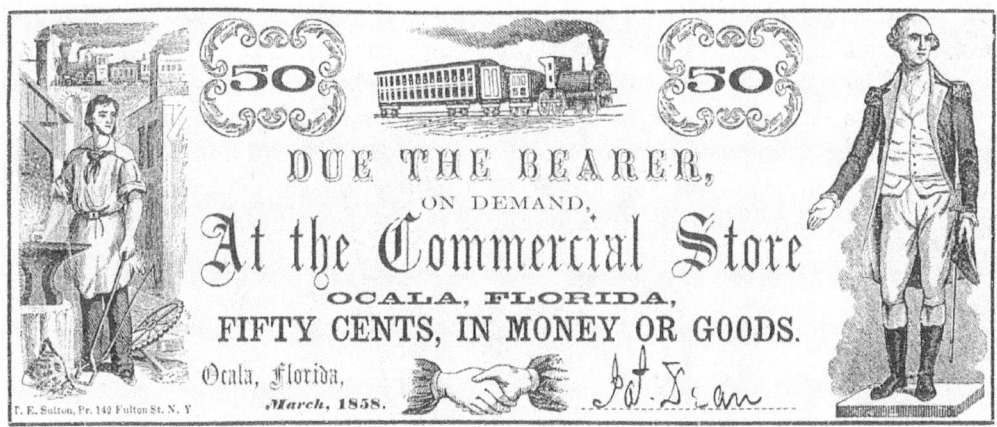

1. 50¢ blacksmith, railroad, Washington R8

ORANGE SPRINGS

Although the town name appears as Orange Spring on most of the scrip, the name has legally been Orange Springs from the establishment of its post office in 1846 straight through to today.

A. G. Bennett

No information was found on this issuer despite the presence of many Bennetts in Marion County in the 1860s.

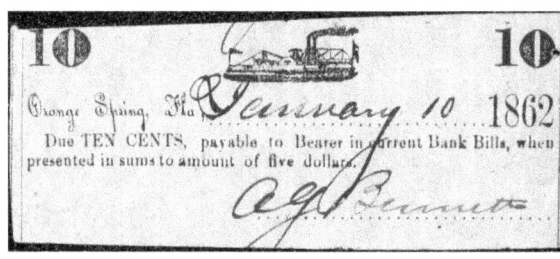

1. 10¢ gunboat R8

J. W. Pearson

John W. Pearson was born in South Carolina on January 19, 1809. In 1843 he and David Levy Yulee bought land around the springs and developed a health resort. By the mid–1850s Pearson owned a hotel, saw mill, grist mill, machine shop, cattle and cotton, and had extensive political connections. During the war he organized and outfitted the 125-man Oklawaha Rangers with muskets and revolvers. He was wounded twice in battle in Virginia and died on September 30, 1864, in Georgia.

Small scrip, usually dated 1862, with a variety of vignettes and type fonts. Printed on poor quality paper or the backs of bonds or other scrip. Each denomination-vignette combination has been given its own number and rarity; type variations are listed as varieties. The illustrations should help identify the vignettes and the differences between the light, medium, heavy, open etc. type fonts used for the denominations.

2. 10¢ Error note dated 1852. small 3-mast sailboat, open type R8
3. 10¢ Correct 1862 date. small 3-mast sailboat R7
3A. open type on 10
3B. thin type
3C. heavy type
4. 10¢ large 3-mast sailboat, medium type R7

5. Obsolete Notes and Scrip — Orange Springs

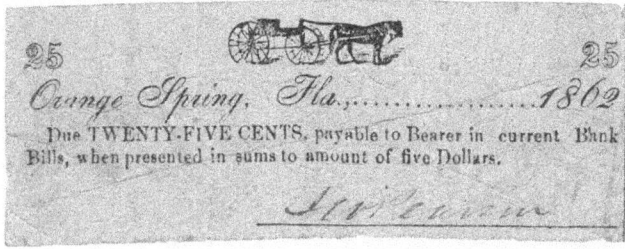

5. 10¢ Orange Springs, 2-mast steamship, light type R7
6. 10¢ gunboat, heavy type R7
7. 10¢ train, heavy type R7
8. 25¢ dated 1861, no vignette R8

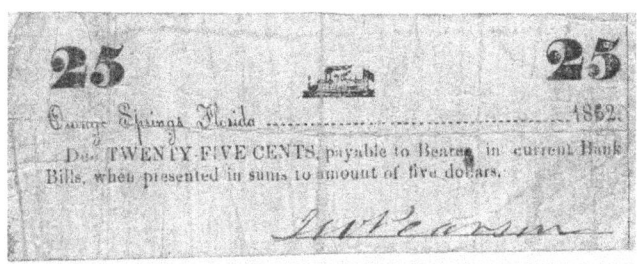

9. 25¢ horse cart, open 25 ....R8
10. 25¢ small steamboat, open type R7

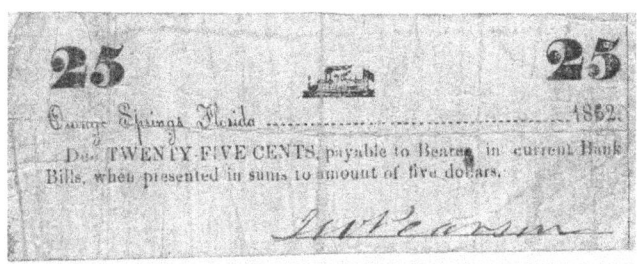

11. 25¢ Orange Springs, small steamboat, heavy type R7
12. 25¢ 2-mast steamship R7
12A. heavy type
12B. medium type
13A. 50¢ no vignette, dated 1861 ....R8
13B. 50¢ no vignette, dated 1862 ....R8

14. 50¢ small 3-mast sailboat, light type R7

15. 50¢ large, 3-mast schooner, heavy type R7

16. 50¢ 3-mast steamship, heavy 5, light 0 ....R7
17. 50¢ 2-mast steamship, medium type R7
18. 50¢ gunboat, light type R7
19. 75¢ small sailboat, medium type R7

20. 75¢ 2-mast sailboat, small type R7
21. 75¢ 3-mast schooner R7

21A. small type
21B. 7 and 5 not aligned
22. $1 gunboat R7
22A. heavy type

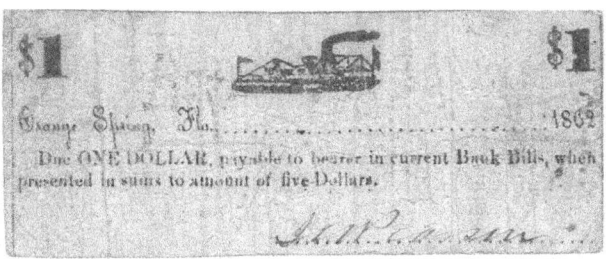

22B. medium type
22C. thin type
23. $2 small 3-mast schooner, heavy type R7
24. $2 large 3-mast schooner, medium type R7

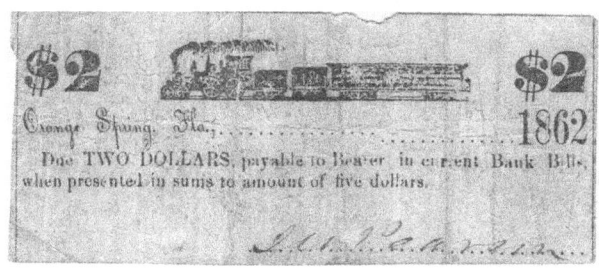

25. $2 train, heavy type R7
Undoubtedly other combinations can be expected to surface.

Panama

Panama, in East Florida, is now part of Jacksonville and should not be confused with Panama City in the Florida Panhandle.

East Florida Steam Saw Mill

Charles F. Sibbald founded Panama and the saw mill on land granted from Spain in 1816. The mill was destroyed by fire in July 1828 and rebuilt a year later.

Notes engraved by Rawdon, Wright & Co. N. York. Signed by William L. Haskins, Agent. Handwritten dates in early 1828.

1. 6¼¢ alligator, Lafayette R8

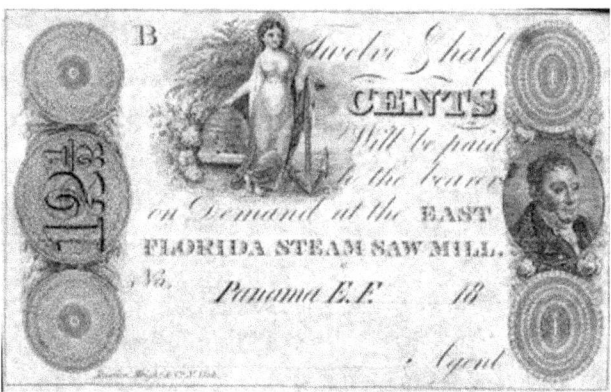

2. 12½¢ standing female with anchor, Lafayette R8
3. 25¢ Prosperity standing, Lafayette R7

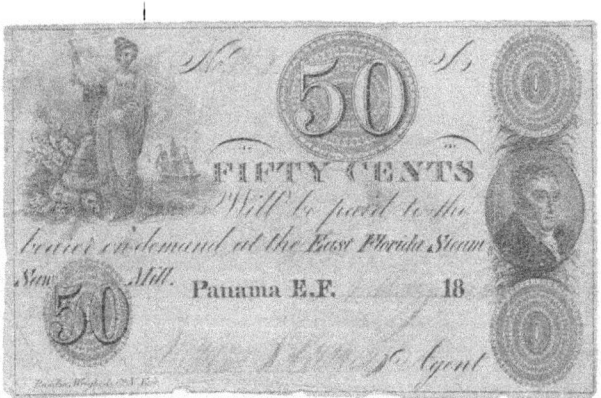

4. 50¢ Allegorical Commerce, Lafayette R7

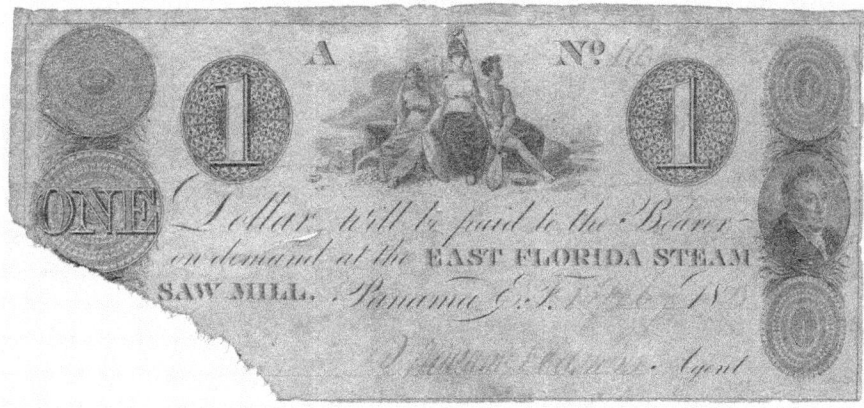

5. $1 Commerce, Athena and male figure, Lafayette R7

Pensacola

Bank of Pensacola

After several unsuccessful attempts, the Territorial Legislative Council approved the incorporation of the Bank of Pensacola over the Governor's veto on January 31, 1831. Capitalization was $200,000. The bank was authorized to issue bonds or notes worth $600,000 more than the amount actually deposited in the bank. Operations began on November 28, 1833. On February 14, 1835, the Governor approved a law increasing capitalization to $2.5 million and authorized an issue of $500,000 in bonds to be guaranteed by the Territory of Florida. In 1836, $131,867 in notes were circulating. On June 5, 1837, specie payments were suspended. They resumed on January 11, 1839, with $202,455 in circulation. The bank folded in 1843.

First issue, with imprint Rawdon, Wright, Hatch & Co. New York, and single plate letters. Handwritten dates between 1834 and 1840. Signed by James Catlin as Cashier. Walter Gregory, the bank's first president, signed all denominations. Subsequent presidents — Thomas Blount, Hanson Kelly and William B. Rochester — signed the $1, 2 and 3 notes.

1. $1 Plate letter A or B, train, Indian with bow, cattle R4

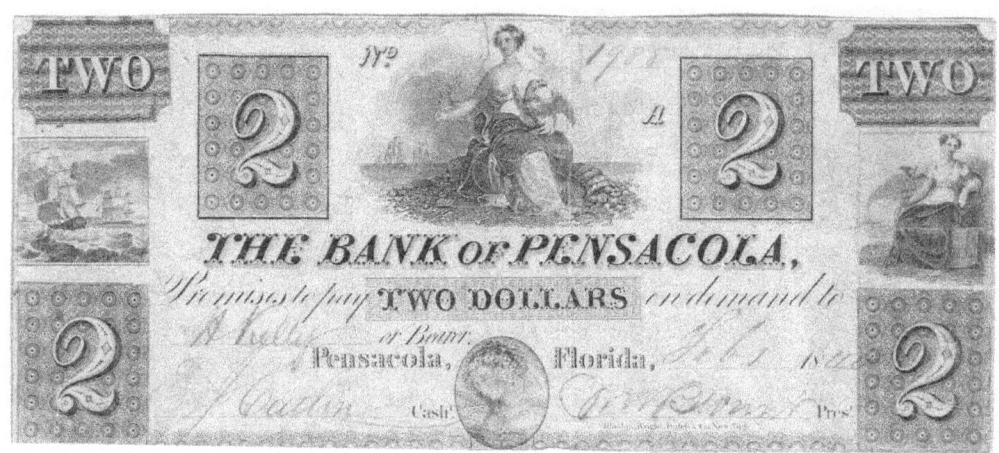

2. $2 Plate letter A, sailboats, allegorical peace and commerce R5

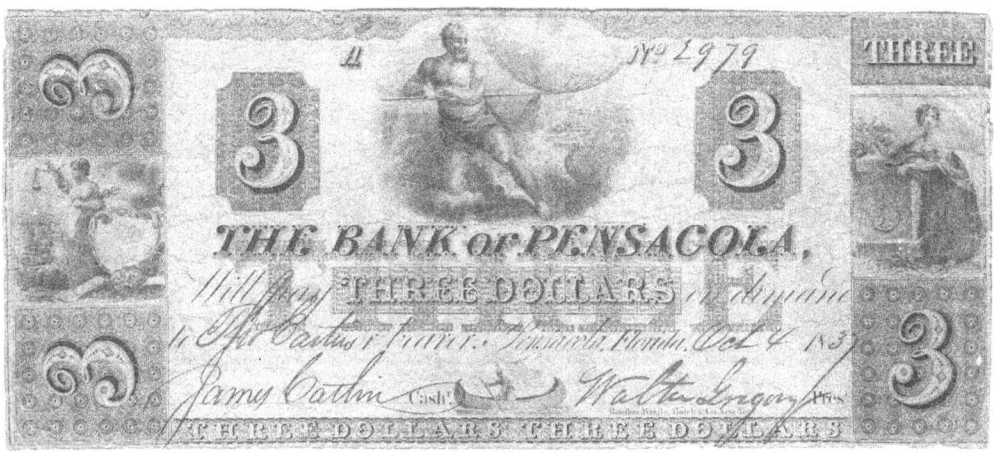

3. $3 Plate letter A, Justice, Archimedes, Ceres' daughter Proserpine R4
4. $5 Plate letter A or B, Indian with rifle, cattle, allegorical America liberty . .R6

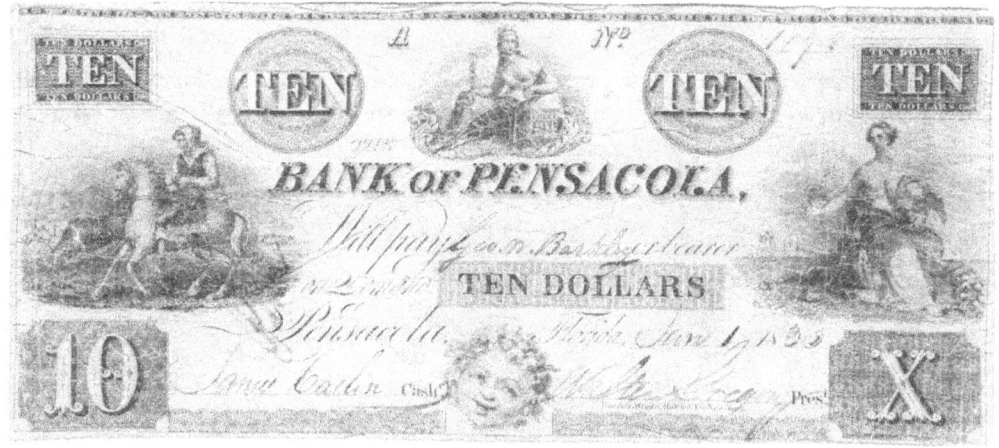

5. $10 Plate letter A, woman on horse, allegorical providence and peace R6
6. $20 Plate letter A, sailboat and providence, justice R7

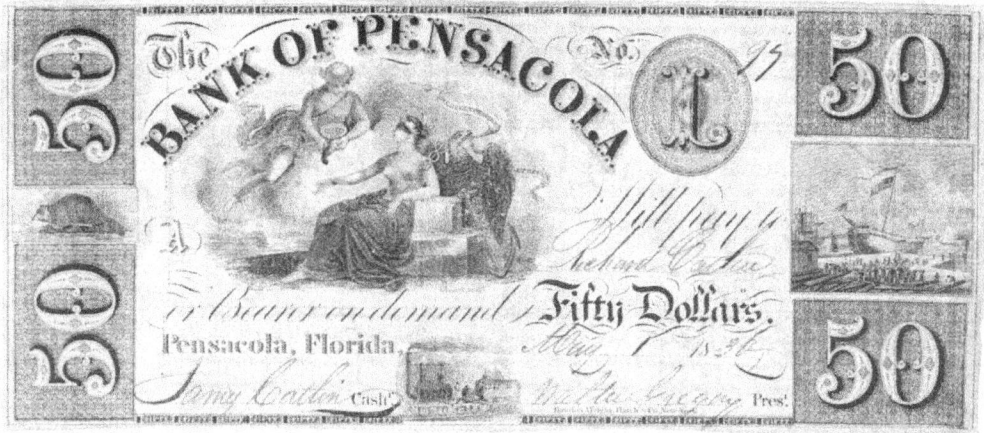

7. $50 Plate letter A, beaver, Mercury, hope and eagle; ship at dock R8

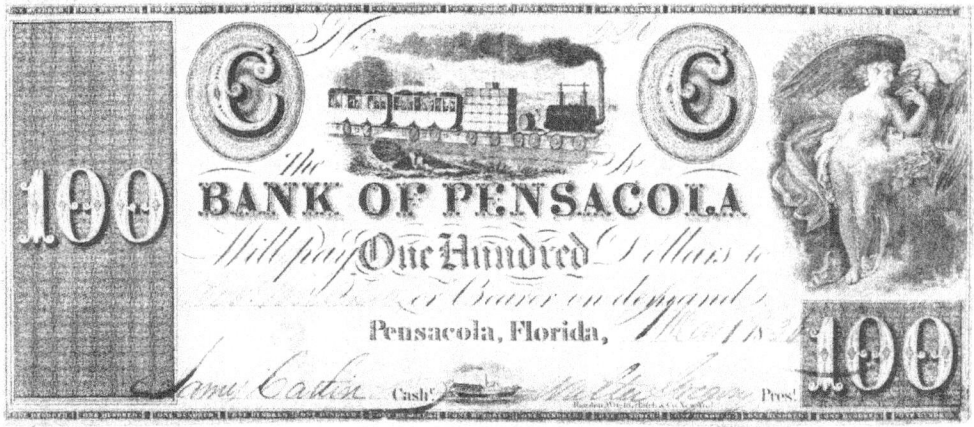

8. $100 Plate letter A, train, Hebe with eagle R7
The $50 and $100 have "Steel Plate TO PREVENT FORGERY" on the back.

Second issue, with imprint Draper Underwood Bald & Spencer. Handwritten date March 10, 1840, signed by J. Catlin, Cashier and Hanson Kelly, President Pro Tem.

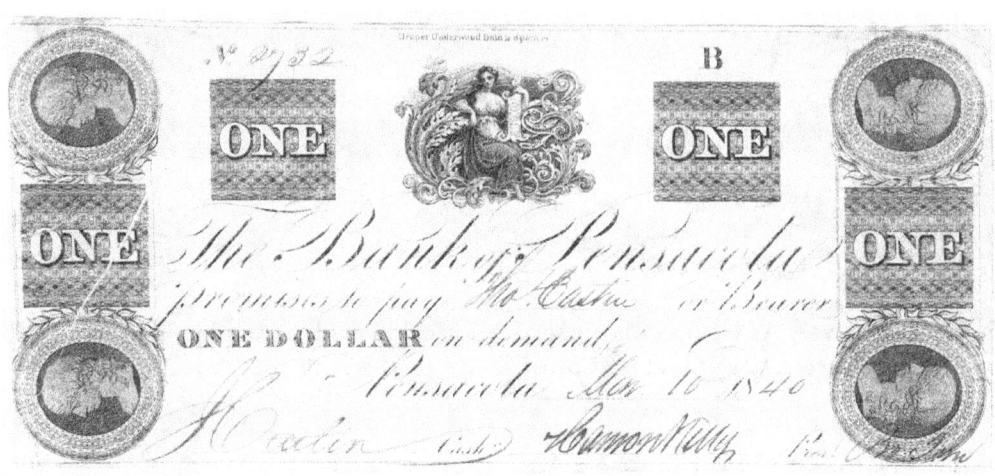

9. $1 Plate A or B, woman holding ornamental 1 ....R5

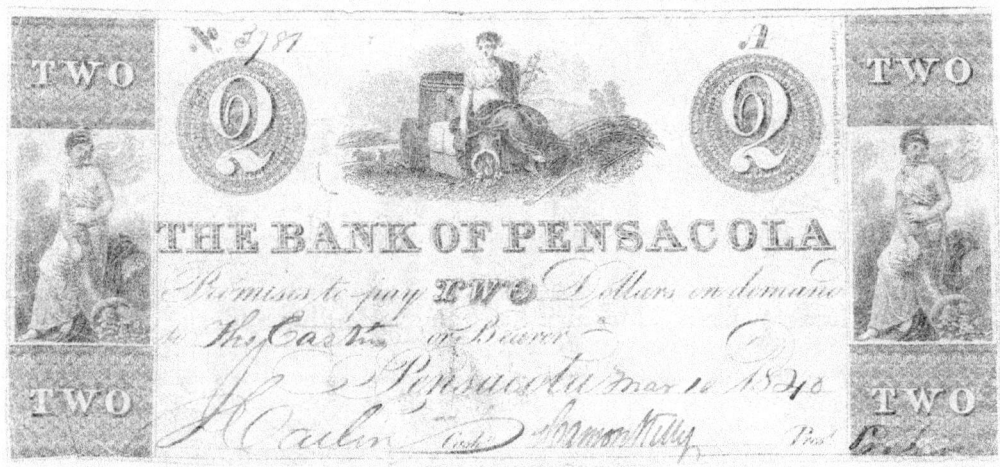

10. $2 Plate A, allegorical plenty, Ceres seated, plenty R6

11. $3 Plate A, Justice, Athena with 3 on shield, Justice R6

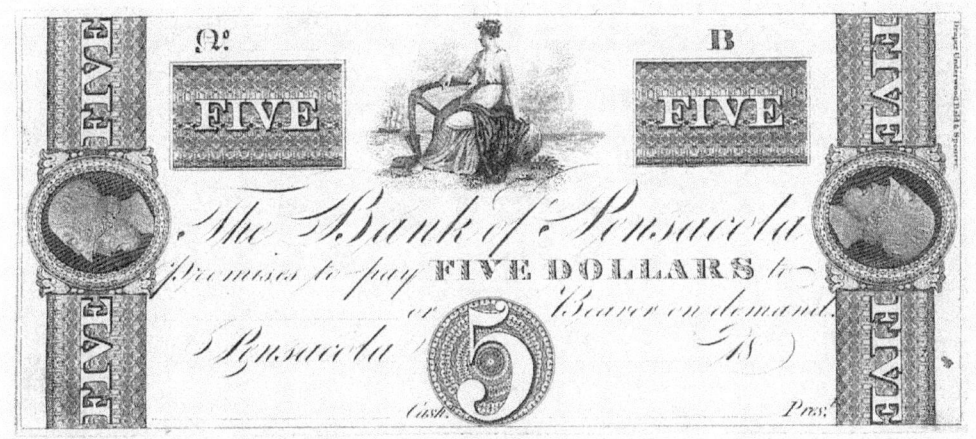

12. $5 Plates A or B, allegorical Hope with ship in background R7

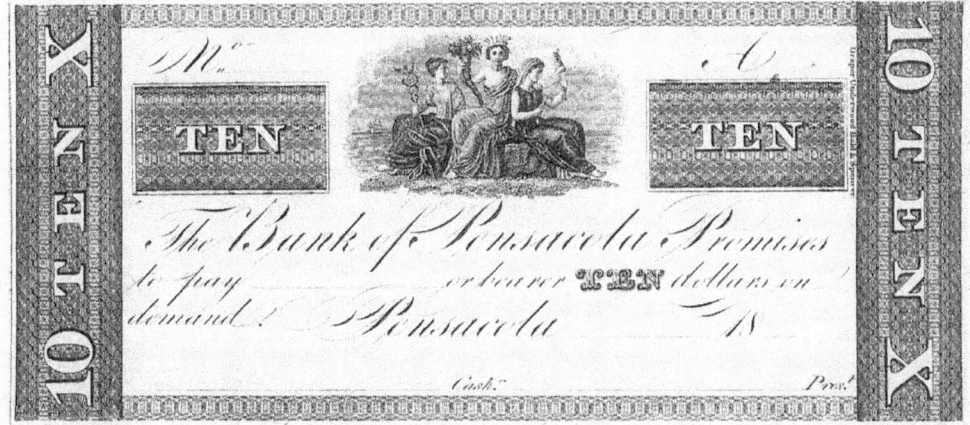

13. $10 Plate A, three seated goddesses R8

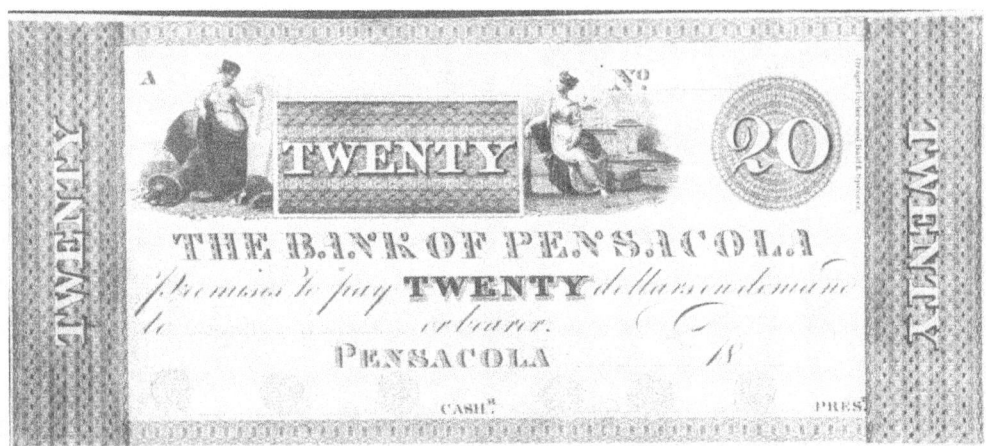

14. $20 Plate A, seated female figures on both sides of TWENTY R7

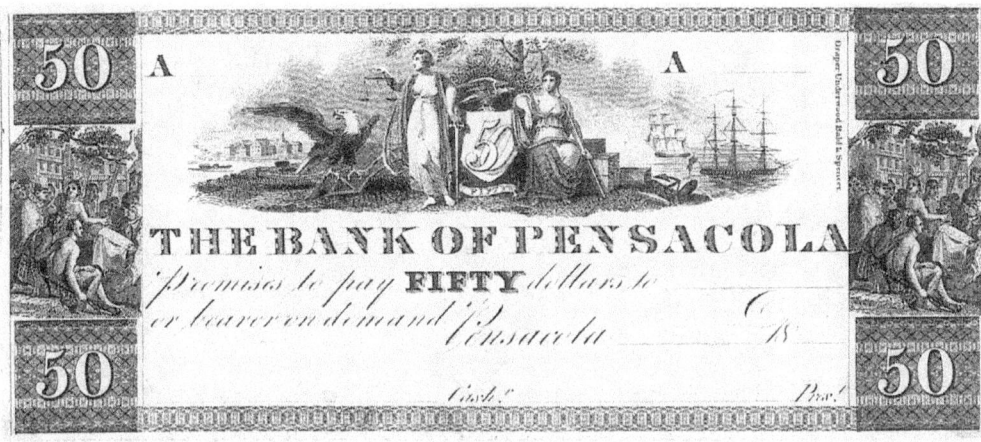

15. $50 Plate A, eagle, Justice, and Liberty around shield with 50 . . . . .R8

Third Issue. Reused plates from first issue with minor changes to some vignettes and addition of double plate letters. Additional imprint Rawdon, Wright, Hatch & Edson, New Orleans. Handwritten date May 4, 1840. Signatures same as second issue.

16. $1 Plates AA, AA-A, BB or BB-B, vignettes same as number 1 above R6

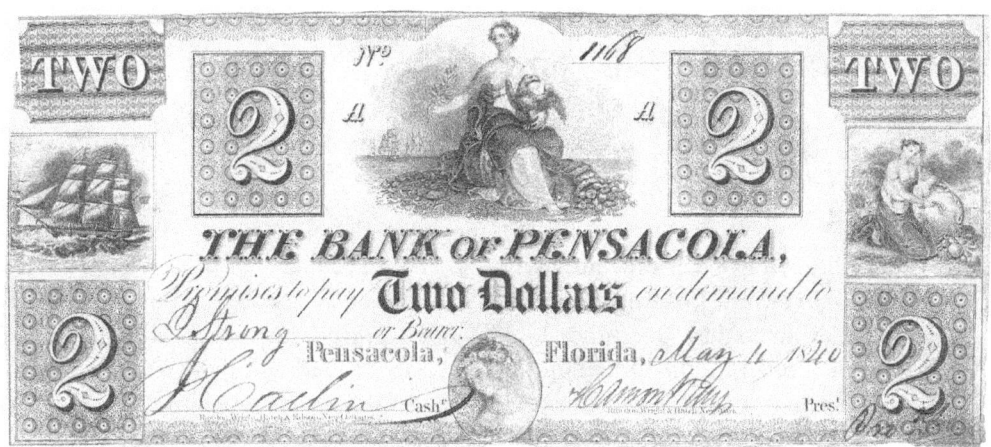

17. $2 Plate A-A, sailboat, peace and commerce, Proserpine kneeling R5
18. $3 Plate A-A, Providence and peace, Archimedes, Proserpine standing R6

Fourth Issue. Actually never issued and may have been printed before the third issue. Notes payable at the Bank of the United States in New York. Engraver's imprint Rawdon, Wright, Hatch & Edson, New Orleans. Unfortunately, the bill authorizing the formation of the third Bank of the United States with headquarters in New York was vetoed by President Tyler. During the Civil War, the blank backs of the sheets were used for other notes. No complete notes are known; our knowledge is limited to fragments on the backs of other southern states notes.

19. $5 woman with liberty cap and scene of commerce and plenty
20. $10 similar, within oval frame

City of Pensacola

There were five issues of scrip: three precipitated by the Panic of 1837; two by the Civil War.

Notes with printed date October 20, 1837. Freeman speculated that a series of denominations was issued, but only one denomination is known.

21. 6¼¢ sailboat vignette, denomination in side borders R8

Notes with printed date January 1, 1838. Signed by Hanson Kelly, Mayor, and Micajah Crupper, Secretary. Only two denominations known.

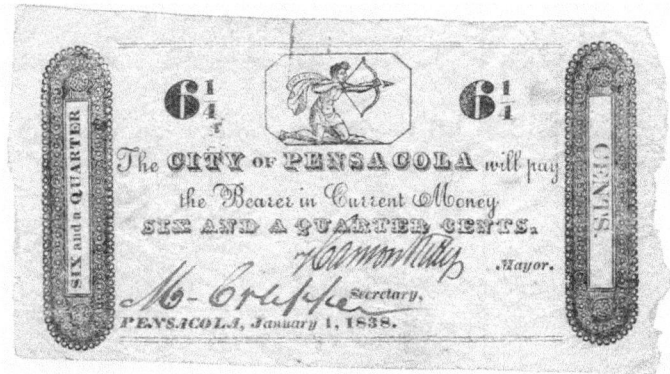

22. 6¼¢ man kneeling with bow and arrow R8
23. 12½¢ woman seated holding flower R8

Notes with printed date December 2, 1839, and engraver's imprint E. Morris, Printer. 45 Chestnut St. Philad. Signed by Hanson Kelly, Mayor, and Micajah Crupper, Secretary. By the summer of 1840, Pensacola had issued $5,000 in change bills.

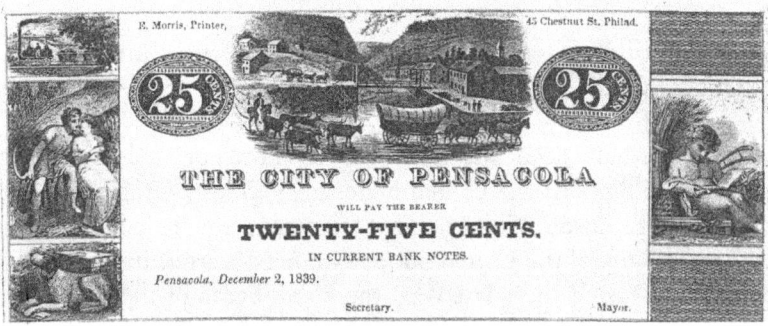

24. 6¼¢ woman with sheaf of grain, man with rod R7

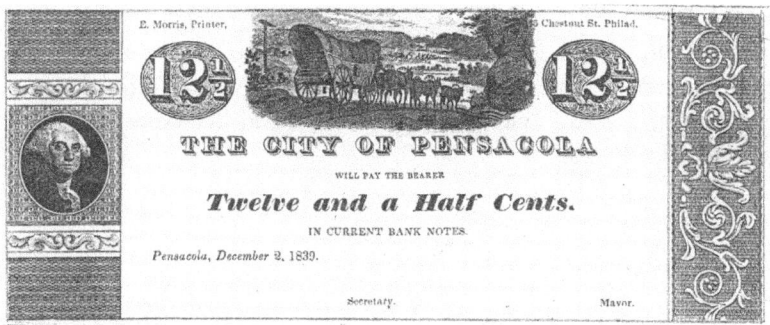

25. 12½¢ Washington, covered wagon R7

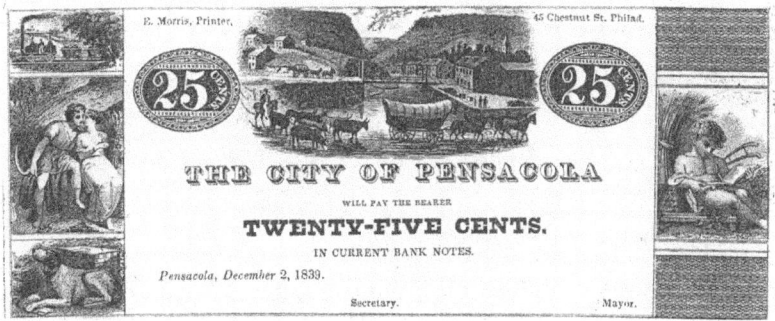

26. 25¢ covered wagon and cattle R8
27. 50¢ same R8
28. 75¢ same R8

Notes with printed date October 1, 1861. Signers are C. H. Gingles, Mayor, and Maximo Posse Rioboo, Secretary.

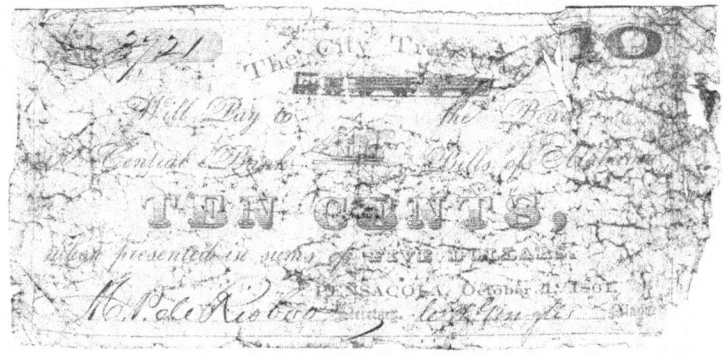

29. 10¢ train and ship R8
30. 25¢ same R8
31. 50¢ flag with 11 stars and 3 bars R8

Notes with printed date February 1, 1862. The Florida General Assembly authorized Pensacola to issue up to $25,000 of 5-, 10-, 25- and 50-cent notes on December 17, 1861.

The city records have been destroyed, so it is unknown whether the three lowest denominations were actually issued. The idea of using a red "L" in the middle of the note to signify the Roman numeral fifty first appeared on Pennsylvania Colonial currency in 1773. Signers were Mayors C. H. Gingles, Francis B. Bobe, and J.B. Gormely. Filo E. de la Rua countersigned as City Clerk.

32. 50¢ red "L" signifying 50 . . . . .R6

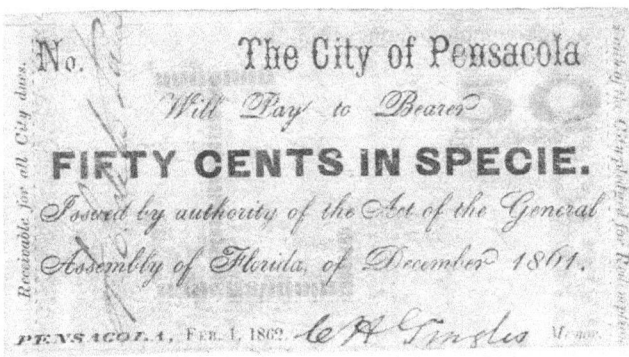

Judah & LeBaron — LeBaron & Son

These notes involve two different firms in two states. William H. Judah and Leonard LeBaron were merchants in Pensacola whose firm Judah & LeBaron was recognized by Bankers Magazine as private bankers. Another branch of the family, headed by Charles LeBaron, were merchants in Mobile. In 1861, the two masted schooner William H. Judah successfully ran the Union blockade bringing in mercury, lead and tin from Canada. Soon thereafter, it was burned and sunk by Union forces.

Scrip with printed date Dec. 15, 1861, signed Judah and LeBaron.

33. 5¢ train, red borders R8
34. 10¢ no vignette, all printing in blue R8
35. 20¢ same R8
36. 25¢ same R7

37. 50¢ same R7
38. 75¢ same R8

Joseph Mitchell

Scrip with printed date Evergreen, Ala., Jan. 25, 1862.

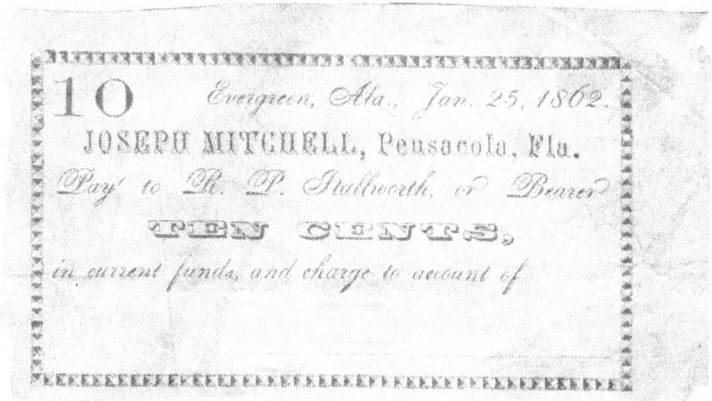

39. 10¢ No vignette. Green printing.	R7
40. 25¢ same	R7
41. 50¢ same	R8

Perdido Bay Lumber Company

George W. Robinson, owner of several mills in Millview (which see), constructed this sawmill with capacity of 90,000 feet of lumber per day in 1873. Eighty people were employed there. Pay scrip with printed date October 1, 1874, and signature of Chas. Courter, President.

42. 25¢ train in front of factory; green lathe work on back	R8
43. 50¢ same	R8
44. $1 same	R8

United States' Navy Yard

Scrip issued and signed by Henry Etting, Purser of the Pensacola Navy Yard. Printed date January 1st, 1838. Apparently he was an independent, self starter. In 1846, Congress voted to reimburse him for personal expenditures on a lawsuit to recover public funds from the Commercial Bank of New Orleans. The word "picayune" in the left border refers to a Spanish coin equal to one-half real, a sixteenth of a dollar, 6¼¢.

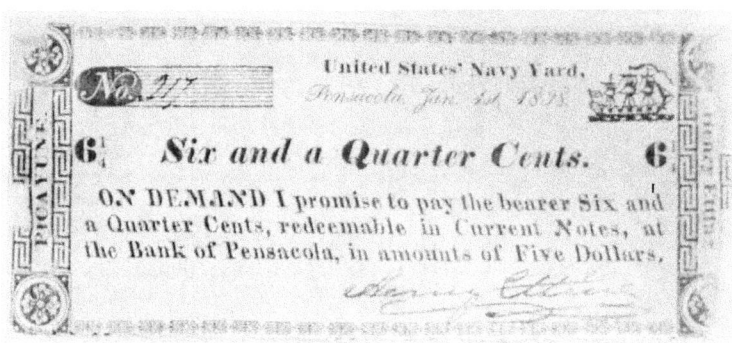

45. 6¼¢ ship in upper right corner R8

Unidentified Colonial Era Fiscal Paper

Blank forms with text, "Pensacola _____ 177__ I promise to pay the bearer the sum of _____ Value Receiv'd _____."

These are blank promissory notes. They were transferable since they were payable to bearer, as would be a check payable to bearer or cash. However, they lack all other attributes of scrip: There is no name of an issuer and no denomination. Panton, Leslie and Company, frequently mentioned as the likely "issuer," was not formed until 1783 and did not open a trading post in Pensacola until 1785. These notes are significant as surviving relics of Colonial Florida.

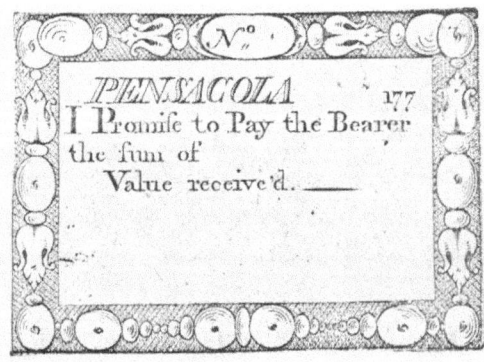

46. No Denomination Ornate red border R8

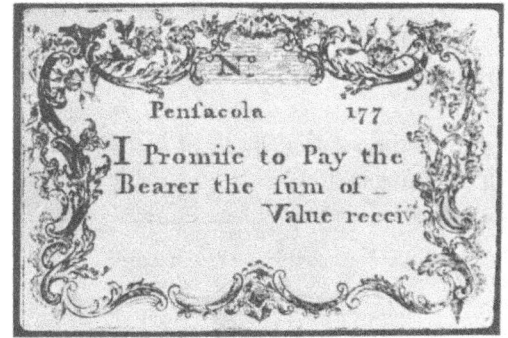

47. No Denomination Ornate green border R8

QUINCY

Forman & Muse

Arthur J. Forman and Hudson Muse were tobacco planters, dealers and exporters.
Notes with imprint Lith. Pub. & Sold by T. & C. Wood 18 Wall St. N. Y. Signed Forman & Muse. Some countersigned John G. Gunn & Co. Handwritten dates in 1840 and 1841.

1. 6¼¢ barrels and cotton bales R7

2. 12½¢ Athena seated R7
3. 25¢ Ceres seated R7
4. 50¢ building R7
5. 75¢ bull R7
6. $1 Liberty seated with eagle R7

E. M. Fraleigh

Scrip with printed date November 1, 1862.

7. 5¢ stagecoach R8

William Monroe & Co.

Scrip payable in notes of the Central Bank of Georgia when presented in the sum of five dollars. Handwritten dates in 1842.
8. 25¢ elaborate side borders, no vignette R8

ST. AUGUSTINE

The Southern Life Insurance & Trust Company

On February 14, 1835, the Territorial Legislature approved formation of the corporation to sell insurance and trade in bills of exchange. Initial capitalization was $2 million, increasable to $4 million. Authorization was given to issue bills up to the amount of paid in capital. The charter was amended on February 11, 1838, to permit ordinary banking. A total $601,000 in notes was printed, and circulation reached $111,595 in 1840. The bank failed in 1842 with much of this and $6,500 in post notes (from the Tallahassee branch) outstanding.

Notes engraved by Rawdon, Wright, Hatch & Edson, New-York. Vignette signed by George W. Hatch. Some $5 and $10 plates have "Flora" in thin hollow letters at the edge above the vignette. Handwritten dates in 1836 and 1837. Authorized signatures are Lot Clark, President, and George Field or Arthur M. Reed as Cashier.

1. $1 Flora seated in a garden R8
2. $2 same R7
3. $3 same R7
4. $5 same R6
4A. with "Flora" at top border above vignette
4B. without "Flora"
5. $10 same R6

5A. with "Flora"

5B. without "Flora"
6. $20 same R7

M. Cook

Margaret Cook owned an inn and store in the building now known as the Ximinez-Fatio house. Cassidy pictures a St. Augustine, East Florida note (see discussion below) hand dated November 9, 1829, with her signature.
7. 12½¢ replica of reverse of 1829 dime modified to 12½¢ R8

Wm. Hamlin Sr.

Scrip with handwritten date Sept. 7, 1838.

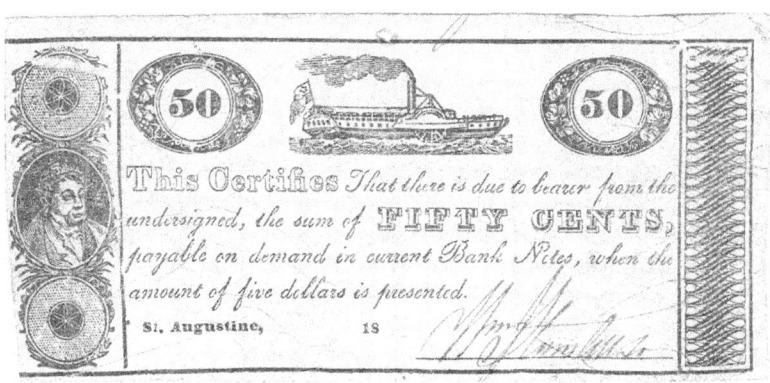

8. 50¢ Lafayette, steamboat R8

St. Augustine, East Florida

On August 12, 1823, St. Augustine City Council authorized issuance of bills in the denominations 6¼-, 12½-, 25-, 50- and 100-cents. Apparently, these were standard blank note forms to be signed by local business people. Apparently also, 5¢ notes were printed instead of 100¢. The plates were re-engraved several times over the years. Very few specimens have survived, and much of what we know about the early notes has been deduced from later notes printed from modified plates. Some notes have the engraver's imprint Wright S.C.; others of the same denomination do not.

9. Notes imprinted 182_. No surviving examples known except for M. Cook above.

10. 6¼¢ Imprinted 183_. Eagle with arrows and olive branch
    Undated and unsigned remainder R7
    Dated 1838 and signed V. Sanchez (see 15 below)
11. 12½¢ 183_.
11A. "UNITED" on coin replica R8
11B. "UNITED" changed to "CONFED" on coin replica R7
12. 25¢ 183_.
12A. same as 11A R8
12B. same as 11B R7
13. 50¢ 183_.
13A. same as 11A. R8
13B. same as 11B. R7
14. Notes imprinted 18__. CONFED on coin replica.
    No surviving examples of 18__ known except Venancio Sanchez below

Venancio Sanchez

Venancio Sanchez operated a hotel and general store for more than 50 years. He served as mayor in 1866. Venancio Street is named after him. Interestingly, there is a tie-in with Apalachicola Lands scrip. In 1845 he became administrator of John Forbes' will and was successfully sued for $2 million in 1876 by the Panton heirs. The judgment was overturned because their claim was "stale."

Scrip from original plates of ST. AUGUSTINE EAST FLORIDA. Hand dated in 1838 and signed.

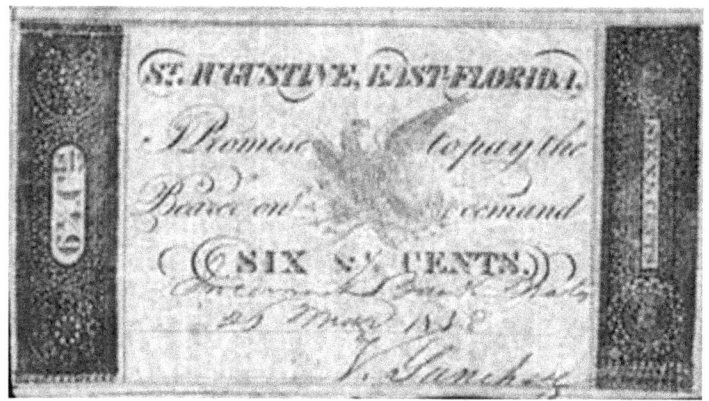

15. 6¼¢ eagle R8

Scrip from CONFED STATES OF AMERICA altered plates of ST. AUGUSTINE, EAST FLORIDA scrip. Hand dated in 1861 and 1862 and signed. Some specimens have Wright S.C. imprint. Some also have handwritten "Payable in current bank bills."

16. 5¢ 5 in round seal R8
17. 6¼¢ eagle R8
18. 10¢ 10 in round seal R8

19. 12½¢ 12½¢ coin with eagle R8
20. 25¢ 25¢ coin with eagle R7
21. 50¢ 50¢ coin with eagle R8

St. Joseph

St. Joseph was a short-lived town with an interesting history. In 1835 the Supreme Court ruled that Panton, Leslie & Co. owned the Apalachicola lands. Many residents of Apalachicola chose to form a new city, St. Joseph, 28 miles away rather than pay. To compete with Apalachicola as a cotton port, the Lake Wimico and St. Joseph Canal Company was formed to open an alternate route from the river. When the dredged route proved too shallow, a 30-mile bypass railroad was built via another new town, Iola. The boom town of St. Joseph hosted the Florida Constitutional Convention in 1838. In the summer of 1841, a yellow fever epidemic caused most residents to leave. In September 1841, a hurricane wiped out the town. On February 27, 1842, the *Niles Register* reported: "A gone city — The city of Apalachicola has bought out the city of St. Joseph, and hereafter all the business of the latter is to be united with that of the former."

Commercial Bank of Florida

Unauthorized branch of Commercial Bank of Florida in Apalachicola.

The plates from Apalachicola #s 18, 19 and 20 were re-engraved with St. Joseph substituted for Apalachicola. Imprinted Chas. Toppan & Co. Phila.

1. $5 Washington; boy with sickle, steamboat, boy; Jackson R7
2. $10 Standing Indian, Sailboat, Standing Washington .R7
3. $20 Justice, Sailboat, Sailboat, Justice R7

The plates from Apalachicola #s 21, 22 and 23 were re-engraved with St. Joseph substituted for Apalachicola. Imprinted Draper, Toppan, Longacre & Co. Phila. & NY. Authentic signatures are William Patrick and J. C. Maclay with dates in 1836 and 1837 written in. In 1847, long after the parent bank had failed and St. Joseph had vanished, remainder notes were released with 1847 dates and fictitious signatures.

4. $5 Portraits of Washington, Marshall, Fulton and Franklin R5
   in the corners, sailboats center

4A. authentic signatures
4B. fraudulent signatures
5. $10 same 4 portraits, steamboat R5
5A. authentic signatures

5B. fraudulent signatures
6. $20 same 4 portraits, sailing ships R5
6A. authentic signatures
6B. fraudulent signatures

7. $100 standing female, allegorical commerce, Ceres standing R7

Merchants & Planters Bank of Florida

This bank was created in Tallahassee by reviving the charter of the failed Merchants and Planters Bank at Magnolia. This roundabout method was required since Congress had taken away the right of the territorial legislature to charter new banks. St. Joseph was a branch location.

Bank notes with imprints Rawdon, Wright & Hatch New-York and Rawdon, Wright, Hatch & Edson, New Orleans. 184_ imprinted for date. After St. Joseph failed, some remainder notes had "Tallahassee" written over "St. Joseph."

8. $1 silver dollar, Hebe pouring drink for eagle, train R7

9. $2 Commerce, cotton plant R7

10. $3 Venus rising from sea, horses pulling plow, cherub R7

Corporation of Saint Joseph

Notes with 183__ engraved and signature spaces for Clerk and Mayor.
11. 6¼¢ seated woman, steamboat and sailboat, man smoking pipe R7
12. 12½¢ same as preceding R7
13. 12½¢ standing woman, woman in farm scene, rowboat and sailboats R7

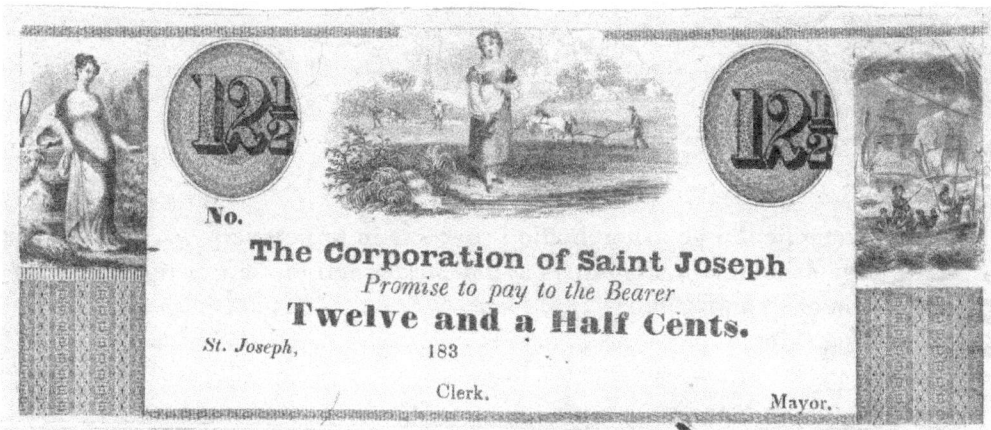

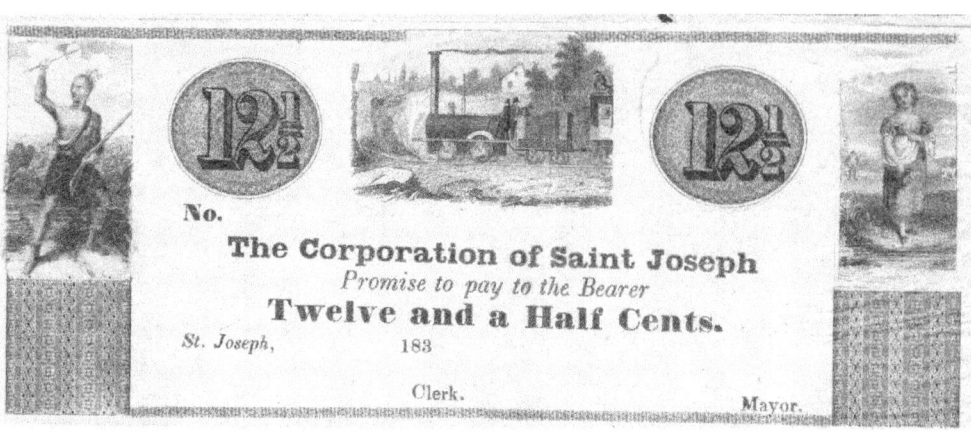

14. 12½¢ Indian with tomahawk, steam engine, standing woman R7
15. 25¢ same as 14 ....R8
16. 50¢ same as 13 ....R8
   Notes with 184__ engraved and signature spaces for Clerk and Mayor.
   Imprint: Juls. Manouvrier & P. Snell Lithogr. N. Orls.

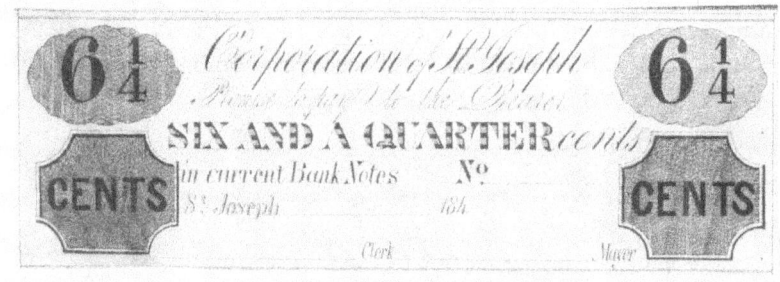

17. 6¼¢ no vignette. Large denomination counters in top corners R8
18. 12½¢ large denomination counters at left border and top left & right R8
19. 25¢ cotton bales and sailboat R8
20. 50¢ sailing ships R7

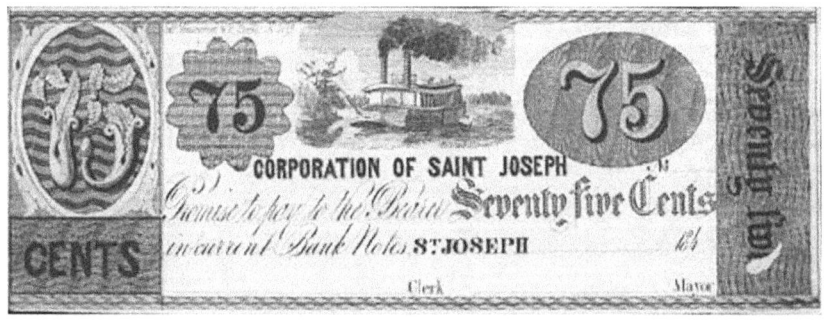

21. 75¢ steamboat R7

22. $1 early railroad train R7

Lake Wimico and St. Joseph Canal & Railroad Company

Printed year 1837 with handwritten dates on six month post notes. Signed by R. C. Allen and R. S. Griggs as president and secretary, respectively.

23. $5 sailboat R8

24. $10 sailboat R8

SILVER SPRINGS

Proskey Brothers

Samuel, A.S. and Winfield Proskey operated a general store, saw mill and hotel. They were reportedly related to the famous early numismatic dealer, auctioneer, writer and editor, David Proskey, 1853–1928, but this has not been substantiated. The items listed below fall outside the usual realm of paper money. The round items are perhaps better classified as tokens; the rectangular items as miscellaneous exonumia. Business name and dates, if any c.1886, stamped on generic good-for blanks.

1. 5¢ round blue cardboard R7
2. 10¢ round pink cardboard R7

3. 25¢ round yellow cardboard R7

The business also issued non-circulating rectangular punch cards: a $1 card with seven 10¢ and six 5¢ punches and a $5 card with two 50¢, eight 25¢, fourteen 10¢ and twelve 5¢ punches.

STARKE

Bank of Fernandina

When Union forces invaded Fernandina in March 1862, the bank moved inland to Starke. Small scrip, payable in current bank bills, with printed date April 1, 1862. Signed by John Hodges as Cashier.

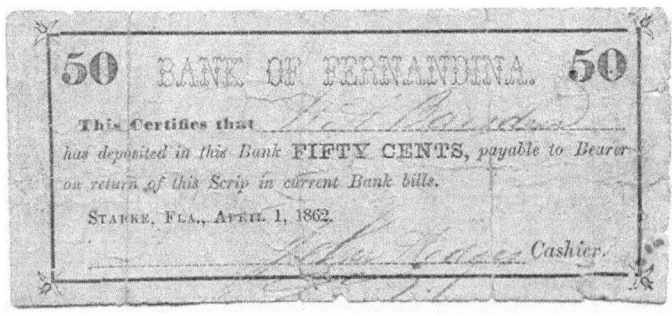

1. 50¢ no vignette R8

Tallahassee

Bank of Florida

On November 23, 1828, the Territorial Legislative Council approved, over the governor's veto, the Bank of Florida with $500,000 in stock and authority to issue $400,000 in notes. The Territory would accept the notes as payment and would deposit public monies in the bank. No stock was sold in the bank, so the legislature passed, over a veto, a replacement law on November 17, 1829. Capital was $600,000, but startup was permitted as soon as $25,000 was received. Notes were not to exceed three times paid in capital.

In April 1833 the Central Bank of Florida bought the assets of the Bank of Florida and assumed responsibility for the outstanding circulation. However, they kept the Bank of Florida's charter alive. On March 15, 1843, the Legislative Council approved reactivating the bank with stricter rules on issuance and redemption of notes. Edwin G. Booth bought the charter and sold it to James G. Graham who subsequently left town with the assets. On July 4, 1844, the bank stopped redeeming its notes for specie and finally, on March 10, 1845, the charter was annulled.

Demand notes imprinted Fairman Draper Underwood & Co. No signed or dated notes known. The imprint indicates they were engraved in the late 1820s.

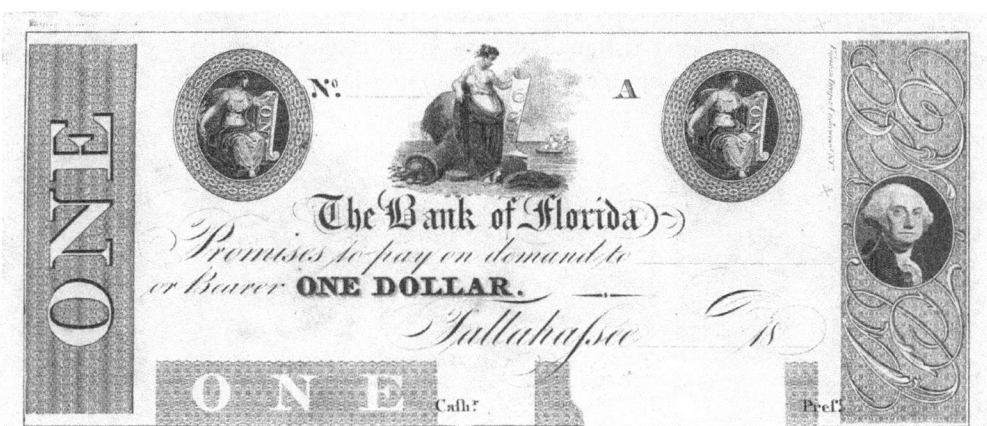

1. $1 standing female, Washington R8
2. $2 Mercury seated, Franklin R8
3. $5 seated female, Raleigh R8
4. $10 female holding TEN, Jefferson R8

Demand note with printed date January 1843, predating legislative approval. Note appears to be printed from set type rather than engraved plate. Signed by Edwin G. Booth.

5. $1 no vignette. "To D. S. Kennedy, New York. Pay the bearer, ...R8
on demand, one dollar."

Demand notes with no mention of Kennedy. Engraved by Rawdon, Wright & Hatch, New York. Handwritten dates in February 1843. Signed by Booth and Henry L. Rutgers.

6. $1 griffin, commerce, Mercury, cherubs in ornamental 1s R8

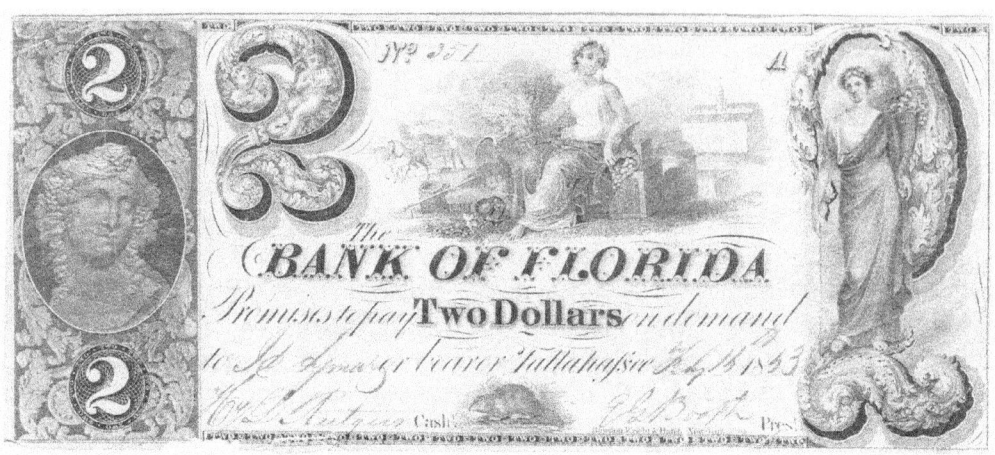

7. $2 Ceres representing commerce, female standing in ornamental 2 . . . . .R8
8. $3 Hope, female standing in ornamental 3 . . . . .R8
9. $4 farmer and hunter R8

Exchange notes to David S. Kennedy, New York. Engraved by Rawdon, Wright & Hatch, New York. Handwritten dates in March 1843. Signed by Booth and Rutgers.

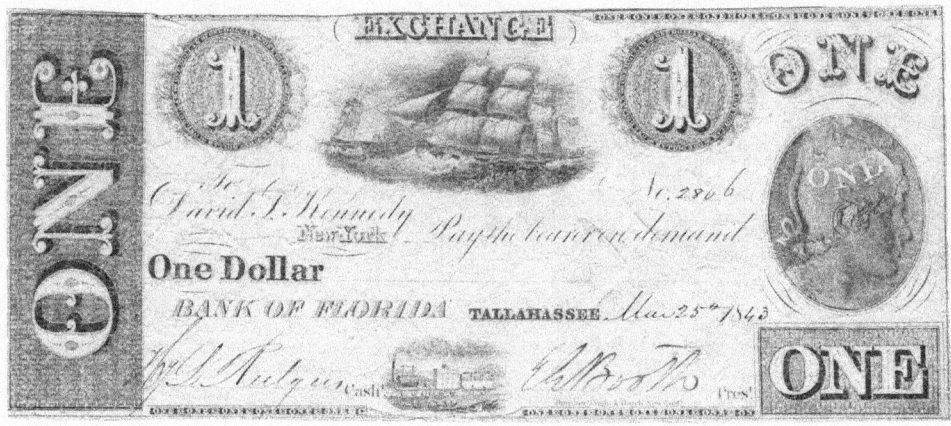

10. $1 sailing ships R5

5. Obsolete Notes and Scrip—Tallahassee

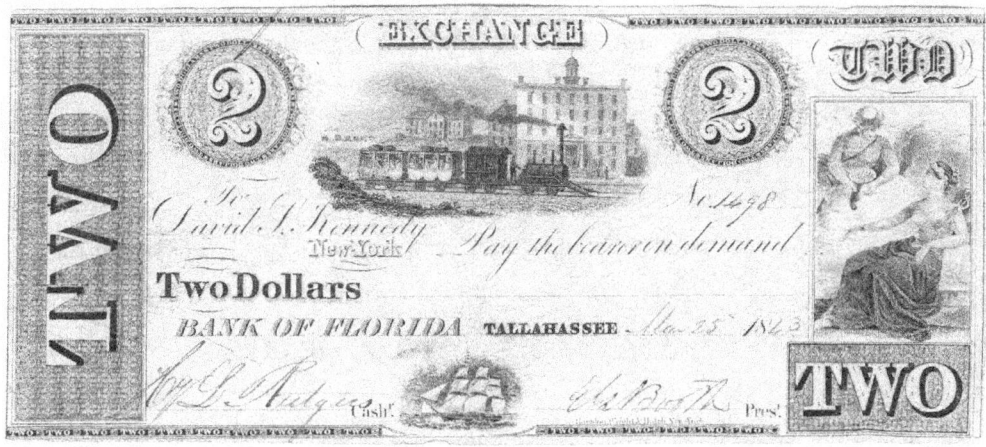

11. $2 early passenger train and buildings R5

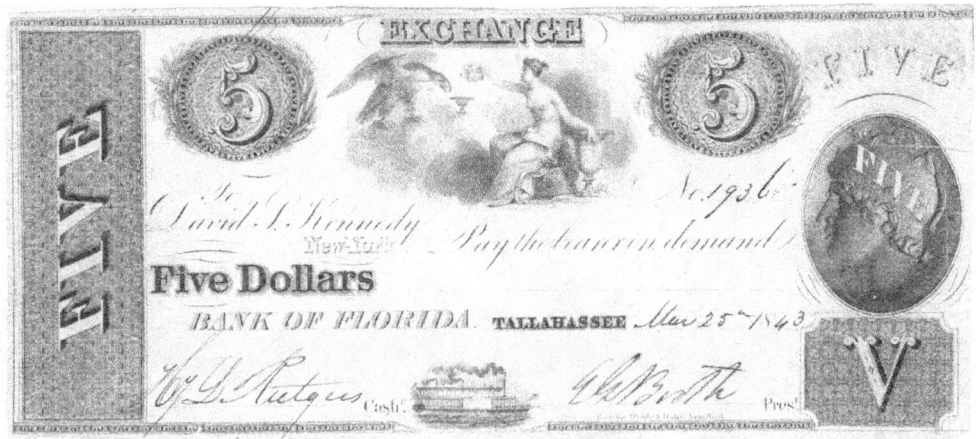

12. $5 Hebe pouring drink for eagle R6

13. $10 steamboat and horsedrawn dray, Athena R5

Demand notes. Imprinted Rawdon Wright & Co. N. York. "at the office of D. S. Kennedy New York" handwritten. Dates in August 1843 written in. Signed by Booth and Rutgers.

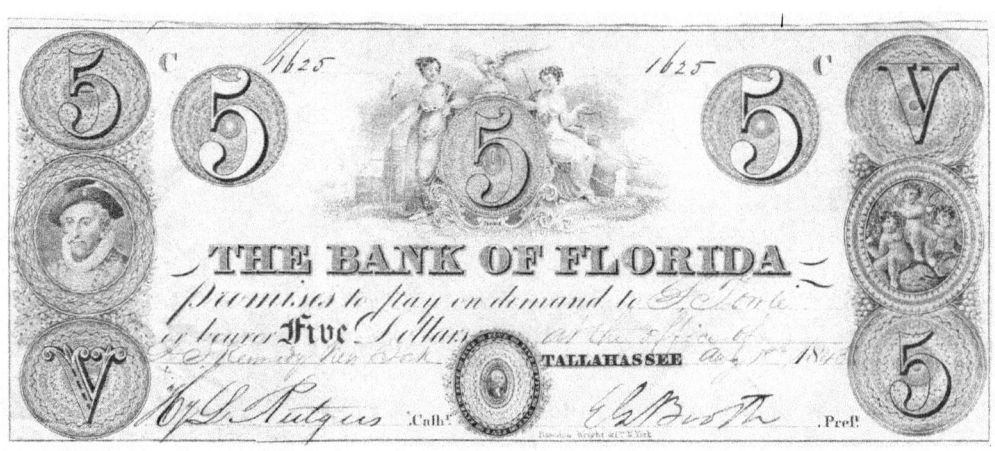

14. $5 Raleigh, Liberty and Justice, 3 cherubs R7
15. $10 Minerva and Justice R6

16. $20 Male portrait, three cherubs and globe R7

Demand notes. Imprinted Rawdon Wright & Co. N. York. "at the office of D. S. Kennedy New York" engraved. Written dates in August 1843 signed by Booth and Rutgers; dates in March 1844 signed by Graham and Rutgers.

17. $5 same as 14 ....R6
17A. Booth signature

17B. Graham signature
18. $10 same as 15 ....R7

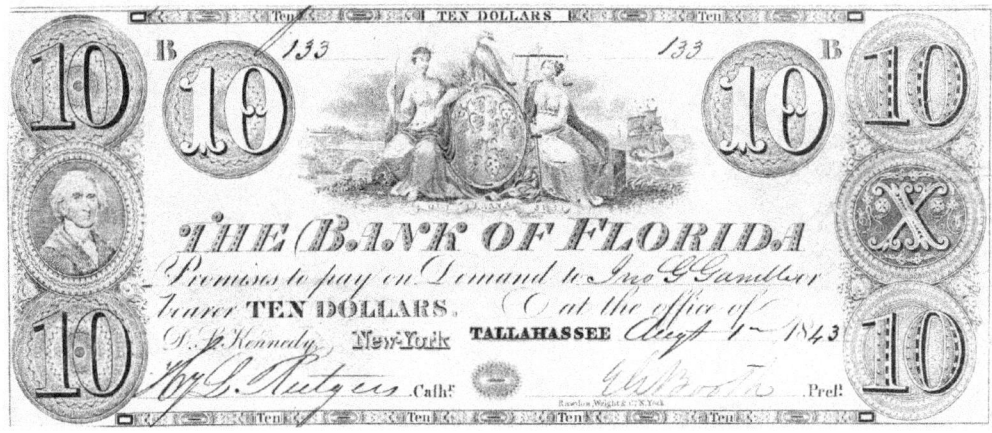

18A. Booth signature
18B. Graham signature
19. $20 same as 16 ....R7
19A. Booth signature
19B. Graham signature

Demand notes with Kennedy engraved. Engraved by Rawdon, Wright & Hatch, New York. Handwritten dates in February 1844. Signed by Graham and Rutgers.

20. $1 same as 6 ....R7
21. $2 same as 7 ....R7

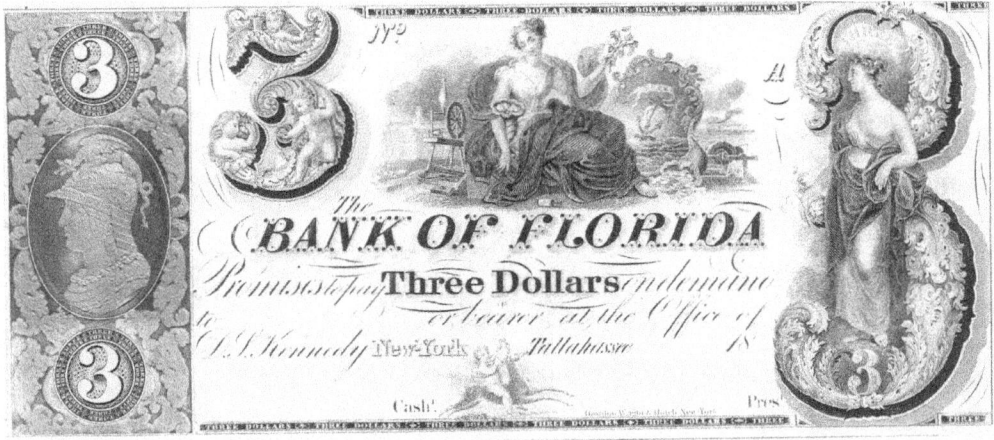

22. $3 same as 8 ....R7

23. $4 same as 9 .... R6

Central Bank of Florida

The bank was approved on February 11, 1832, apparently to bail out the Bank of Florida. The law provided that notes on the Bank of Florida could be used to buy stock in the Central Bank. Capitalization was set at $1,000,000 and notes were limited to three times the capital actually paid in. Remarkably, on February 12, 1837, a law was passed increasing the capitalization to $2 million, half of which was reserved for the Territory, and removing the requirement that notes issued by the bank be redeemable at the bank. Legislation in 1841 forbade selling the bank or branching east of the Apalachicola River. Notes totaling $93,458 were outstanding at year end 1837.

Notes imprinted Draper Underwood Bald & Spencer. "The President, Directors & Co. of the Central Bank of Florida promise to pay ... on demand." Signed by Benjamin Chaires as President and Leslie A. Thompson as Cashier. Handwritten dates in 1834 or 1835.

24. $1 Ceres standing R8

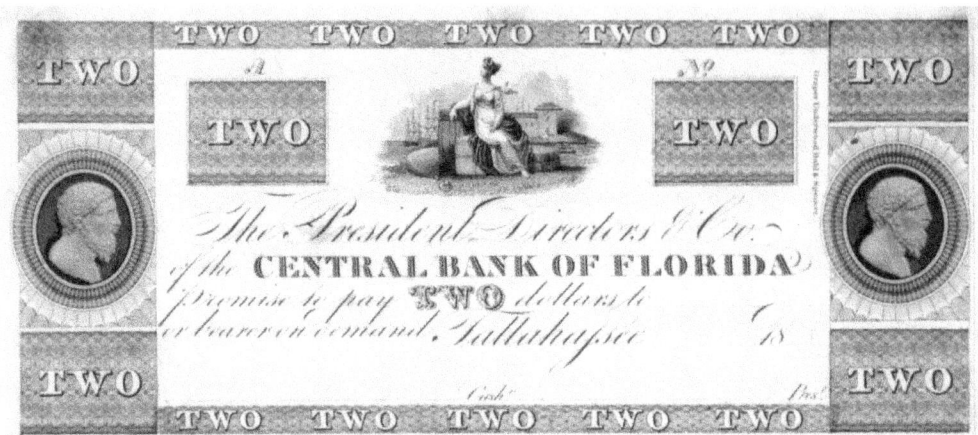

25. $2 Commerce seated R8

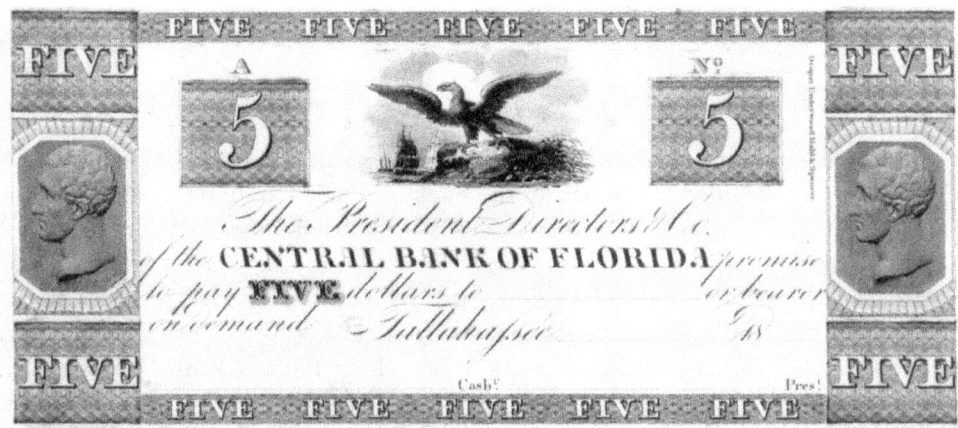

26. $5 Eagle R8

27. $10 Liberty with young woman and man R8

Notes imprinted Rawdon Wright Hatch & Edson New York. Same text as preceding. Known only by surviving proofs.

28. $20 Hebe serving drink to eagle R8
29. $50 Female holding eagle; ships in background R8
30. $100 Eagle R8

Merchants & Planters Bank of Florida

This bank started as the Merchants & Planters Bank of Magnolia which failed early in 1834. On February 15, 1834, the Legislative Council authorized relocation to Tallahassee and a change in name, provided that the new bank redeemed the outstanding circulation of the failed bank.

Notes printed for the bank's branch in St. Joseph (See St. Joseph notes #s 8, 9 and 10.) with St. Joseph crossed out by hand and Tallahassee written above the old place name. Imprinted Rawdon, Wright & Hatch New-York and Rawdon, Wright, Hatch & Edson, New Orleans. 184__ printed.

31. $1 silver dollar, Hebe pouring drink for eagle, train .R7
32. $2 Commerce, cotton plant R7
33. $3 Venus rising from sea, horses pulling plow, cherub R7

Notes printed for the Tallahassee location. Engraved by Rawdon Wright & Hatch New York. No New Orleans engraver imprint.

34. $3 tree, Ceres kneeling, standing female R7
35. $5 two children with wheat, steamboat, standing female R7

36. $10 Commerce and Mercury, 2 horses and plowman, Washington R7

37. $20 Farm woman with sheaves of wheat, Providence, Hope R7

Southern Life Insurance & Trust Company

The Southern Life Insurance and Trust Company was a territorial chartered bank headquartered in St. Augustine, but authorized to operate a branch in Tallahassee. Post notes with handwritten dates in 1841 used the same design and engraver as the lower denomination demand notes issued in St. Augustine (#s 1–6).

38. $50 Flora seated in a garden R8
39. $100 Flora seated in a garden R8

State Bank of Florida

On January 21, 1851, the state legislature authorized the incorporation of the State Bank of Florida, but it was never organized because the constraints on operation were too onerous. In 1853 the law was changed allowing notes to be furnished by the comptroller, secured by bonds. But it was not until 1855 that the legislature approved a viable bank, and Florida's first bank after statehood raised money and opened in early 1859.

Demand notes printed by the American Bank Note Company. Handwritten dates in 1859. William Bailey was president; William R. Pettes was cashier, and T. W. Brevard was Comptroller. At secession, there were $85,265 in notes circulating. Denomination overprinted in large red letters except on proofs.

40. $5 Henry Clay, mule drawn wagons, Comptroller seal R7

40A. FIVE overprinted in red
40B. no overprint
41. $10 John C. Calhoun, train, Comptroller seal R7
41A. TEN overprinted in red
41B. no overprint
42. $20 two Indians, two farm workers, Comptroller seal R7
42A. 20 overprinted in red
42B. no overprint

Specie payment was suspended after war broke out. Certificates of deposit were circulated with printed date July 1, 1862. No engraver imprint. Same president and cashier signers as preceding plus B. C. Lewis signing for the president.

43. $1 flying eagle with three arrows R5
44. $2 same R4

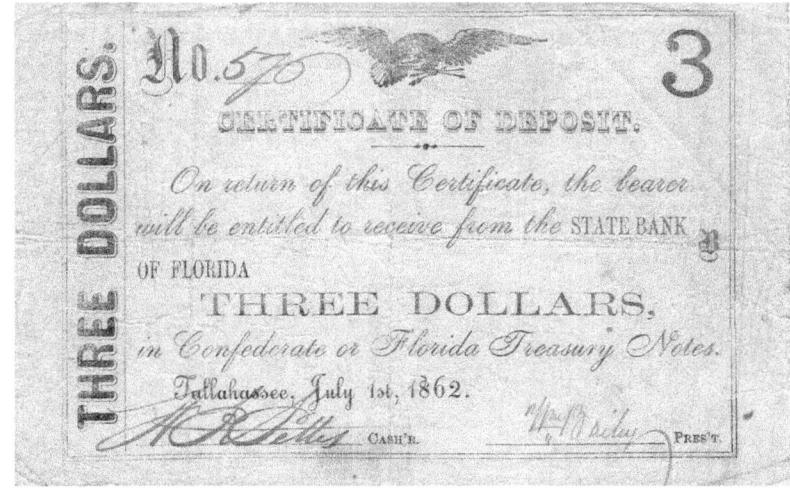

45. $3 same R5
46. $5 same R4

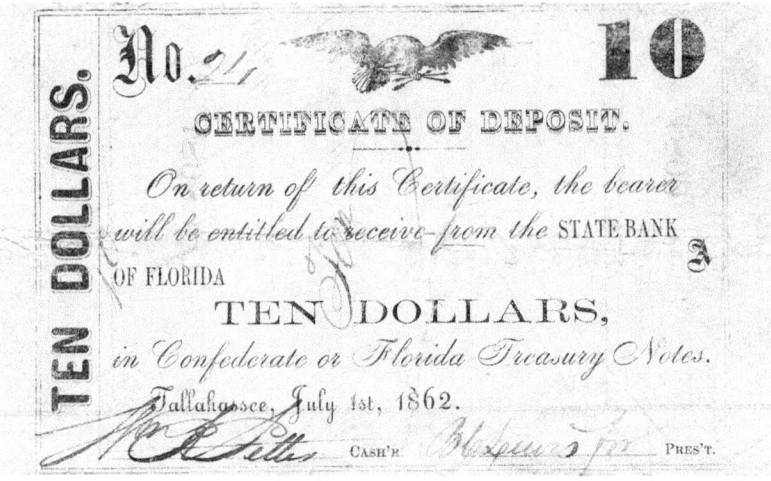

47. $10 same R6
48. $20 same R7

State Stock Bank

The State Stock Bank was a fictitious bank. The perpetrators of the fraud took advantage of the legislative approval of a State Bank of Florida. The notes were produced by modifying the plates of notes of the Government Stock Bank of Ann Arbor, Michigan. The Michigan comptroller's seal was not changed to the Florida seal. The backs of unissued notes were later used to print scrip for South Carolina and Florida. Whole $5 notes exist with plain or South Carolina backs, but most are reconstructed from two or more pieces of 1861 South Carolina scrip. Imprinted Danforth, Bald & Co. New York & Philada. except for $10 which is Danforth, Wright.

49. $1 eagle, Jackson. Fragments only reported, not confirmed R8
50. $2 Indian, shield, women, Fillmore. Fragments reported, not confirmed ..R8

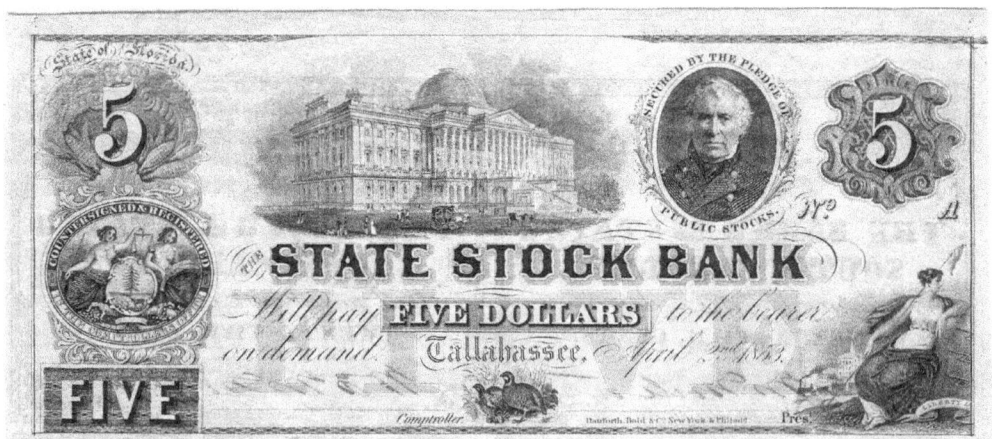

51. $5 U. S. Capitol, Taylor. R7
52. $10 Commerce, Prosperity & Navigation; Sailboat. Fragments confirmed...R8

Union Bank of Florida

Unlike the other territorial banks, the Union Bank of Florida was approved by Governor Duval. It was the largest and most fraudulent of the chartered territorial banks.

On February 13, 1833, legislation was approved to establish the bank with initial capitalization of $1,000,000 increasable to $3,000,000. Stock in the bank was sold in exchange for mortgages with no money down. Then the buyer (typically a farmer) could borrow against the stock! The bank was to be financed by issuing bonds guaranteed by the faith of the Territory and sold in New York and Europe. More bonds were sold in 1837. The assets of the Central Bank were acquired. The bank couldn't make its interest payments in 1841 and shut down in 1842. In 1842 the Territorial Legislature passed a resolution stating that it never had the authority to guarantee the bonds. Then, on March 16, 1843, the legislature suspended the bank and called for liquidation, including foreclosing property that had been mortgaged to buy stock. Attempts to get the United States to make good on the bonds were unsuccessful.

The bank's circulation was $365,111 at the end of 1841. Most of the demand notes were redeemed with proceeds from liquidation. Another $102,573 in post notes was still outstanding at year-end 1844. The five issues of notes are categorized by their engravers and whether they are demand notes or post notes.

Demand notes with imprint Rawdon, Wright, Hatch & Co. New York. Handwritten dates 1834 to 1838. Signed by John Parkhill, Cashier, and John Gamble, President.

53. $1 young man with cattle R7

54. $2 Washington, Archimedes lifting globe, Lafayette R7

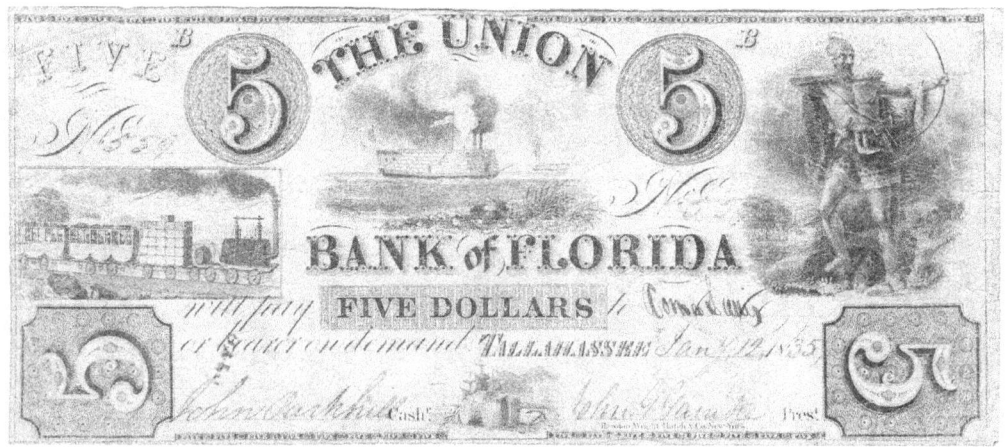

55. $5 Train, steamboat, Indian with name Nehamathla right R5

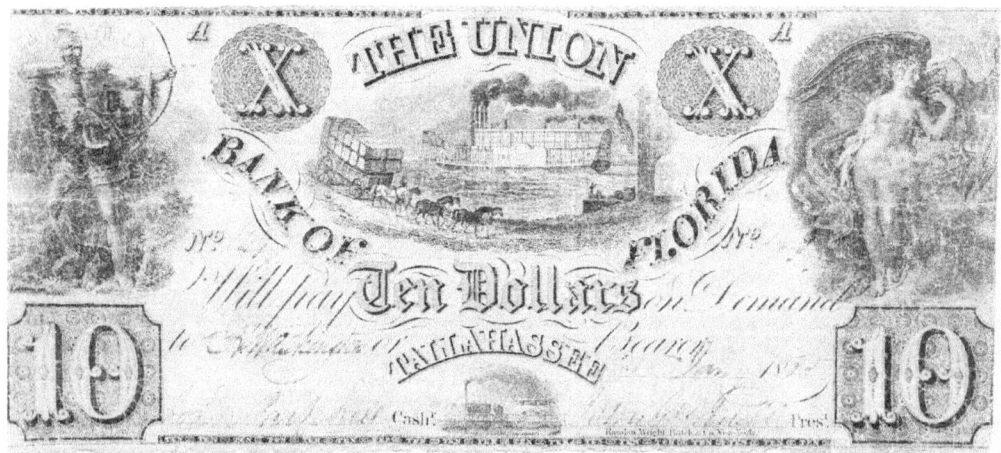

56. $10 Indian with Nehamathla left, horsedrawn wagon & steamboat, Hebe ..R7

57. $20 Mule train, Wisdom with eagle & Washington portrait, Hebe R6

Demand notes with imprint Rawdon, Wright, Hatch & Edson, New York. Handwritten dates in 1836. Signed by John Parkhill, Cashier and John Gamble, President. Place payable handwritten.

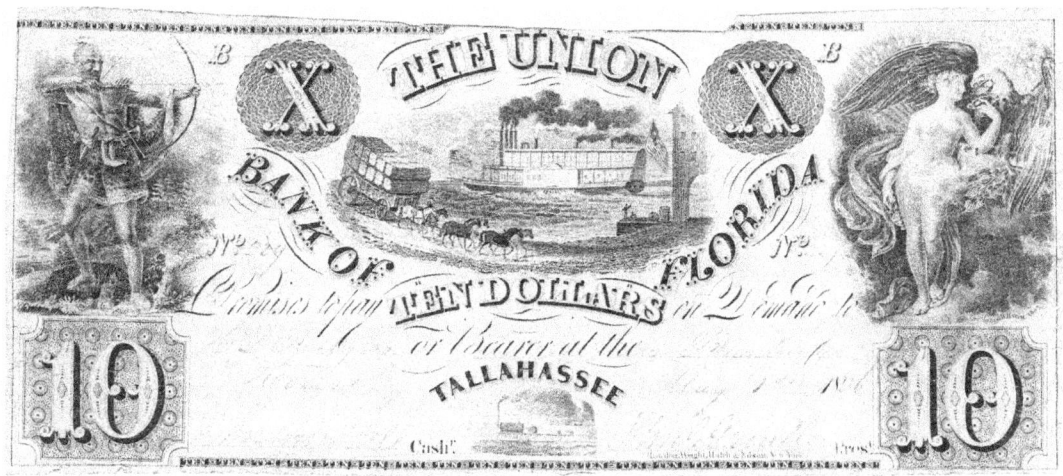

58. $10 similar to #56, but "Nehamathla" missing and different R8
fonts on Ten Dollars and Tallahassee

Post notes with imprint Rawdon, Wright, Hatch & Edson, New York. Handwritten dates in 1836. Signed by John Parkhill, Cashier and John Gamble, President. Place payable handwritten.

59. $20 similar to #57, but new fonts on Twenty Dollars and Tallahassee R8

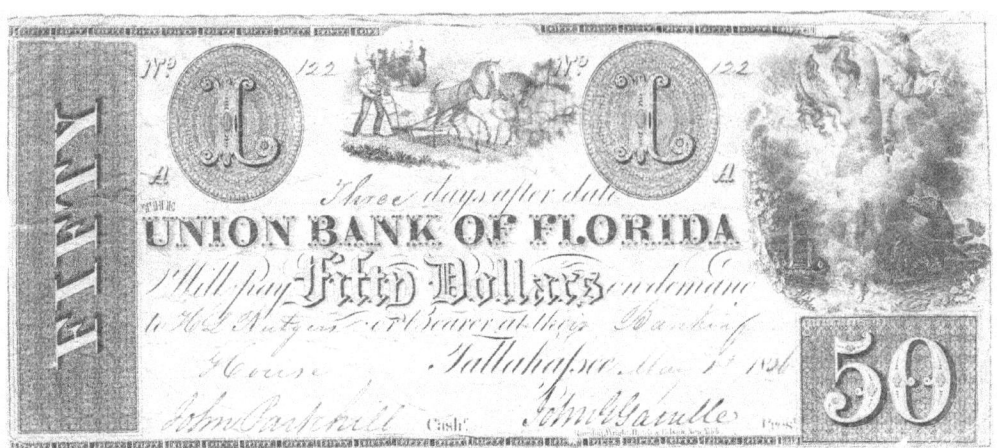

60. $50 farmer plowing with two horses, Venus rising from the sea R7

Post notes with imprints Rawdon, Wright, Hatch & Co. New York and Rawdon, Wright, Hatch & Edson, New Orleans. Handwritten date January 1, 1840. Signed by C. F. Mercer, Cashier and John Gamble, President.

61. $10 Justice, horse drawn wagon, Ceres R8
(Center vignette reversed from #s 56 and 58)

"Post notes" with imprints Rawdon, Wright, Hatch & Co. New York and Rawdon, Wright, Hatch & Edson, New Orleans. Handwritten dates in 1840. Signed by C. F. Mercer, Cashier, and John Gamble, President. Amounts, time period and place payable handwritten. Endorsements on back show that these notes, which have characteristics of checks and promissory notes, circulated.

5. Obsolete Notes and Scrip—Tallahassee

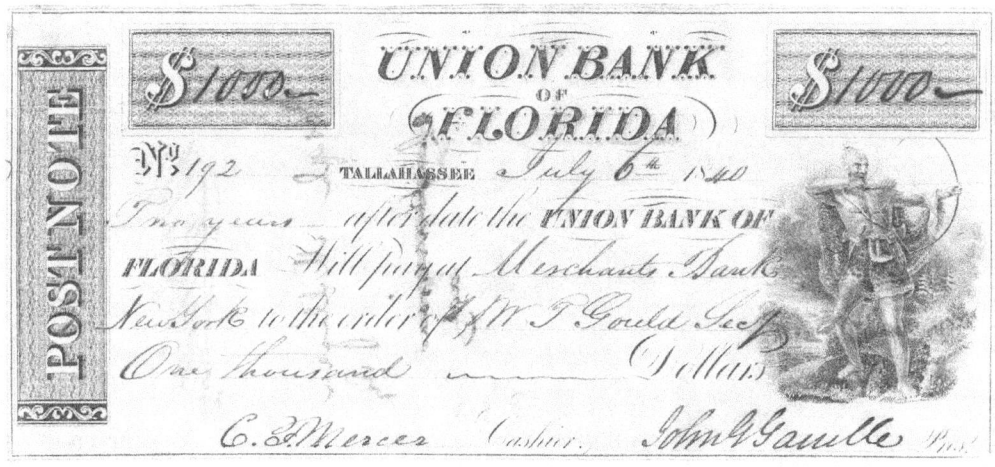

62. various "Nehamathla" without name above vignette R6

Corporation of Tallahassee

Scrip redeemable at the Union Bank of Florida. Imprinted Lowe, B'way N.Y. Handwritten dates between 1837 and 1841.

63. 6¼¢ Justice, Commerce, Sailboat R8
64. 12½¢ Locomotive, leaves, seated Indian R8
65. 25¢ Juno & Mercury, sailboat R8
66. 50¢ surviving example not confirmed
67. 75¢ early locomotive and cars R8

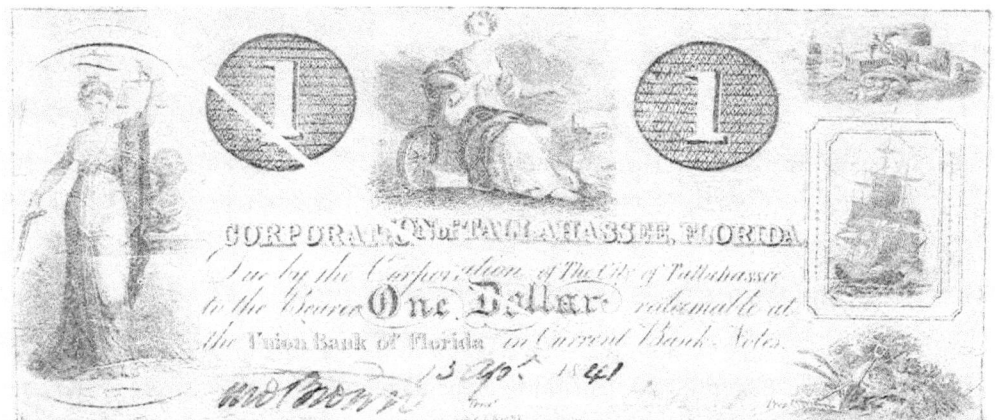

68. $1 same as number 63 .... R8
69. $2 same as number 63 .... R8

Scrip redeemable at the State Bank of Florida. Printed date March 1, 1862. Signed by William Bailey, B.C. Lewis or W. R. Pettes.

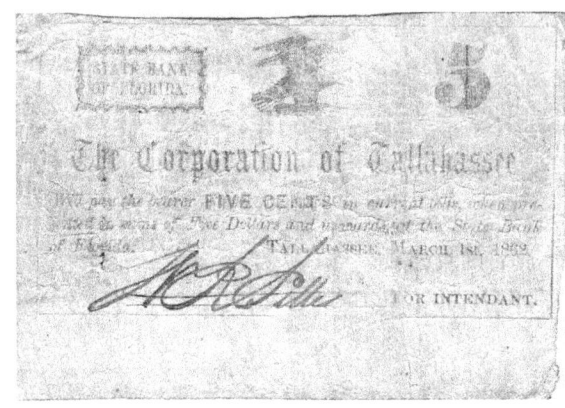

70. 5¢ eagle R4
71. 5¢ sailboat with two masts R5
72. 5¢ steamship with three masts and side wheel R4
73. 10¢ eagle R4
74. 10¢ steamship with three masts and side wheel R4
75. 25¢ steamship with three masts and side wheel R3

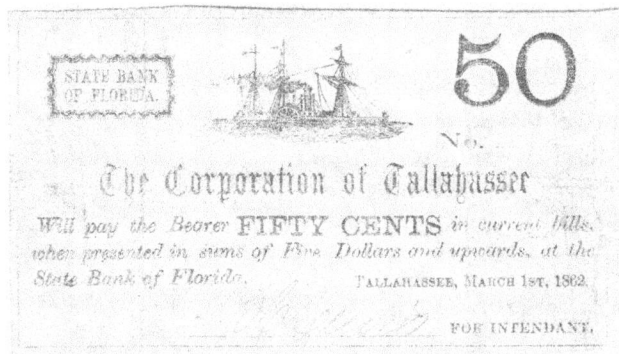

76. 50¢ steamship with three masts and side wheel R3
77. 75¢ steamship with three masts and side wheel R4

Generic Scrip Notes

Generic scrip notes with no issuer name, city or date, containing a "promise to pay the bearer [printed denomination] in trade or bankable bills." Tallahassee and date are handwritten on a blank line at top; the notes are signed at the bottom. Printer's imprint: Sold at Smith's 774 Bd.Way N.Y. Known signers are Ambrose Cook & Sons, 1836, and Jonathan Ashe, 1837.

78. 6¼¢ Seated Liberty with flag (Ashe signature known) R8
79. 12½¢ Eagle with olive branch (Cook signature known) R8

R. Hayward's Store

Scrip payable to bearer in specie or current money. Handwritten dates in 1834. Known examples signed by Willis Alston. No engraver's imprint.

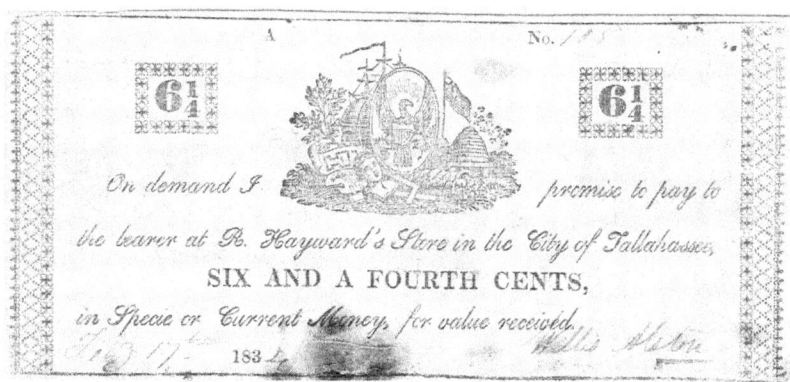

80. 6¼¢ Eagle on shield with olive branch, beehive, cornucopia, etc. R8
81. 12½¢ Wheat sheaf, plow, sickle, rake, hoe, etc. R8

82. 25¢ same as on 12½¢ R8
83. 50¢ same as on 6¼¢ R8

E. Loockerman's Store

Edward Loockerman was one of the founders of the Bank of Florida. Scrip payable on demand in specie or current money at his store. Printed date March 1, 1834. Known example signed by Achille Murat, a nephew of Napoleon.

84. 12½¢ Woman seated with an assortment of farm implements R8

Robinson's Store

Scrip imprinted American Bank Note Co. Philadelphia. Printed location is Leon County Florida rather than Tallahassee. Printed date October 1, 1877. Signed W. L. Robinson.

85. 25¢ beehive R8

Henry L. Rutgers

Henry L. Rutgers served as treasurer of Florida Territory and as cashier of the Bank of Florida. Two series of scrip payable in Union Bank notes on demand at the Union Bank of Florida. No vignettes. Ornamental borders same on all denominations within each issue.

Handwritten dates in November 1841.

86. 6¼¢ R8

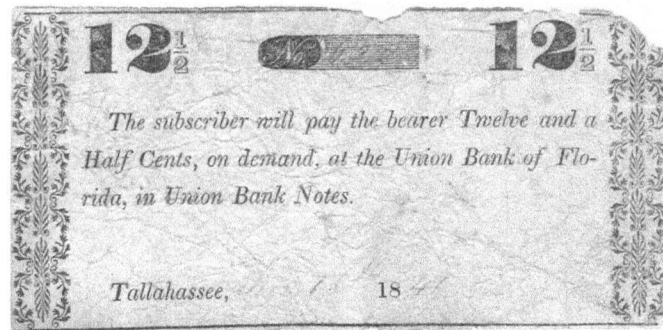

87. 12½¢ R7
88. 25¢ R8

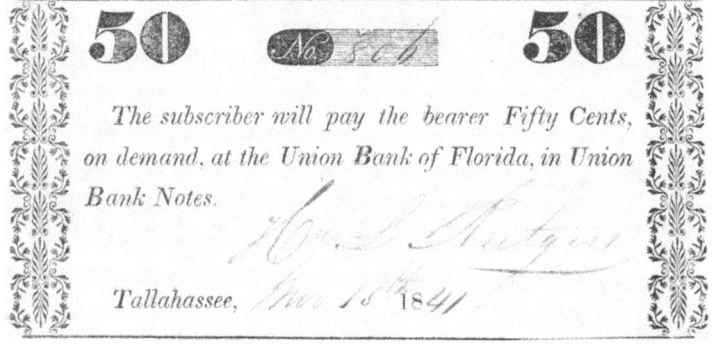

89. 50¢ R4

Handwritten dates in January 1842. Notes and borders wider than 1841 series.

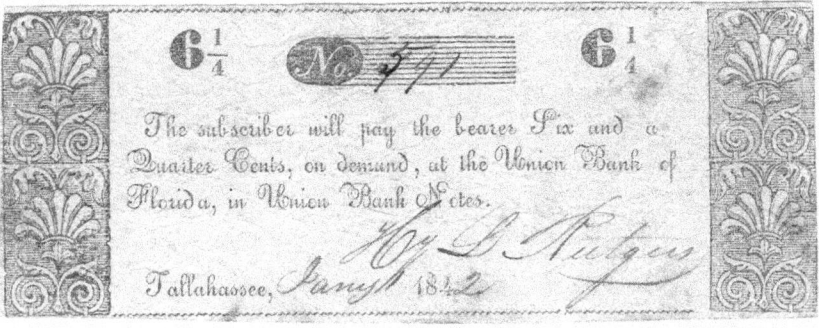

90. 6¼¢	R8
91. 12½¢	R7

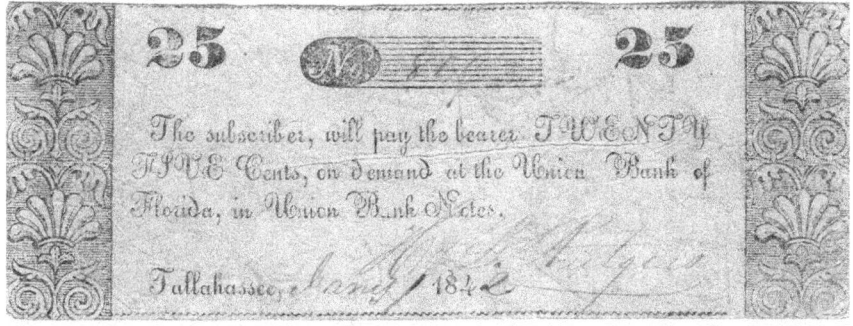

92. 25¢	R7
93. 50¢	R7

Tallahassee Post Office

Scrip, payable in postage, with the imprint Morris Printer Philadelphia in the left and right borders. 1837 printed, month and day handwritten. Signed by William Hilliard. Interestingly, U.S. Government records do not show Hilliard ever being postmaster! No vignettes. Proofs are known with only 183_ of date printed.

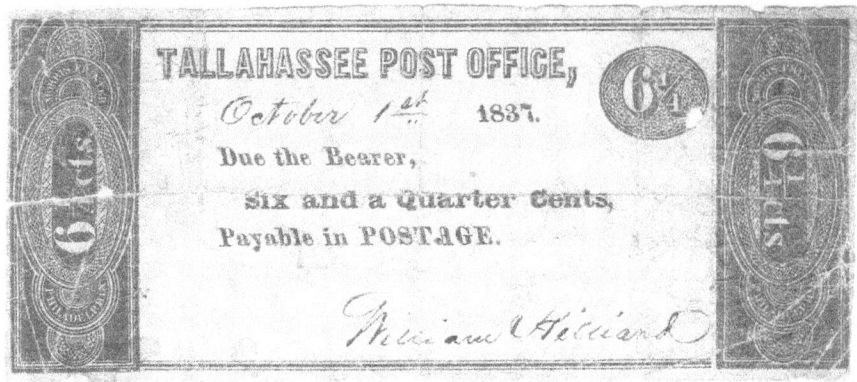

94. 6¼¢ R8
95. 12½¢ R8
96. 18¾¢ R8
97. 25¢ R8
98. 50¢ R8

Scrip, payable in postage. No imprint. Date 18__ printed, remainder handwritten. Dates in 1839. Signed by Hilliard.

99. 75¢ **Franklin, Battle of Lake Erie scene, Washington** R8

Scrip payable in postage or current bank notes. Imprinted New England Bank Note Co. Boston. No date. Signed by Hilliard.

100. 6¼¢ **Shepherdess and seated man** R8

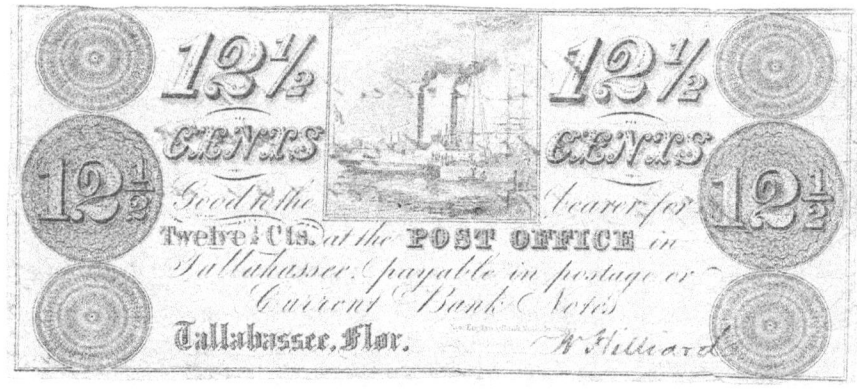

101. 12½¢ steamboat at wharf R8
102. 25¢ eagle R8
103. 50¢ woman with sheaf of wheat R8

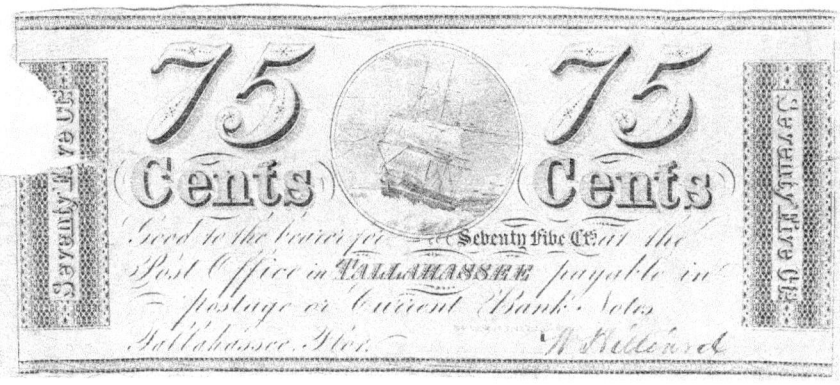

104. 75¢ sailboat R8
105. $1 sailboats, steamship and covered wagon R8

Tallahassee Rail Road Company

The Tallahassee Rail Road Company was incorporated by an act of the Territorial Legislature on February 10, 1834. The legislation gave the company half a million acres of land and broad authority to take whatever land, lumber or stones they needed along the route provided the owners received just compensation. The company prospered and expanded.

Demand notes payable in transportation. Printed by Rawdon, Wright, Hatch & Edson. New York. Signed by Richard K. Call or Edward Houstoun as president. Various signers as Secretary. Handwritten dates between 1852 and 1856. Sheet structure was $1A-$1B-$2A-$2B; no $3 notes were printed.

106. $1 Dockside scene with train, wagon, ships R7

107. $2 same R7

Demand notes payable in transportation. Printed by American Bank Note Company. Handwritten dates between 1859 and 1870. Early issue, with plain backs, signed by F. H. Flagg as Secretary and E. Houstoun as President. Later issue with elaborate printed backs (and some late plain backs) signed by Flagg and either J. S. Stone or M.L. Littlefield as President. Both issues have green overprint on face.

108. $1 plain back; group of people waving at train R5

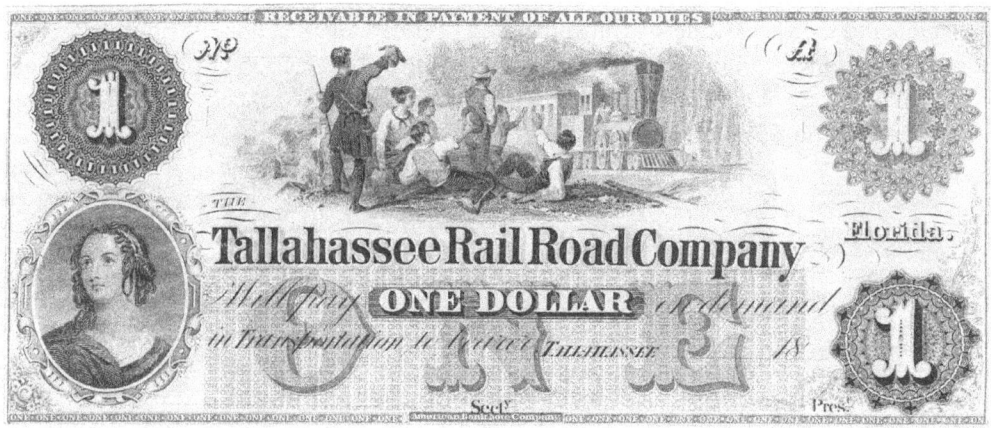

109. $1 elaborate green back; same vignette R4

5. Obsolete Notes and Scrip—Tallahassee

110. $2 plain back; train crossing bridge R5

111. $2 elaborate green back; same vignette R4

112. $3 plain back; sailor and anchor on land R5
113. $3 elaborate green back; same vignette R4

Small scrip payable on demand in transportation. 186_ of date printed. Handwritten date in 1861. No imprint. Signed by F. H. Flagg, Treasurer.

114. 25¢ railroad engine and two cars R8

TAMPA

The village around Fort Brooke became known as Tampa Bay in 1831. It was legally shortened to Tampa in 1834, but the Post Office continued referring to the old name until at least 1843.

Burr & Lynch

Joseph Burr and James Lynch operated a general store. Scrip payable on demand in goods or current money. Tampa Bay, Florida printed on notes. Handwritten date of September 18, 1837, on only note seen. Issuer name handwritten. No imprint.

1. 6¼¢ seated woman holding a flower R8

Several people signed scrip of the same types issued in Alafia, Brooksville, Orange Springs and other area towns. The scrip has Tampa, Florida printed on it but no issuers' names are preprinted. In many cases the signatures have faded and cannot be read. Known signers are Claiborne R. Mobley (drugstore), Jackson S. Redbrook (groceries) and Jose Vigil (general store). 1862 printed. Space for month and day to be written usually blank or faded.

C. R. Mobley

2. 50¢ small sailboat R8
3. $1 three-mast schooner R8

4. $1 gunboat R8
5. $1 1863 printed; gunboat R8

J. S. Redbrook

6. 50¢ larger size; sailboat, gunboat, two-mast steamship R8

Jose Vigil

Jose Vigil signed scrip similar to preceding, but also issued notes with Jose Vigil printed on the notes and with printed date June 26, 1862.

7. 5¢   Jose Vigil printed; two three-mast ships R8
8. 10¢ Jose Vigil printed; gunboat R8
9. 25¢ Vigil signature only; horse and cart R8
10. 25¢ Vigil signature only; two-mast ship R8

11. 50¢ Jose Vigil printed; gunboat R8
12. 50¢ Vigil signature only; two-mast ship R8
13. 50¢ Vigil signature only; three-mast ship R8

6

Advertising Notes

Advertisements that look like paper money certainly got attention when they were distributed. They've received less attention from currency collectors over the years. Consequently they've remained an inexpensive and enjoyable adjunct to obsolete paper money collections.

Because they are inexpensive and appeal to a small audience, they are not featured in auction catalogs. When they appear, it is frequently with minimal description or as part of a group lot. They are rarely pictured. The first catalog was written by Robert A. Vlack in 2001. Its 360 pages cover 19th century notes that imitate obsolete or federal notes, and notes printed by several advertising companies. Future books will include advertisements printed on facsimiles of real notes and 20th century notes. He recognizes that his listings are not complete, but they provide a great start for collectors or future researchers.

I am listing here the advertising notes that I know about from Florida. None are in Vlack's catalog. They cover the entire range from Federal and Confederate look-alikes down to some that only marginally qualified for inclusion. I am sure my listing is not complete. Too little is known to attempt assigning rarity numbers to these notes at this time. I have arbitrarily excluded advertising notes printed after World War II where the face of the note is not a facsimile or close imitation of a real note.

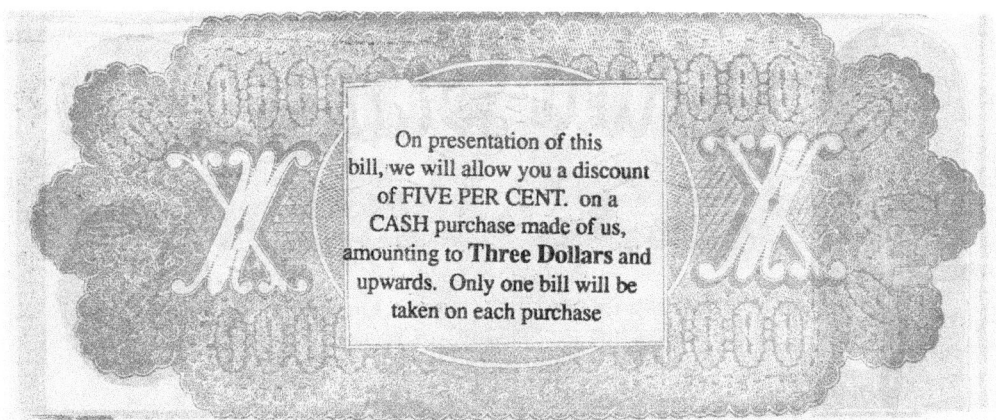

1. 1862 United States Legal Tender Look-alike

B. Genovar, St. Augustine. Circa 1876. The story of Bartolo Genovar and his store, including photographs, can be found in my article in the July/August 2005 issue of *Paper Money*.

2. 1864 Type 60 Confederate States facsimile

Bettelini's Hotel, Jacksonville. Circa 1898. Fred Bettelini also owned a hotel in Cedar Key.

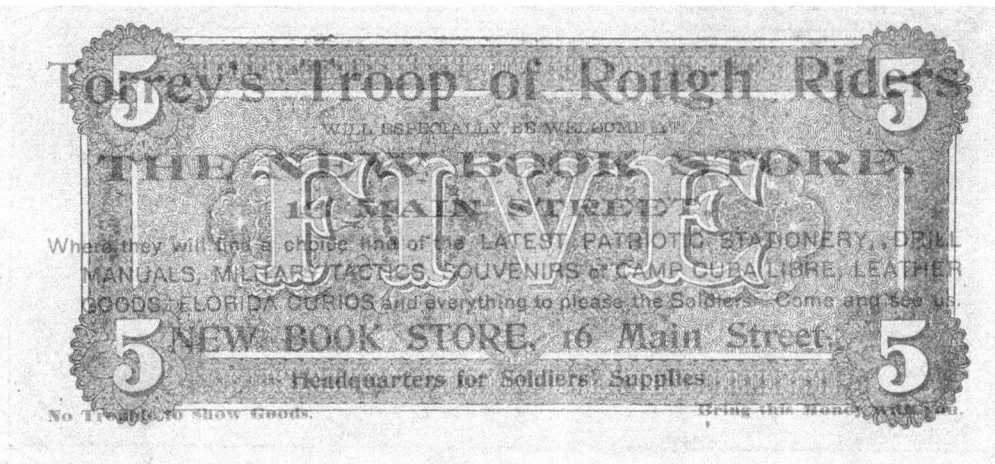

3. 1864 Type 60 Confederate States facsimile

The New Book Store, Jacksonville, 1898. Torrey's Troop of Rough Riders was based at Camp Cuba Libre in Jacksonville during the Spanish American War.

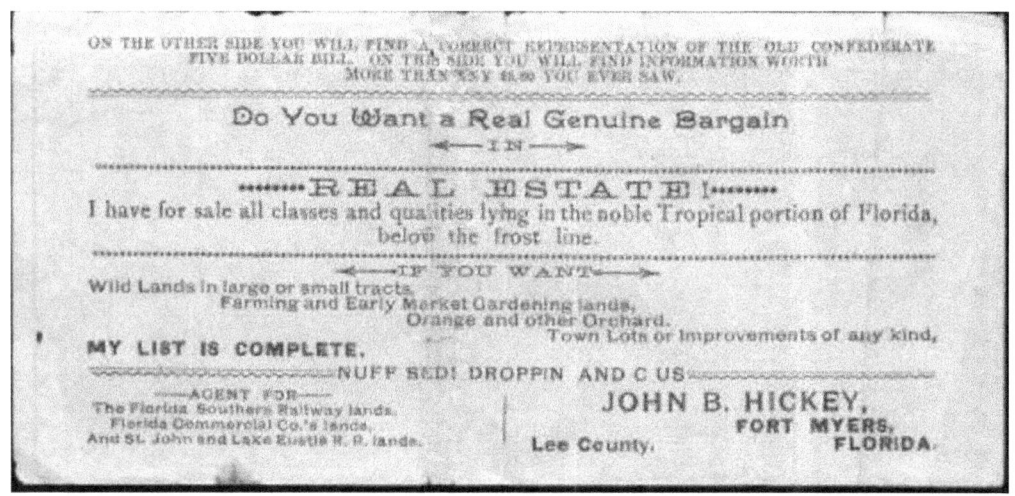

4. 1864 Type 60 Confederate States facsimile

John B. Hickey, Fort Myers, circa 1890s. Real estate for sale.

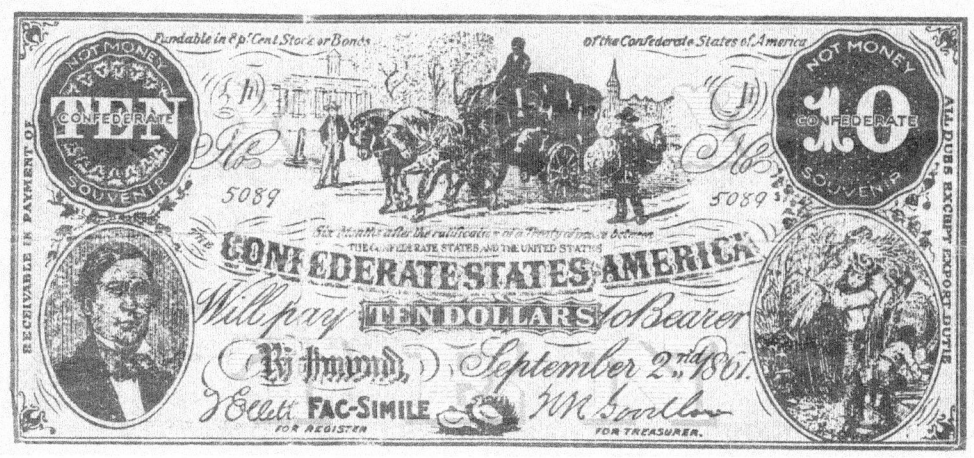

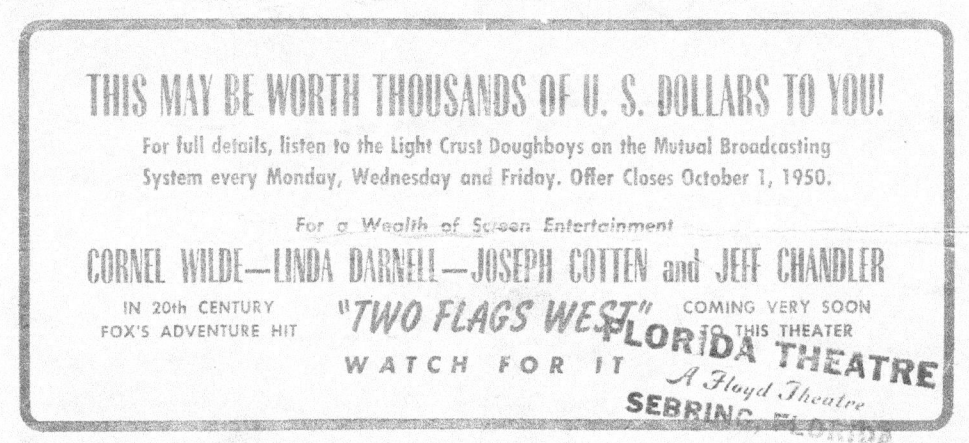

5. 1861 Type 23 Confederate States facsimile

Two Flags West movie advertisement, 1950. Stamped overprint: Florida Theatre, Sebring, Florida.

6. 1844 Bank of Florida $4 facsimile

William P. Donlon, Utica N.Y., early 1970s. An author and dealer in U.S. paper money, died in 1978.

7. $5 fantasy note with elaborate green back
   Capital City Business College, Tallahassee, 1890s.

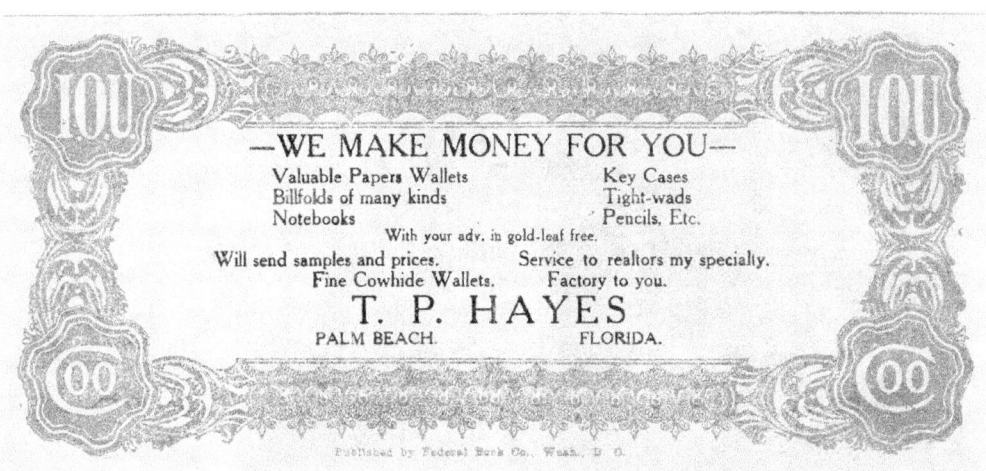

8. **I.O.U. fantasy note with green border and orange back.**
   T.P. Hayes, Palm Beach, circa 1900 (?).

6. Advertising Notes

9. Elaborate lathe work — brown front with elk vignette; blue back
   Overprinted with advertising for Elks Home Benefit. Pensacola, December 1925.

7

Financial Panic and Depression Scrip

Much of the small denomination scrip listed in this catalog was issued to relieve shortages of coins. These shortages may have resulted from remoteness from cities or banks. But, frequently the cause of the shortage was a financial panic during which specie was hoarded. This explains the 1837–1840, 1861–1863 and 1873 clusters of scrip issues in the Obsolete Notes and Scrip section of this book.

1873

In some cases the scrip was issued pursuant to some governmental authorization or was issued under the auspices of a clearing house association or chamber of commerce. The earliest Florida example of privately issued scrip bearing a reference to governmental authorization is the C. W. Denny scrip from Jacksonville in 1873. (Illustrated as Jacksonville #31 in this book.)

1907

The Panic of 1907 led to the issuance of Clearing House Certificates. I have listed below the certificates known to me.

Jacksonville Clearing Association

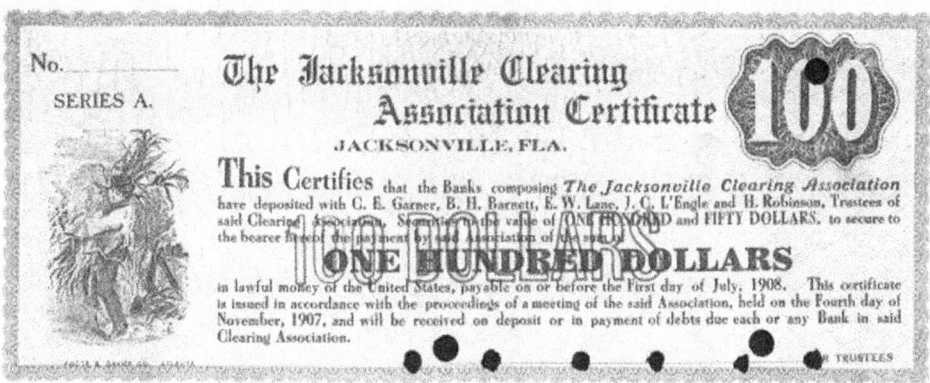

$100 Nov. 4, 1907 red and brown, man harvesting corn

Key West Clearing House
$2 Nov. 27, 1907 green, Hope

Citizens National Bank of Pensacola
Payable through the Pensacola Clearing House

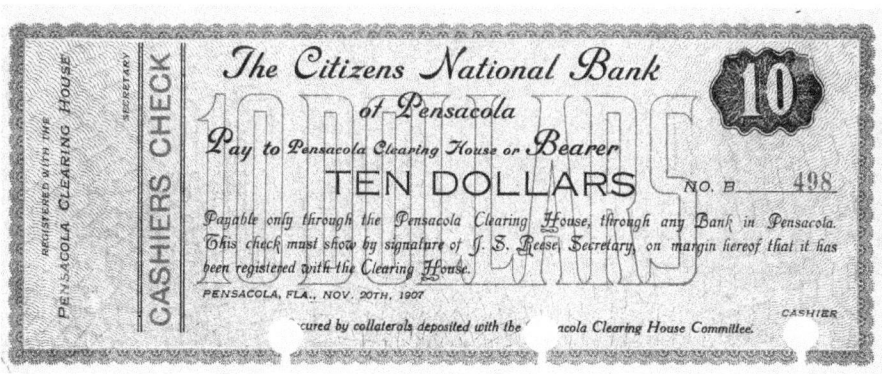

$5 Nov. 20, 1907 red and green, no vignette
$10 Nov. 20, 1907 red and green, no vignette

First National Bank of Pensacola
Same design and clearing house as Citizens Bank.

$1 Nov. 20, 1907 red and green, no vignette
$2 Nov. 20, 1907 red and green, no vignette
$5 Nov. 20, 1907 red and green, no vignette
$10 Nov. 20, 1907 red and green, no vignette

Pensacola Bank & Trust Co.

Same design and clearing house as Citizens Bank
$1 Nov. 20, 1907 red and green, no vignette

Tampa Clearing House Association

$100 Nov. 6, 1907 red and green, man and woman with basket

1933

The Great Depression and the 1933 Bank Holiday led to the issuance of scrip by many banks and communities. A tutorial on the depression and how and why the various forms of scrip were created can be found in Mitchell and Shafer (1984). I have not included payroll warrants, merchant punch cards, or scrip valid only within a school since these were not intended to circulate as currency.

Drew Issues

The most widely issued scrip was printed by The H. & W. B. Drew Co. of Jacksonville, Fla. The notes all have the same elaborate underlying design on the fronts and backs (common back design shown below) of all denominations. An Indian, palm tree, steamboat and all or part of the words "In God We Trust" appear seven times surrounded by a lathe work border. The $1 notes are green; $2, brown; $5, blue; and $10, orange. The bank name and denomination are overprinted in black. Most surviving specimens are unissued remainders, and it is widely believed that few were actually circulated.

7. Financial Panic and Depression Scrip

The following Drew issues have been documented:

Apalachicola State Bank

Scenic Highlands State Bank, Babson Park
Bank of Blountstown

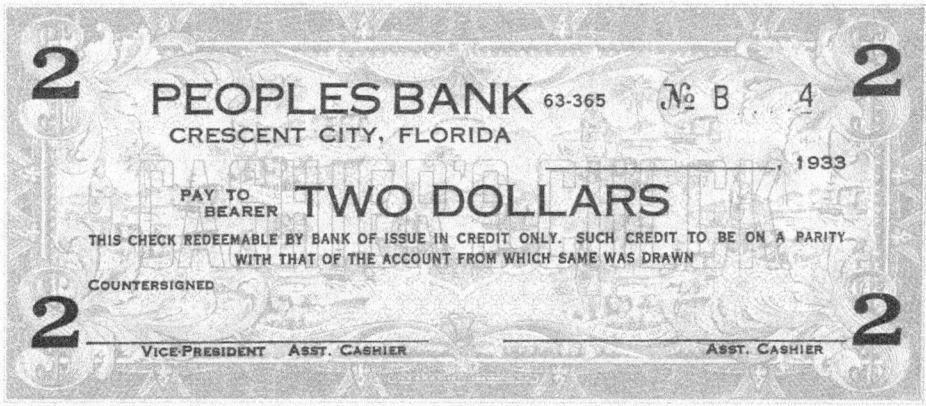

Peoples Bank, Crescent City

Cawthorn State Bank, DeFuniak Springs
Bank of Dunedin
First State Bank, Eustis
First State Bank, Fort Meade
Fort White Bank
Phifer State Bank, Gainesville
Bank of Green Cove Springs
Bank of Greensboro
High Springs Bank

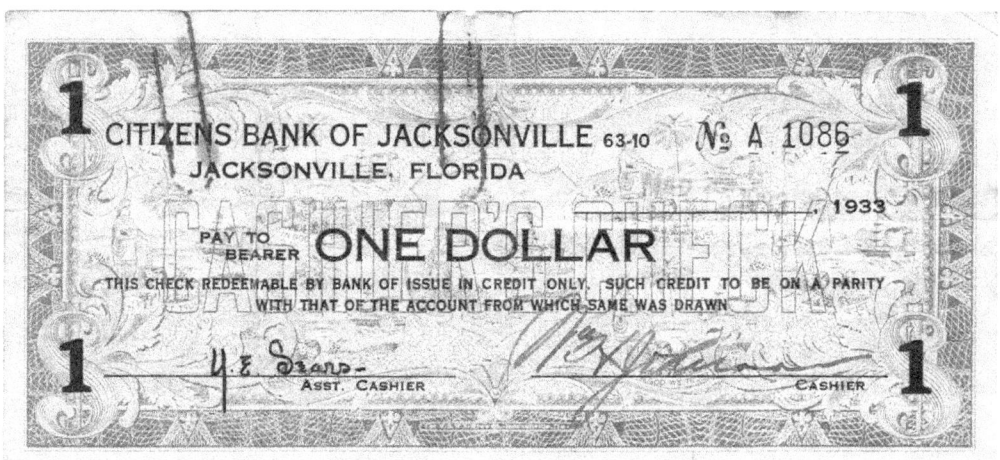

Citizens Bank of Jacksonville
Mayo State Bank
Farmers and Merchants Bank, Monticello
Bank of Mulberry
Bank of Newberry
Commercial Bank and Trust Company, Ocala
Bank of Pahokee
First Bank and Trust Company, Pensacola
Hillsboro State Bank, Plant City
Citizens Bank and Trust Company, Quincy
Quincy State Bank
Gadsden County State Bank, River Junction
Bank of Starke
Capital City Bank, Tallahassee

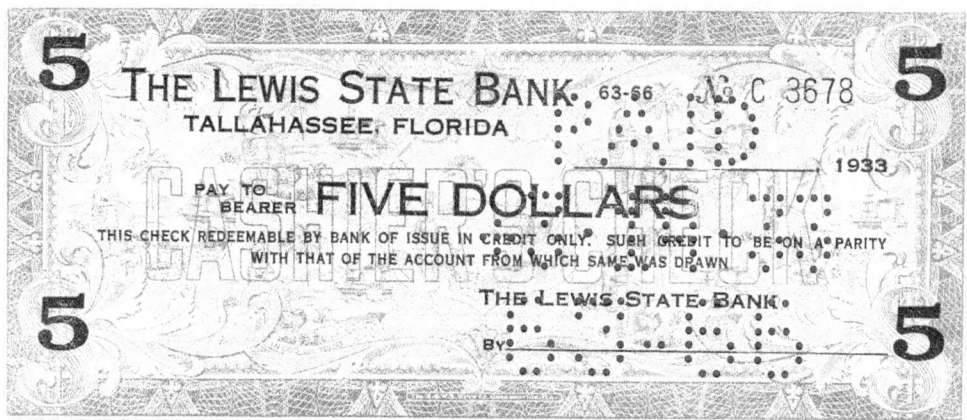

Lewis State Bank, Tallahassee
Farmers and Merchants Bank, Trenton
Wewahitchka State Bank
Bank of Wildwood

City of Fort Pierce

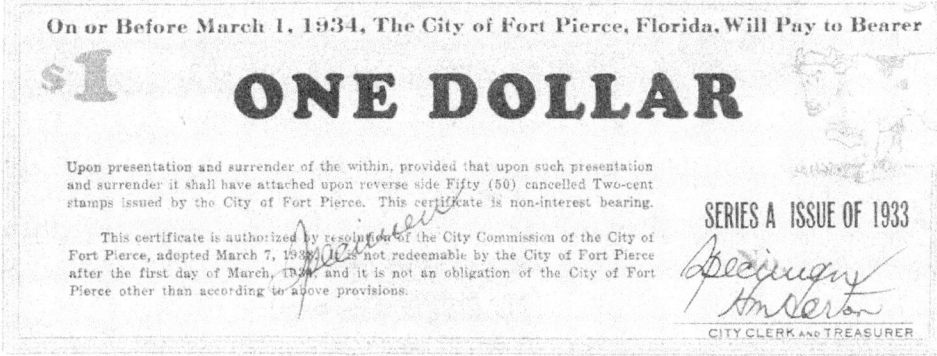

50¢ (green paper, rooster vignette) and $1 (yellow paper, bull vignette) certificates redeemable when the back is filled with the appropriate number of 2¢ stamps. Plain back. Authorized by City Commission on March 7, 1933.

Gainesville Chamber of Commerce

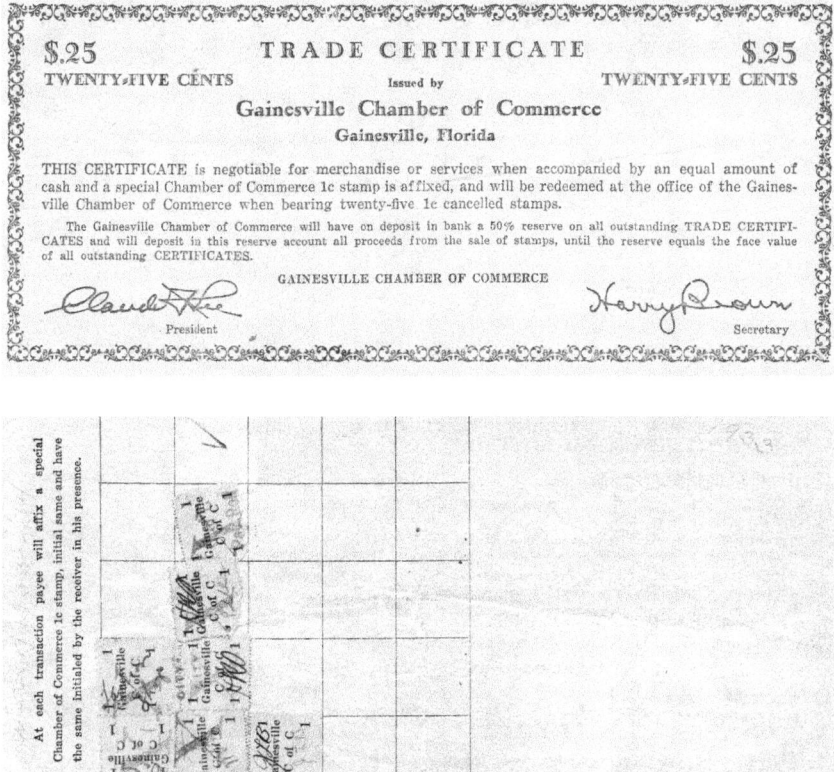

25¢ (yellow), 50¢ (blue) and $1 (pink) trade certificates with spaces on back for affixing small 1¢ stamps (on the 25¢ and 50¢) or small 2¢ stamps (on the $1). The scrip was self-liquidating since one stamp was affixed with each transaction. Printed on Hammermill safety paper.

City of Key West Florida

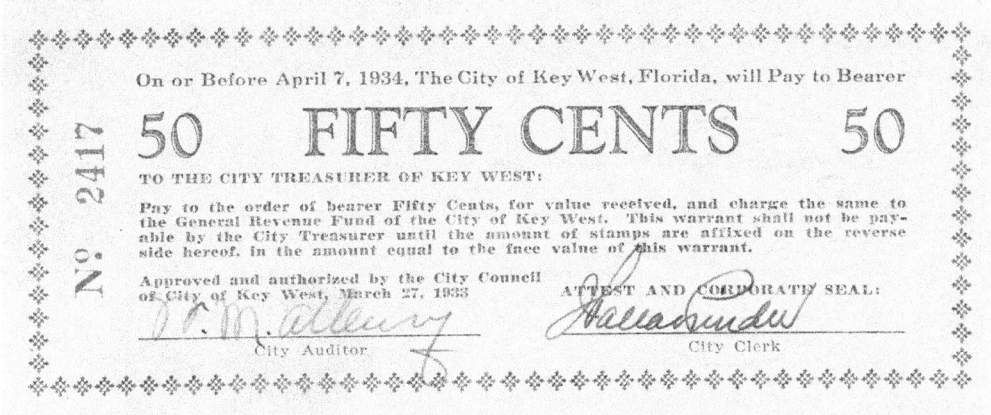

50¢ and $1 scrip with spaces for stamps on back. Serially numbered, signed by city auditor and clerk, and embossed with city seal.

City of St. Petersburg

$1 Time Warrants dated November 1, 1933, payable to bearer on or before April 1, 1934, with interest. Black on green face, elaborate green back.

St. Petersburg Citizens Emergency Committee

Change scrip issued in exchange for collateral deposited with the committee. After the emergency was over, unissued certificates were overprinted with a brief history and sold as souvenirs.

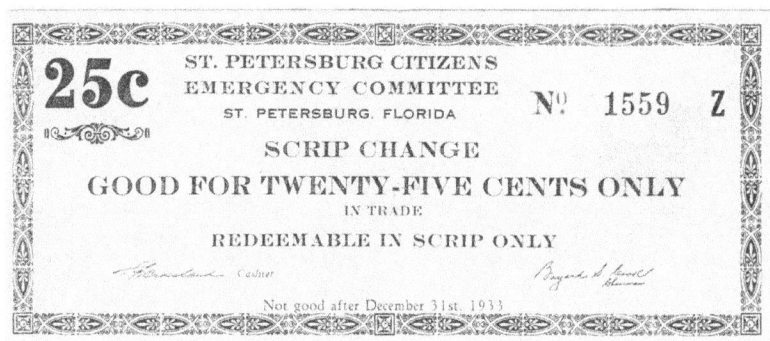

5¢, 10¢ and 25¢ scrip with same design

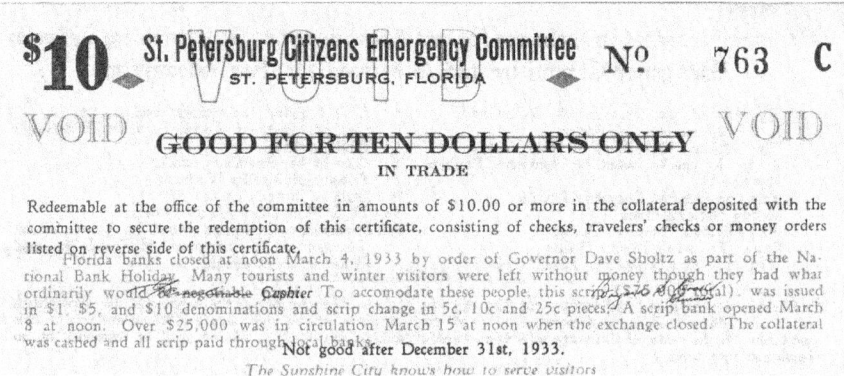

$1, $5 and $10 scrip with same design

City of West Palm Beach

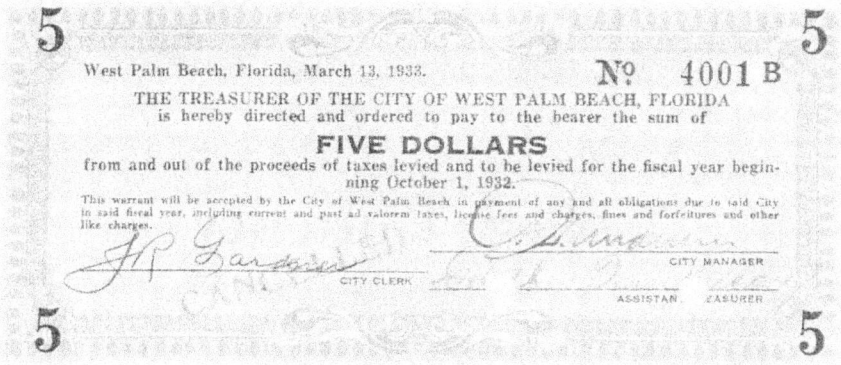

Treasurer warrants payable on demand out of taxes collected or usable to pay taxes or fees. Dated March 13, 1933. 50¢, $1, $5 and $10 with orange background. City and denomination on back of notes in green.

District of West Palm Beach

Treasurer warrants dated January 3, 1934. 50¢, $1, $5 and $10 on Todd security paper with gray background and watermarked PROTOD-GREENBAC. District seal with 1933 at left, plain back.

8
College Currency

Since the mid–19th century, business colleges taught the basics of everyday commerce. Courses included penmanship, letter writing, accounting and legal principles. To simulate actual experience in bookkeeping or banking skills, the colleges used "play money" rather than real currency. The banknotes developed for this purpose typically bore the name of the institution and resembled real money.

Since the notes had no real value, they were usually not saved by students or when the institution closed. They have been ignored by most paper money collectors, who consider them play money rather than real money. Consequently the notes used by smaller, short-lived local business colleges are scarce and little is known about them.

Florida Normal College, White Springs

Notes from this school are the only college currency known from Florida. They were issued circa 1887–1890. Printed by William B. Burford, lithographer, Indianapolis.

1. 10 Cents, blue with brown pattern back. Soldier and family, men working in field with palm tree.

[There is no depiction of this note.]

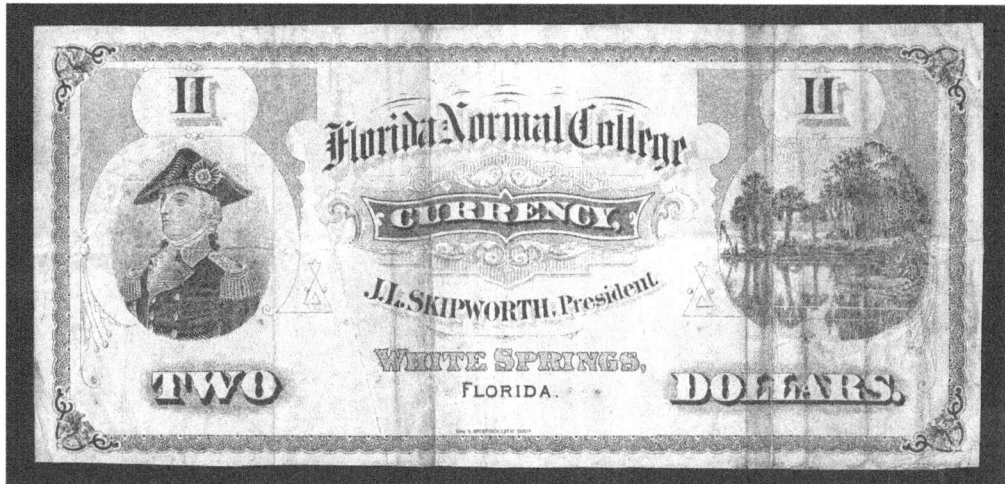

2. 2 Dollars, black with brown pattern back, General Anthony Wayne, lake and trees

3. 10 Dollars, black with brown pattern back, Sailboat, woman with rake

Other denominations were undoubtedly issued.

A college-related note from the Capital City Business College, Tallahassee, is illustrated in this book as number 7 in the section on Advertising Notes.

Herb and Martha Schingoethe, in their book *College Currency—Money for Business Training* (Port Clinton, Ohio: BNR Press, 1993) erroneously attributed notes issued by the First National Bank of Jacksonville Business College to Florida. Although there was a Jacksonville Business College in Florida, my research has established that R. C. Crampton, whose name appears on these notes as president, founded this Jacksonville Business College in Jacksonville, Illinois, in 1866.

Bibliography

Abbey, Kathryn T. "The Union Bank of Tallahassee: An Experiment in Territorial Finance." *Florida Historical Quarterly*, April 1937.

Acts and Resolutions Adopted by the General Assembly of Florida. Tallahassee: Dyke & Carlisle, 1861–1865.

Acts and Resolutions Adopted by the Legislature of Florida. Tallahassee: Charles H. Walton, State Printer, 1868–1877.

Acts and Resolutions of the Legislative Council of the Territory of Florida 1822–1845. Pensacola: Floridian Press, 1823–1845.

Arends, Tulio. *La Republica de las Floridas 1817–1818*. Caracas: Academia Nacional de la Historia, 1986.

Ares, Robert. "Florida Governor Believed in States' Rights." *Bank Note Reporter*, May 1997, pages 24–28.

The Bankers' Magazine and Journal of the Money Market (London). 1861–1866.

The Bankers' Magazine and Statistical Register (New York). 1861–1865.

Battey, F. A. *Biographical Souvenir of the States of Georgia and Florida*. Chicago: F. A. Battey, 1889.

Benice, Ronald J. "An Early Florida Advertising Note." *Paper Money*, July/August 2005, pages 286–289.

_____. "Florida Currency During Reconstruction." *Paper Money*, January/February 1999, pages 3–9.

_____. "Florida's Civil War Currency." *Paper Money*, May/June 2002, pages 131–154.

_____. "Florida's First Civil War Currency: 1861 Essays." *Paper Money*, March/April 2000, pages 35–39.

_____. "J. R. Powell's Multi-State Notes." *Paper Money*, March/April 2004, pages 85–91.

_____. "The Numismatic Legacy of Gregor MacGregor." *Paper Money*, March/April 2006, pages 83–88.

_____. "Recycling Paper Money in Florida." *FUN Topics*, Winter 1996, pages 18–21.

Blakey, Arch Frederick. *Parade of Memories: A History of Clay County, Florida*. Green Cove Springs, Fla.: Clay County Bicentennial Commission, 1976.

Bradbeer, William West. *Confederate and Southern State Currency*. Mt. Vernon, N.Y.: by the author, 1915.

Briggs, Deane R., Editor. *Florida Stampless Postal History 1763–1861*. North Miami: Phillips, 1999.

Brown, Canter, Jr. *Tampa in Civil War and Reconstruction*. Tampa: University of Tampa Press, 2000.

Bruton, Quintilla Geer, and David E. Bailey, Jr. *Plant City: Its Origin and History*. Winston-Salem, N.C.: Hunter, 1984.

Bushnell, David. *La Republica de las Floridas*. Mexico City: Pan American Institute of Geography and History, 1986.

Carter, Farish. Collected Papers, Southern Historical Collection, University of North Carolina at Chapel Hill.

Cassidy, Daniel G. *The Illustrated History of Florida Paper Money*. Jacksonville, Fla.: Cassidy, 1980.

Coker, William S., and Thomas D. Watson. *Indian Traders of the Southeastern Spanish Borderlands: Panton Leslie & Company and John Forbes & Company, 1783–1847*. Pensacola: University of West Florida Press, 1986.

Comptroller's and Treasurer's annual reports to the Governor and Legislature, January 1, 1861–January 1, 1877. In the collection of the State Library of Florida, Tallahassee.

Criswell, Grover C., Jr. *Confederate and Southern States Currency*. 4th ed. Port Clinton, Oh.: BNR, 1992.

Davis, T. Frederick. *History of Jacksonville, Florida and Vicinity*. Gainesville: University of Florida Press, 1964.

―――. *MacGregor's Invasion of Florida, 1817*. Jacksonville: Florida Historical Society, 1928.

Davis, William Watson. *The Civil War and Reconstruction in Florida*. New York: Columbia University Press, 1913.

Dees, Jesse Walter, Jr., and Vivian Flannery Dees. *Off the Beaten Path: The History of Cedar Key, Florida 1843–1990*. Chiefland, Fla.: Rife, 1990.

Dietz, August. *The New Dietz Confederate States Catalog and Handbook*. Miami: Bogg & Laurence, 1986.

Dovell, J. E. *History of Banking in Florida 1828–1954*. Orlando: Florida Bankers Association, 1955.

Durand, Roger H. *Interesting Notes about Allegorical Representations*. Rehoboth, Mass.: Durand, 1994.

―――. *Interesting Notes about Portraits*. Vols. I, II and III. Rehoboth, Mass.: Durand, 1996, 1997 and 2004.

―――. *Interesting Notes about Territories*. Rehoboth, Mass.: Durand, 1992.

Federal Brand Enterprises. *The Sixth Annual Northeast Ohio Numismatic Show Auction*. Cleveland: 1966.

Fishburne, Charles C., Jr. *The Cedar Keys in the Civil War and Reconstruction*. Cedar Key: Seahawk, 1982.

Freeman, Harley L. *Florida Obsolete Notes and Scrip*. Society of Paper Money Collectors, 1967.

Governor's annual messages to the Legislature, 1861–1877. In the collection of the State Library of Florida, Tallahassee.

Grismer, Karl H. *Tampa: A History of the City of Tampa and the Tampa Bay Region of Florida*. St. Petersburg: St. Petersburg Printing Company, 1950.

Hartman, David. *Biographical Roster of Florida's Confederate and Union Soldiers, 1861–1865*. Wilmington, N.C.: Broadfoot, 1996.

Harvey, Karen. *St. Augustine and St. Johns County: A Pictorial History*. Virginia Beach, Va.: Donning, 1979.

Haxby, James A. *United States Obsolete Banknotes 1782–1866*. Iola, Wis.: Krause, 1988.

Jahoda, Gloria. *River of the Golden Ibis*. New York: Holt, Rinehart and Winston, 1973.

Johannes, Jan H. *Yesterday's Reflections: Nassau County Florida, A Pictorial History*. Callahan, Fla.: T. O. Richardson, 1976.

Journal of the Proceedings of the Senate of the State of Florida. Tallahassee: Charles H. Walton, State Printer, 1865–1877.

Kappen, Charles V., and Ralph A. Mitchell. *Depression Scrip of the United States, Period of the 1930s*. San Jose, Calif.: Globe Printing Company, 1961.

Keuchel, Edward F. *A History of Columbia County, Florida*. Tallahassee: Sentry, 1981.

Knauss, James Owen. "St. Joseph: An Episode in the Economic and Political History of Florida." *Florida Historical Quarterly*, April and July, 1927.

Levy County Archives Committee. *Search for Yesterday: A History of Levy County, Florida*. Bronson, Fla.: Levy County, 1977.

Lewis, G. E. *Florida Banks*. Tallahassee: Florida Bankers Association, 1942.

Marckhoff, Fred R. "The Development of Currency and Banking in Florida." *Coin Collectors Journal*, September–October 1947, pages 118–123; and November–December 1947, pages 138–141.

Martin, John H. *Columbus, Geo.: From Its Selection as a "Trading Town" to its Partial Destruction by Wilson's Raid in 1865*. Columbus, Ga.: T. Gilbert, 1874.

McKethan, Alfred A. *Hernando County, Our Story*. Brooksville, Fla.: McKethan, 1989.

Mitchell, Ralph A., and Neil Shafer. *Depression Scrip of the United States, the 1930s*. Iola, Wis.: Krause, 1984.

Ordinances Adopted by the Constitutional Convention. Tallahassee: Dyke & Carlisle, 1861–1862.

Ott, Eloise Robinson. *Ocali Country, Kingdom of the Sun: A History of Marion County, Florida*. Oklawaha, Fla.: Marion, 1966.

Owens, Harry P. *Apalachicola before 1861*. Tallahassee: Florida State University, 1966.

Pfeiffer, Philip A. *Pensacola's Currency Issuing Banks and Their Bank Notes 1833–1935*. Pensacola: Pfeiffer Printing, 1975.

Pizzo, Anthony P. *Tampa Town 1824–1886*. Miami: Hurricane House, 1968.

Powell, Evanell Klintworth. *Tampa That Was: History and Chronology through 1946*. Boynton Beach: Star, 1973.

RARCOA. *Central States Numismatic Society Annual Convention Auction Sale*. Chicago: RARCOA, 1977.

Rerick, Rowland H. *Memoirs of Florida*. Atlanta: Southern Historical Association, 1902.

Rice, Foster Wild. "Antecedents of the American Bank Note Company of 1858." *Essay Proof Journal*, Vol. 18 (1961), Nos. 71, 72.

Rogers, William W. *At the Water's Edge: A Pictorial and Narrative History of Apalachicola and Franklin County*. Virginia Beach, Va.: Donning, 1997.

―――. *Outposts on the Gulf: St. George Island and Apalachicola from Early Exploration to World*

War II. Pensacola: University of West Florida Press, 1987.

Rosenbleeth, Arnie. "Pensacola Mayors Sign City Scrip in 1861." *Bank Note Reporter*, October 1985.

Shofner, Jerrell H. *History of Jefferson County*. Tallahassee: Sentry, 1976.

Sims, Elizabeth H. *A History of Madison County, Florida*. Madison, Fla.: Madison County Historical Society, 1986.

Stanaback, Richard J. *A History of Hernando County 1840–1976*. Brooksville, Fla.: Action '76 Steering Committee, 1976.

Stanley, J. Randall. *History of Gadsden County*. Quincy, Fla.: Gadsden County Historical Commission, 1948.

Thomas, David Y. "Florida Finance in the Civil War." *Yale Review*, November 1907, pages 311–318.

_____. *A History of Banking in Florida*. Gainesville: University of Florida, 1907.

VanLandingham, Kyle S. "The Life and Career of Perry Green Wall." *Journal of the Tampa Historical Society*, December 1997.

Vlack, Robert A. *An Illustrated Catalogue of Early American Advertising Notes*. New York: R. M. Smythe, 2001.

Warrant books and treasury certificate registers, January 1, 1866–January 1, 1877. In the collection of the Florida State Archives, Tallahassee.

Waters, Zack C. "Florida's Confederate Guerillas: John W. Pearson and the Oklawaha Rangers." *Florida Historical Quarterly*, October 1991, pages 133–149.

Webb, Wanton S. *Webb's Historical, Industrial and Biographical Florida*. New York: W. S. Webb, 1885.

Willoughby, Lynn. *Fair to Middlin': The Antebellum Cotton Trade of the Apalachicola/Chattahooche River Valley*. Tuscaloosa: University of Alabama Press, 1993.

Windhorn, Stan, and Wright Langley. *Yesterday's Key West*. Miami: E. A. Seemann, 1973.

Womack, Miles Kenan, Jr. *Gadsden, a Florida County in Word and Picture*. Quincy: Gadsden County Bicentennial Committee, 1976.

Worsley, Etta B. *Columbus on the Chattahoochee*. Columbus, Ga.: Columbus Office Supply Co., 1951.

Index

Aberdeen, Miss. 105
advertising notes 166–173
agriculture 44, 54, 63, 98
Alabama 42, 103–107
Alachua County 100
Alafia 41–42, 96, 164
Allen, R.C. 137
alligator 114
Alligator Town 89
Allison, Abraham K. 33–34
Alston, Willis 157
Alverson, L.M. 80
Amelia, Princess 6
Amelia Island 5–6
America 102, 116
American Bank Note Company 70, 72–73, 77, 82, 90, 148, 157, 162
Amphitrite 78
anchor 45, 114, 163
Apalachicola 42–60, 76, 96, 104, 131–132
Apalachicola Lands 54, 76, 130–131
Apalachicola River 42, 145
Apalachicola State Bank 177
archer 122
Archimedes 45, 58, 94, 116, 121, 152
Ares, Robert 13
art 53
Ashe, Jonathan 156
Athena 115, 119, 127, 141
Aury, Luis 6
Austin, Charles H. 13–34

Babson Park 177
Bailey, William 148, 155
Balch, Stiles & Co. 96
Baldwin, Dr. Abel Seymour 89

Ball, Douglas 32
Baltimore 62
Bank of Blountstown 177
Bank of Charleston 82
Bank of Columbus 59, 77–78
Bank of Commerce 68–69
Bank of Dunedin 178
Bank of Fernandina 70–71, 138
Bank of Florida 139–145, 157, 170
Bank of Green Cove Springs 178
Bank of Greensboro 178
Bank of Jacksonville 79–82, 87
Bank of Mulberry 178
Bank of Newberry 178
Bank of Pahokee 178
Bank of Pensacola 115–122, 126
Bank of St. Johns 82–88
Bank of St. Marys 55–57, 104
Bank of Starke 178
Bank of the United States 121
Bank of West Florida 42–47, 77, 96–98
Bank of Wildwood 179
Bankers Magazine 124
barrels 87–88, 127
Bartow 74
Battle of Lake Erie 160
Bay Port 42, 60–61, 74
Beach, M.Y. 80
beaver 117
beehive 67, 76, 89, 157
Bennett, A.G. 110
Bertram, Thomas 43–45, 96
Bettelini's Hotel 167
Beveridge, Robert 96
Birmingham, Alabama 103
Bisbee, Cyrus 85
Bisbee & Canova 85–86

blacksmith 109
Blount, Riley Redding 74
Blount, Thomas 115
Bobe, Francis B. 124
Bolivar, Simon 5
Booth, Edwin G. 139–143
Bours, J.H.H. 84–86
bow and arrow 122
Bradbeer 11, 28
Bradenton 96
Brevard, Theodore W. 82, 148
Brooks, Martin 43–45
Brooksville 42, 61–62, 74, 164
Brown, William C. 65
Brunswick & Florida Steam Boat & Stage Line 62–63
Bryant, George L. 82
Bucki, Louis 66–68
bull 53, 66–67, 127, 179
Burford 184
Burr, Joseph 164
Burr & Lynch 164

Calhoun 69, 149
Call, George 72
Call, Richard K. 161
Camp Cuba Libre 168
Campbell, J.W. 96
Canova, Lawrence 85
Capital City Bank 178
Capital City Business College 171, 185
Caracas 7
carpetbagger notes 11
Carter, Farish 58
Casilear, Durand, Burton & Edwards 98
Cassidy, Daniel G. 1, 74, 99, 101, 129
Catlin, James 115, 118

Index

cattle 72, 81, 91, 99–100, 116, 121, 123, 151
Cawthorn State Bank 178
Cedar Key 63–64, 68, 71, 167
Central Bank of Florida 139, 145–147, 151
Central Bank of Georgia 128
Ceres 17–20, 29–32, 38–39, 45, 53, 59, 63, 94–100, 116, 118, 127, 134, 140, 145, 147, 154
Chaires, Benjamin 145
Charleston 62–63
Chas. Toppan 47, 132
Chattahoochee River 42, 58
cherub 46, 57, 135, 142, 144, 147
children 72–73, 77, 79, 147
Chipola River 76
Citizens Bank and Trust Company 178
Citizens Bank of Jacksonville 178
Citizens National Bank of Pensacola 175
City Council of Apalachicola 57
City of Pensacola 122–124
Civil War 11–34, 63, 68, 74, 89, 93, 121–122
Clark, Edward A. 61, 65, 74
Clark, Lot 128
Clark, M. 47
Clay 148
Clearing House Certificates 174
coins 47, 58, 129–131, 147
Cole, Archibald H. 70, 72
College Currency 184–185
Colombia 6
Colonial era fiscal paper 126–127
Columbia County 73
Columbus 76–79
Columbus, Georgia 55, 57–60, 66, 77–79, 105
commerce 21–24, 43–45, 48, 54, 60, 63, 77, 79, 95, 97, 99, 114–116, 121–122, 134, 140, 146–147, 150, 155
Commercial Bank and Trust Company 178
Commercial Bank of Florida 47–52, 77, 132–134
Commercial Bank of New Orleans 126
Commercial Store 109
comptroller seal 69, 83, 148–150
comptroller's warrants 35–37

Confederate facsimile 167–169
Confederate gunboat 87
Confederate notes 103, 167–169
Confederate packing-house 87–88
Conover, Simon B. 36
Conover, Simon P. 36, 40
Cook, Ambrose 156
Cook, Margaret 129–130
cork 61, 64–65, 74
Corlies, Macy & Co. 75
Corporation of St. Joseph 135–137
Corporation of Tallahassee 155–156
cotton 64, 70, 83, 90, 127, 134, 136, 147
County Treasurer 107
Courter, Chas. 125
covered wagon 63, 123, 161
Coweta Falls Manufacturing 58–59
Cowgill, Clayton A. 39–40
Crampton, R.C. 185
Crescent City 177
Criswell, Grover C. 1, 11, 20, 28
Crocker, Elijah E. 98
Crupper, Micajah 122
Cuba 92

Danforth, Bald 150
Danforth, Underwood 55, 63
Danforth, Wright 68, 82, 150
Dean, I.L. 106
Decatur 105
deer 57, 83
DeFuniak Springs 178
de la Rua, Filo E. 124
Del Pino, Antonio & brothers 92
Denham, William 108
Denny, C.W. 88, 174
Denny and Brown 88
Depression Scrip 174–183
De Soto 48
dog 55–57, 67, 72, 107
Donlon, William P. 170
Doty & Bergen 59
Douglas, B.M. 11
Douglas Engravers & Lithographers 101
Draper Underwood Bald & Spencer 44, 95, 97, 118, 145
Draper, Toppan, Longacre 50, 132
Drew, George F. 66
Drew & Bucki 66–68
Drew Issues 176–179

Durand 52
Durand, Roger 2
Dutton 65–66, 68
Duval, Gov. William P. 8, 42, 96, 151

eagle 43, 44, 46, 48, 55, 57–58, 60, 63, 66–67, 81, 97–98, 100, 102, 104–105, 109, 117, 120, 127, 130–131, 141, 146, 149–150, 153, 156–157, 160
Eagle Manufacturing 59–60
Early, Eleazer 96
East Florida Steam Saw Mill 113–115
elk 29, 31, 102
Elks Home 173
Ellaville 66–68
Elwyn, Rev. Alfred L. 28, 30
engravers and printers: American Bank Note Company 70, 72–73, 77, 82, 90, 148, 157, 162; Balch, Stiles & Co. 96; Burford 184; Casilear, Durand, Burton & Edwards 98; Chas. Toppan 47, 132; Corlies, Macy & Co. 75; Danforth, Bald 150; Danforth, Underwood 55, 63; Danforth, Wright 68, 82, 150; Doty & Bergen 59; Douglas Engravers & Lithographers 101; Draper, Toppan, Longacre 50, 132; Draper Underwood Bald & Spencer 44, 95, 97, 118, 145; Durand 52; Fairman Draper Underwood 139; Florida Union Printing 88; Hatch, George W. 128; Hoyer and Ludwig 13–23; Jocelyn, N. & S.S. 9; Keatinge & Ball 28–32; Keefe & Bro. 103; Lowe 155; Major & Knapp 66, 68; Manouvrier, Juls. & Snell, P. 136; Milwaukee Lithographing 102; Morris, E. 122, 159; National Bank Note Company 37–39; New England Bank Note Co. 79, 160; North, Sherman & Co. 89; Pelletreau & Raynor 67; Rawdon, Wright 113, 142–143; Rawdon, Wright & Hatch 43, 45–47, 51, 57, 77, 93, 115, 134, 140, 144, 147, 151, 154; Rawdon, Wright, Hatch & Edson 121, 124, 134,

147, 153–154, 161; Rollinson 54; Smith's 156; Sutton, T.E. 109; Underwood, Bald, Spencer & Huffy 53, 63; Verelst & Co. 64; Wood, T. & C. 127; Wright 130–131
Escambia County 101
essays 12–13
Etting, Henry 126
Eustis 178
Evergreen, Alabama 125
Exchange and Banking Company 52–53

Faber, Eberhard 63
factory 66, 92, 125
Fairbanks, Samuel 85
Fairman Draper Underwood 139
farm implements 94, 107, 132, 157
farm scene 38–39, 63, 95, 135, 140, 147–148, 154, 175
Farmers and Merchants Bank 179
Farmers Bank of Florida 98–100
Fernandez, Don Domingo 68
Fernandina 6, 63, 68–73, 138
Field, George 128
Fillmore 150
financial panic 174–183
First Bank and Trust Company 178
First National Bank of Jacksonville 185
First National Bank of Pensacola 175
First State Bank 178
flag 123
Flagg, F.H. 162–164
Flint River 42
Flora 128–129, 148
Florida Atlantic & Gulf Central Railroad 82, 84, 89–91, 93
Florida Internal Improvement Commission 89
Florida Normal College 184–185
Florida Railroad 63, 65, 68, 71–73, 75
Florida Theatre 169
Florida Union Printing 88
flower 122, 164
Floyd, Davis 8–10
Forbes, John 54, 130
Forcheimer, Abraham & Gershon 103
Forman, Arthur J. 127

Forman & Muse 127
Fort Blount 74
Fort Brooke 41, 164
Fort Meade 41, 178
Fort Myers 168
Fort Pierce 179
Fort White Bank 178
Fraleigh, E.M. 127
Franklin 48, 50–51, 94, 133, 139, 160
Freeman, Harley L. 1, 74, 99, 101
Friebele, Christopher B. 61–62, 74
Fulton 50–51, 133

Gadsden County State Bank 178
Gainesville 71, 178
Gainesville Chamber of Commerce 180
Gamble, John 151–155
Gamble, Robert H. 36–38, 40
Garey, John 8–10
Gaston 64
Generic Scrip 156
Genovar, Bartolo 166
Georgia 6, 42, 103–107, 110
Gingles, C.H. 123–124
Goddess 119
Gordon, Thomas G. 93
Gormely, J.B. 124
Government Stock Bank of Ann Arbor 150
Graham, James G. 139, 143–145
Great Depression 176
Green Cross Republic 5–6
Gregory, Walter 115
Griffin 52, 140
Griggs, R.S. 137
Grothe, William 86
Gulf of Mexico 42, 54, 63, 68
gunboat 42, 61–62, 65, 75, 110–113, 164–165
Gunn, John G. 127
Gutterson, J. 80
Gwynn, Walter 20–24

Hamlin, William, Sr. 129
Hammermill safety paper 180
Hartridge, Theodore 86
Haskins, William L. 113
Hatch, George W. 128
Hawes, Peter 12–13, 17
Haxby, James A. 2, 99
Hayes, T.P. 172
Hayward's Store 157
Hebe 9, 43, 45, 58, 60, 63,

97–98, 100, 117, 134, 141, 147, 152–153
Hernando County 42, 60–61, 74–75
Hickey, John B. 168
High Springs Bank 178
Highland 75–76
Hilliard, William 159–161
Hillsboro State Bank 178
Hillsborough County 41, 73, 96
Hodges, John 138
Honduras 7
Hope 45, 53–54, 97, 117, 118, 140, 148, 175
horse and wagon 42, 51, 62, 70, 78–79, 111, 141, 152, 154, 161–162, 165
horses 66, 80–82, 90, 108, 117, 135, 147
Houstoun, Edward 161–162
Howell, John D. 57
Hoyer and Ludwig 13–23
Hughes, B.H. 11
Hughes, Daniel 64
hunter 83, 140
Huntsville 105

Ichepucksassa 64
Indian 29, 31–32, 46–49, 53, 58–59, 77, 79, 81–83, 85, 90–91, 93–94, 103, 116, 121, 132, 136, 149, 150, 152–153, 155, 176–179
inverted overprint 27
Iola 76–79, 132

Jackson 48–49, 81, 96, 132, 150
Jacksonville 66, 79–92, 167–168, 174–175, 178, 185
Jacksonville Business College 185
Jacksonville Clearing Association 176
Jacksonville, Illinois 185
Jacksonville, Pensacola & Mobile Railroad 93
Jefferson 139
Jefferson County 107
Jemison, Robert Jr. 103
Jocelyn, N. & S.S. 9
Johnson, J.B. 101
Johnston, R.E. 100–101
Judah, William H. 124
Judah & LeBaron 124
Juno 97, 155
justice 10, 44, 46, 49, 63, 94, 116–117, 119–120, 132, 142, 154–155

Index

Karlsruhe, Germany 61
Keatinge & Ball 28–32
Keefe & Bro. 103
Kelly, Hanson 115, 118, 122
Kennedy, David S. 139–145
Kennedy, Thomas 41
Key West 92, 175, 181
Key West Clearing House 175
Keystone Mills 75–76
King George II 6

Lafayette 47, 63, 98, 100, 114–115, 129, 152
Lake City 82, 89, 93
Lake Wimico 76
Lake Wimico and St. Joseph Canal & Railroad Company 131, 137
Larkin, J. E. 72
LeBaron & Son 124
Lee, Robert E. 34
Leon County 157
Leslie 54
Levy County 64
Lewis, B.C. 149, 155
Lewis State Bank 179
liberty 44, 47, 59, 63, 88, 97–98, 102, 116, 120, 122, 127, 142, 146, 156
literature 58
Littlefield, M.L. 162
Loockerman's Store 157
Louisiana 104–107
Lowe 155
lumbermen 102
Lynch, James 164
lyre and horn 108

MacGregor, Gregor 5–7
Maclay, John C. 47–49, 132
MacRae, Alex 72
Madison 93
Magnolia 93–95
Major & Knapp 66, 68
Manatee 42, 96
Manouvrier, Juls. & Snell, P. 136
Marianna 42, 96–100
Marion County 110
Marshall 50–51, 98, 133
Mayo, Anderson 74
Mayo State Bank 178
Mercer, C.F. 154
Merchants and Planters Bank at Magnolia 93–94, 134
Merchants and Planters Bank of Florida 95, 134–135, 147–148
Merchants and Planters Bank of Magnolia 95, 147

Mercury 10, 52, 58, 89, 94, 117, 139–140, 147, 155
Mexico 5–6
Micanopy 100–101
Millview 101–102, 125
Milton, John 12–20, 25–32, 34, 103
Milwaukee Lithographing 102
Minerva 142
Mississippi 104–107
Mitchell, Joseph 125
Mitchell and Shafer 176
Mobile 62–63, 124
Mobley, Claiborne, R. 164
Moneta 29, 32
Monroe, James 6
Monroe, William & Co. 128
Montgomery Insurance Company 105–107
Montgomery, Alabama 103–107
Monticello 107–109, 178
Mooney, George 87
Morgan, J.B. 79–80
Morris, E. 122, 159
Morris, James D. 107
mortar & pestle 92
mules 148–149, 153
Murat, Achille 157
Muse, Hudson 127

Napoleon 157
Nashville 103
National Bank Note Company 37–39
navigation 21–24, 150
Nehamathla 152–153, 155
Neptune 78
New Book Store 168
New England Bank Note Co. 79, 160
New Orleans 12, 62–63, 105
New York State shield 107
Nicaragua 7
Niles Register 42, 76, 132
North, Sherman & Co. 89
Nueva Grenada 5

obsolete notes 41–165
Ocala 106, 178
Ogelthorpe, James 6
Oklawaha Rangers 110
Orange Springs 42, 96, 109–113, 164

Palm Beach 172
palm trees 69, 90, 176–179
Palmer, Joseph 108
Pan American Union 6

Panama 113–115
Panic of 1837 122
Panton 54, 130
Panton, Leslie and Company 126, 131
Paper Money 7, 12, 35, 40, 103, 167
Parkhill, John 151, 153
Parsons, Maj. John B. 60–61
Patrick, William 47, 132
peace 116–117, 121
Pearson, J.W. 110–113
Pelletreau & Raynor 67
Pennsylvania Colonial Currency 124
Pensacola 103, 115–127, 173, 178
Pensacola and Georgia Railroad 93
Pensacola Bank & Trust Co. 176
Pensacola Clearing House 175
Pensacola Gazette 42, 47
Pensacola Lodge B.P.O. Elks 173
Pensacola Navy Yard 126
Peoples Bank 177
Perdido Bay Lumber Company 125
Perry, Georgia 98–100
Perry, Madison Starke 12–17
Pettes, William R. 148, 155
Phifer State Bank 178
Phoebe 72
Phoenix Bank 78
Picayune 126
Pittman, James J. 98
Plant City 64, 178
Planters and Mechanics Bank 79
Plenty 63, 118, 122
plow 107
Pony Express 103
Powell, James Robert 103–107
Powell, Jeremiah 93, 95
Poyais 7
printers *see* engravers and printers
Progress 59
Proserpine 116, 121
Proskey, David 138
Proskey Brothers 138
Prosperity 21–24, 77, 79, 114, 150
Providence 45, 52, 117, 121, 148

Quincy 127–128, 178
Quincy State Bank 178

Raleigh 10, 139, 142–143
Rarcoa 74, 101
Rarity Scale 1
Rawdon, Wright 113, 142–143
Rawdon, Wright & Hatch 43, 45–47, 51, 57, 77, 93, 115, 134, 140, 144, 147, 151, 154
Rawdon, Wright, Hatch & Edson 121, 124, 134, 147, 153–154, 161
Reconstruction 35–40, 66
Redbrook, Jackson S. 164
Reed, Arthur M. 82–83, 128
Reed, Gov. Harrison 36, 38–39
Remington, J. 87–88
Republic of the Floridas 5–7
Revere, Paul 66
Rio de la Plata 5
Rioboo, Maximo Posse 123
River Junction 178
Rixford, George 65
Rob Roy 5
Roberts, Wm. S. 73
Robinson, George W. 102, 125
Robinson, W.L. 157
Robinson's Store 157
Rochester, William B. 115
Rollinson 54
Roman heads 44, 55–57, 97–98, 140–141, 144, 146
Rome, Ga. 105
rooster 179
Roux, George S. 70
Rutgers, Henry L. 140–145, 158–159

safe 107
sailor 46, 66, 163
St. Augustine 82, 128–131, 148, 166–167
St. Augustine Herald 79
St. Catherine of Alexandria 29, 31
St. Joseph 47, 54, 62–63, 76, 131–137, 147
St. Marys River 65
St. Petersburg 181–182
St. Petersburg Citizens Emergency Committee 182
Sanchez, Venancio 130–131
Savannah 56–57
Scenic Highlands State Bank 177
Schingoethe 185
Scotland 5, 7
Sebring 169
Seixas, E. 93
Seminole Wars 41, 54, 60, 74

Sheldon scale 1, 11
shepherd 80, 160
ships 29–33, 42, 48–52, 57–58, 60–66, 69–70, 73, 75, 77–83, 87, 90, 106–107, 110–113, 116–117, 119–122, 126, 129, 132–137, 140–141, 147, 150, 152–156, 160–162, 164–165
Shull, Hugh, 11
Sibbald, Charles F. 113
signers: Allen, R.C. 137; Allison, Abraham K. 33–34; Alston, Willis 157; Alverson, L.M. 80; Ashe, Jonathan 156; Austin, Charles H. 13–34; Bailey, William 148, 155; Bennett, A.G. 110; Bertram, Thomas 43–45, 96; Beveridge, Robert 96; Blount, R.R. 74; Blount, Thomas 115; Bobe, Francis B. 124; Booth, Edwin G. 139–143; Brevard, Theodore W. 82, 148; Brooks, Martin 43–45; Brown, William C. 65; Bryant, George L. 82; Bours, J.H.H. 84–86; Burr, Joseph 164; Call, George 72; Call, Richard K. 161; Campbell, J.W. 96; Catlin, James 115, 118; Chaires, Benjamin 145; Clark, Lot 128; Clark, M. 47; Cole, Archibald H. 70, 72; Conover, Simon B. 36; Cook, Ambrose 156; Cook, Margaret 129; Courter, Chas. 125; Cowgill, Clayton A. 39–40; Crocker, Elijah E. 98; Crupper, Micajah 122; Dean, I.L. 106; de la Rua, Filo E. 124; Denham, William 108; Early, Eleazer 96; Etting, Henry 126; Field, George 128; Flagg, F.H. 162–164; Floyd, Davis 8–10; Forman & Muse 127; Friebele, Christopher B. 61–62; Gamble, John 151–155; Gamble, R.H. 36, 38; Gingles, C.H. 123–124; Gordon, Thomas G. 93; Gormely, J.B. 124; Graham, James G. 139, 143–145; Gregory, Walter 115; Griggs, R.S. 137; Gunn, John G. 127; Gutterson, J. 80; Gwynn, Walter 20–24; Hamlin, Wm. 129; Haskins, William L. 113; Hilliard, William 159–161; Hodges, John 138; Houstoun, Edward 161–162; Johnston, R.E. 100–101; Judah & LeBaron 124; Kelly, Hanson 115, 118, 122; Larkin, J.E. 72; Lewis, B.C. 149, 155; Littlefield, M.L. 162; Lynch, James 164; Maclay, John C. 47–49, 132; MacRae, Alex 72; Mayo, Anderson 74; Mercer, C.F. 154; Milton, John 12–20, 25–32, 34; Mobley, Claiborne, R. 164; Mooney, George 87; Morgan, J.B. 80; Murat, Achille 157; Palmer, Joseph 108; Parkhill, John 151, 153; Parsons, John B. 60–61; Patrick, William 47, 132; Pearson, J.W. 110–113; Perry, Madison Starke 13–16; Pettes, William R. 148, 155; Pittman, James J. 98; Powell, James Robert 103–107; Powell, Jeremiah 93, 95; Redbrook, Jackson S. 164; Reed, Arthur M. 82–83, 128; Reed, Harrison 36, 38–39; Remington, J. 87–88; Rioboo, Maximo Posse 123; Roberts, Wm. S. 73; Robinson, G.W. 102, 125; Robinson, W.L. 157; Rochester, William B. 115; Rome, Ga. 105; Roux, George S. 70; Rutgers, Henry L. 140–145, 158–159; Sanchez, Venancio 130–131; Seixas, E. 93; Smith, I.B. 85; Stevenson, H. 97; Stevenson, J.E. 100–101; Stone, J.S. 162; Thompson, Leslie A. 145; Vigil, Jose 165; Wall, Perry Green 74; Webster, E.P. 91–92; Wellborn, Carlton 98; White, Thomas M. 98; Wiggins, J.C. 46, 97; Williams, Darius 108; Winter, John G. 55–57; Wordehoff, A. 41–42; Young, William H. 59–60
Silver Springs 138
slaves 21–24, 28, 30, 32
Smith, I.B. 85
Smith's 156
South Carolina 103, 110, 150
Southern Life Insurance & Trust Co. 82, 128–129, 148
Spanish American War 168
stagecoach 81, 104–108, 127
Starke 70, 138

State Bank of Florida 148–150, 155–156
State seal 27–32
State Stock Bank 150
Stephenson, Hugh 47
Stevenson, H. 97
Stevenson, J.E. 100–101
Stone, J.S. 162
Summerlin, Jacob 64
Supreme Court 54, 76, 131
Sutton, T.E. 109
Suwannee River 66
Suwannee Steam Saw Mills 67–68
Swamp Land Act 89

Tahcoloquiot 48
Tallahassee 8–10, 62–63, 93, 95, 128, 134, 139–164, 171, 178, 185
Tallahassee Post Office 159–161
Tallahassee Railroad 93, 161–164
Tampa 41–42, 61, 65, 74, 164–165, 176
Tampa Clearing House Association 176
Taylor 150
Taylor, William 104
El telégrapho de las Floridas 6
Tellus 14–16
territorial notes 8–10
Texas 105–107
Thompson, Leslie A. 145
Todd security paper 183
Torrey's Troop of Rough Riders 168
trains 29, 31, 41, 53, 61, 64, 69, 71–73, 78–79, 81, 83, 89–91, 96, 104–106, 109, 111, 113, 116–117, 125, 134, 136–137, 141, 147, 149, 152, 155, 161–164
treasury certificates 35–36
Trenton 179
Tucker, James 63
Tucker, Gaston & Co. 63–64
Two Flags West 169
Tyler, John 121

Underwood, Bald, Spencer & Huffy 53, 63
Union Bank 77, 127, 151–155, 158
United States Capitol 150
United States Navy Yard 126

Venezuela 5–7
Venus 135, 147, 154

Verdie 65
Verelst & Co. 64
Vigil, Jose 165
vignettes: agriculture 44, 54, 63, 98; alligator 114; America 102, 116; Amphitrite 78; anchor 45, 114, 163; archer 122; Archimedes 45, 58, 94, 116, 121, 152; Art 53; Athena 115, 119, 127, 141; barrels 87–88, 127; Battle of Lake Erie 160; beaver 117; beehive 67, 76, 89, 157; blacksmith 109; bow and arrow 122; bull 53, 66–67, 127, 179; Calhoun 69, 149; cattle 72, 81, 91, 99–100, 116, 121, 123, 151; Ceres 17–20, 29–32, 38–39, 45, 53, 59, 63, 94–100, 116, 118, 127, 134, 140, 145, 147, 154; cherub 46, 57, 135, 142, 144, 147; children 72–73, 77, 79, 147; Clay 148; coins 47, 58, 129–131, 147; Columbus 76–79; commerce 21–24, 43–45, 48, 54, 60, 63, 77, 79, 95, 97, 99, 114–116, 121–122, 134, 140, 146–147, 150, 155; comptroller seal 69, 83, 148–150; cotton 64, 70, 83, 90, 127, 134, 136, 147; covered wagon 63, 123, 161; deer 57, 83; De Soto 48; dog 55–57, 67, 72, 107; eagle 43, 44, 46, 48, 55, 57–58, 60, 63, 66–67, 81, 97–98, 100, 102, 104–105, 109, 117, 120, 127, 130–131, 141, 146, 149–150, 153, 156–157, 160; elk 29, 31, 102; Elwyn, Rev. Alfred L. 28, 30; factory 66, 92, 125; farm implements 94, 107, 132, 157; farm scene 38–39, 63, 95, 135, 140, 147–148, 154, 175; Fillmore 150; flag 123; Flora 128–129, 148; flower 122, 164; Franklin 48, 50–51, 94, 133, 139, 160; Fulton 50–51, 133; Goddess 119; Griffin 52, 140; gunboat 42, 61–62, 65, 75, 110–113, 164–165; Hebe 9, 43, 45, 58, 60, 63, 97–98, 100, 117, 134, 141, 147, 152–153; Hope 45, 53–54, 97, 117, 118, 140, 148, 175; horse and wagon 42, 51, 62, 70, 78–79, 111, 141, 152, 154, 161–162, 165; horses 66, 80–82, 90, 108, 117, 135, 147; hunter 83, 140; Indian 29, 31–32, 46–49, 53, 58–59, 77, 79, 81–83, 85, 90–91, 93–94, 103, 116, 121, 132, 136, 149, 150, 152–153, 155, 176–179; Jackson 48–49, 81, 96, 132, 150; Jefferson 139; Juno 97, 155; justice 10, 44, 46, 49, 63, 94, 116–117, 119–120, 132, 142, 154–155; Lafayette 47, 63, 98, 100, 114–115, 129, 152; Liberty 44, 47, 59, 63, 88, 97–98, 102, 116, 120, 122, 127, 142, 146, 156; literature 58; lumbermen 102; lyre and horn 108; Marshall 50–51, 98, 133; Mercury 10, 52, 58, 89, 94, 117, 139–140, 147, 155; Minerva 142; Moneta 29, 32; mortar & pestle 92; mules 148–149, 153; Navigation 21–24, 150; Nehamathla 152–153, 155; Neptune 78; New York shield 107; palm trees 69, 90, 176–179; Peace 116–117, 121; Phoebe 72; Plenty 63, 118, 122; plow 107; Progress 59; Proserpine 116, 121; Prosperity 21–24, 77, 79, 114, 150; Providence 45, 52, 117, 121, 148; Raleigh 10, 139, 142–143; Revere, Paul 66; Roman heads 44, 55–57, 97–98, 140–141, 144, 146; rooster 179; safe 107; sailor 46, 66, 163; St. Catherine of Alexandria 29, 31; shepherd 80, 160; ships 29–33, 42, 48–52, 57–58, 60–66, 69–70, 73, 75, 77–83, 87, 90, 106–107, 110–113, 116–117, 119–122, 126, 129, 132–137, 140–141, 147, 150, 152–156, 160–162, 164–165; slaves 21–24, 28, 30, 32; stagecoach 81, 104–108, 127; State seal 27–32; Tahcoloquiot 48; Taylor 150; Tellus 14–16; train 29, 31, 41, 53, 61, 64, 69, 71–73, 78–79, 81, 83, 89–91, 96, 104–106, 109, 111, 113, 116–117, 125, 134, 136–137, 141, 147, 149, 152, 155, 161–164; U.S. Capitol 150; Venus 135, 147, 154; Washington 9–10, 12, 14–16, 45, 47, 49–51, 63, 66, 68, 76, 93, 96, 98, 100, 109, 123, 132–133, 139, 147, 152–153, 160; water god or goddess 10,

98; Wayne, Gen. Anthony 185; Winter, John G. 55–56, 66; wisdom 153; woodsmen 69, 72, 102
Virginia 110
Vlack, Robert A. 166

W.T. & Co. 28, 30–32
Wall, Perry Green 61, 74
Washington 9–10, 12, 14–16, 45, 47, 49–51, 63, 66, 68, 76, 93, 96, 98, 100, 109, 123, 132–133, 139, 147, 152–153, 160

water god or goddess 10, 98
Wayne, Gen. Anthony 185
Webster, Dr. Edward P. 91–92
Weeki Wachee River 60
Weekly Floridian 37
Wellborn, Carlton 98
West Palm Beach 183
Wewahitchka State Bank 179
White, Thomas M. 98
White Springs 184–185
Wiggins, J.C. 46, 97
Wiggins, Teape & Co. 32
Williams, Darius 108
Williams, James 96

Williams, Robert C. 20
Winter, John G. 55–57, 66, 104
Wisdom 153
Wood, T. & C. 127
woodsmen 69
Wordehoff, Antoine 41–42
Wright 130–131

Ximinez-Fatio house 129

Young, William H. 59–60
Yribarren, Joseph de 6
Yulee, David Levy 71, 110

www.ingramcontent.com/pod-product-compliance
Lightning Source LLC
Chambersburg PA
CBHW081557300426
44116CB00015B/2919